Praise for *The Future of Power*

"Whether it's navigating the political waves of the Middle East or the diplomatic dance with China, the book offers a generous batch of insights. . . . Nye is a savvy and respected analyst, and he doesn't disappoint here. He's grappling with the hardest of questions." —*LA Times*

"Nye's writing style is accessible even when his subject grows more complex. . . . A helpful primer to better understand the tools available to those formulating America's foreign policy." —*Washington Times*

"Illuminating analysis of the mechanisms of power shaping global politics. . . . Nye Jr.'s latest book steers the traditional debate over power politics into a new direction. . . . The author's sober, rigorous analysis anchors a debate that seems to be squirming from the grip of most media. A great reminder that fear and hate are not the only tools used to sell books these days—a substantial work that should be read by anyone with an interest in how politics works." —*Kirkus*

"As power moves from west to east and from the palaces of dictators to the street, it is not just the identities of power brokers that are changing: so is the very meaning of power. No one is better placed to explain these trends than the scholar-statesman Joe Nye. . . . *The Future of Power* contains important essays on both 'cyber power' and 'American decline,' but what is most useful is Nye's subtle exegesis of the mechanics of more conventional forms of power." —*New Statesman*

"Nye has a lot of interesting points to make against conventional wisdom in matters geopolitical and cultural." —*Guardian*

"A concise, forceful statement of what Nye refers to as the liberal realist positioning the U.S. academy and in U.S. politics . . . [which] paints a plausible scenario for the continuance of the U.S. at the heart of the international system." —*Times Higher Education Supplement*

"[A] fully-fledged global guru. . . . Nye's genius—and good fortune—was to encapsulate quite a complex constellation of ideas in a single phrase, at a time when there was a hole in the academic and political landscape just waiting for it."   —Mary Dejevsky, *Independent* (UK)

"Power once came from controlling the sea lanes. In the future, Joe Nye explains, it will come from the ability to navigate the information lanes of cyberspace and control the narrative that influences people. Sweeping in its themes but specific in its examples, this book is exciting to read and fascinating to contemplate."

—Walter Isaacson, president and CEO
of The Aspen Institute

"If you are searching for a brilliant and original analysis of cyberpower, read chapter five of Joseph S. Nye's *The Future of Power*. If you are looking for the best available comprehensive analysis of power in world politics, read the whole book."

—Robert O. Keohane, professor of public
and international affairs, Woodrow Wilson School
of Public and International Affairs, Princeton University

"In this magisterial book Joseph Nye offers a highly readable synthesis of more than two decades of conceptually innovative scholarship. He provides an incisive probing of different types of power, analyzes transitions between states that rise and fall, and explores the diffusion of power away from state to non-state actors. Nye's liberal-realist strategy is persuasive: America can stem political decline and extend economic prosperity by adhering to a small power strategy that refuses to seek primacy and prefers to be aligned with other nations. This book should become required reading for anybody who is interested in international affairs."

—Peter J. Katzenstein, Walter S. Carpenter, Jr.
Professor of International Studies, Cornell University

"Joseph Nye has crystallized decades of disciplined, pragmatic, and influential thinking about what power is and how it should be used. With his trademark combination of lucidity and persuasiveness, Nye has provided an antidote to apprehensions about newly powerful nations and fears about American decline."

—Strobe Talbott, author of *The Great Experiment:
The Story of Ancient Empires, Modern States,
and the Quest for a Global Nation*

THE FUTURE OF POWER

ALSO BY JOSEPH S. NYE, JR.

The Powers to Lead (2008)

The Power Game: A Washington Novel (2004)

Power in the Global Information Age:
From Realism to Globalization (2004)

Soft Power: The Means to Success in World Politics (2004)

The Paradox of American Power: Why the
World's Only Superpower Can't Go It Alone (2002)

Understanding International Conflicts: An Introduction
to Theory and History, 7th ed. (2009)

Bound to Lead: The Changing Nature of American Power (1990)

Nuclear Ethics (1986)

Hawks, Doves, and Owls: An Agenda for
Avoiding Nuclear War, coauthored with Graham Allison
and Albert Carnesale (1985)

Power and Interdependence: World Politics
in Transition, coauthored with Robert O. Keohane
(1977; 3rd ed. with additional material, 2000)

Peace in Parts: Integration and Conflict in
Regional Organization (1971)

Pan-Africanism and East African Integration (1965)

The FUTURE of POWER

JOSEPH S. NYE, Jr.

PUBLICAFFAIRS
New York

Copyright © 2011 by Joseph S. Nye, Jr.
Published in the United States by PublicAffairs™,
a member of the Perseus Books Group.
All rights reserved.

Printed in the United States of America.

PublicAffairs books are available at special discounts for bulk
purchases in the U.S. by corporations, institutions, and other
organizations. For more information, please contact the Special
Markets Department at the Perseus Books Group, 2300 Chestnut
Street, Suite 200, Philadelphia, PA 19103, call (800) 810-4145,
ext. 5000, or e-mail special.markets@perseusbooks.com.

Library of Congress Cataloging-in-Publication Data
Nye, Joseph S.
  The future of power / Joseph S. Nye. — 1st ed.
    p. cm.
  Includes bibliographical references and index.
  ISBN 978-1-58648-891-8 (alk. paper)
  1. Power (Social sciences) I. Title.
  JC330.N92 2011
  303.3'3—dc22
                                        2010044581
E-book ISBN: 978-1-58648-892-5
PB ISBN: 978-1-61039-069-9
First Edition
10 9 8 7

To Molly, as always;

to our sons, John, Ben, and Dan;

and to their children—Tupper, Hannah, Sage, Avery, Cole, Maggie, Ellie, Brooke, and Molly— who will live in this century

CONTENTS

PREFACE

In his inaugural address in 2009, President Barack Obama stated that "our power grows through its prudent use; our security emanates from the justness of our cause, the force of our example, the tempering qualities of humility and restraint." Similarly, Secretary of State Hillary Clinton said, "America cannot solve the most pressing problems on our own, and the world cannot solve them without America. We must use what has been called 'smart power,' the full range of tools at our disposal."[1] Earlier, in 2007, Secretary of Defense Robert Gates had called for the U.S. government to commit more money and effort to soft power tools including diplomacy, economic assistance, and communications because the military alone could not defend America's interests around the world. He pointed out that military spending then totaled more than half a trillion dollars annually compared with a State Department budget of $36 billion. In his words, "I am here to make the case for strengthening our capacity to use soft power and for better integrating it with hard power."[2] What does this mean? How will power work, and how is it changing in the twenty-first century?

To answer such questions, we need to have a better understanding of power than is typical in most current discussions. Let me give two examples, one personal and one public.

In the mid-1970s, France agreed to sell Pakistan a nuclear repro-
cessing plant that could extract plutonium, a material that could be
used either for civilian purposes or for bombs. Concerned about the
spread of nuclear weapons, the Ford administration tried to stop
the plant by buying off Pakistan with high-performance aircraft, but
Pakistan refused the deal. Both the Ford and Carter administrations
tried to prevail upon France to cancel the sale, but the French refused on the grounds that it was a legitimate sale for civilian purposes only. Nothing seemed to work until June 1977, when I was
in charge of Jimmy Carter's nonproliferation policy and was allowed
to present French officials with new evidence that Pakistan was
preparing a nuclear weapon. A top French official looked me in the
eye and told me that if this were true, France would have to find a
way to cancel the completion of the plant. Subsequently, he was as
good as his word, and the plant was not completed. How did the
United States accomplish this major objective? No threats were issued. No payments were made. No carrots were dangled or sticks
brandished. French behavior changed because of persuasion and
trust. I was there and saw it happen. This hardly fits the usual model
of power that is prevalent in most editorials or in recent foreign policy books that do not consider persuasion a form of power because
it "is essentially an intellectual or emotional process."[3]

More recently, in August 2008, China and Russia provided sharp
contrasts in the use of power. As French analyst Dominique Moisi
wrote at the time, "Whereas China intends to seduce and impress
the world by the number of its Olympic medals, Russia wants to
impress the world by demonstrating its military superiority—
China's soft power versus Russia's hard power." Some analysts concluded that the Russian invasion of Georgia proved the "irrelevance"
of soft power and the dominance of hard military power.[4] In reality,
the story turned out to be more complicated for both countries in
the long run.

Russia's use of hard power undercut its claims to legitimacy and
sowed fear and mistrust in much of the world. European neighbors

became more wary. An immediate cost was Poland's reversal of its resistance to an American antiballistic missile system. When Russia appealed for support on its Georgian policy to other members of the Shanghai Cooperation Organization, China and others withheld their support. An analysis one year later concluded that Russia's appeal to its neighbors did not sound very seductive. "Ideally, it would present an attractive model for its neighbors, politically and economically. Young generations would learn Russian because they wanted to, and the post-Soviet alliances would be clubs its neighbors are lining up to join." As Russian analyst Alexei Mukhin summed the matter up, "Love bought with money will not last long. That is purchased love. It is not very reliable."[5]

In contrast, China ended August with its soft power enhanced by its successful staging of the Olympic Games. In October 2007, President Hu Jintao declared China's intent to increase its soft power, and the Olympics were an important part of that strategy. With the establishment of several hundred Confucius Institutes to promote Chinese culture around the world, increased international broadcasting, attraction of foreign students to its universities, and softer diplomacy toward its neighbors in Southeast Asia, China made major investments in soft power. Opinion polls showed an increase in its international reputation. By accompanying its growth in hard power with an attractive soft power narrative, China was trying to use smart power to convey the idea of its "peaceful rise" and thus head off a countervailing balance of power.

AMERICAN POWER IN THE TWENTY-FIRST CENTURY

More generally, as the U.S. economy floundered and China continued to grow in the great recession of 2008–2009, Chinese authors launched "a flood of declinist commentary about the US." One expert claimed that the high point of U.S. power projection had been 2000.[6] The Chinese were not alone in such statements. In a 2009

Pew Research Center poll, majorities or pluralities in thirteen of twenty-five countries believed that China would replace the United States as the world's leading superpower.[7] Even the U.S. government's National Intelligence Council projected that American dominance would be "much diminished" by 2025. Russian president Dmitri Medvedev called the 2008 financial crisis a sign that America's global leadership was coming to an end, and even a sympathetic observer, Canadian opposition leader Michael Ignatieff, suggested that Canada should look beyond North America now that the "the noon hour of the United States and its global dominance are over."[8]

How can we know if they are correct or not? That question has fascinated me for two decades, and this book is the culmination of my exploring the sources and trajectory of American power. To answer the question, we need to understand better what we mean when we speak of power and how it is changing under the conditions of a burgeoning revolution in information technology and globalization in the twenty-first century. We also need to avoid certain pitfalls.

First, we must beware of misleading metaphors of organic decline. Nations are not like humans with predictable life spans. For example, after Britain lost its American colonies at the end of the eighteenth century, Horace Walpole lamented Britain's reduction to "as insignificant a country as Denmark or Sardinia."[9] He failed to foresee that the Industrial Revolution would give Britain a second century of even greater ascendency. Rome remained dominant for more than three centuries after the apogee of Roman power. Even then, Rome did not succumb to the rise of another state, but died a death of a thousand cuts inflicted by various barbarian tribes. Indeed, for all the fashionable predictions of China, India, or Brazil surpassing the United States in the next decades, the greater threats may come from modern barbarians and nonstate actors. Moreover, as we shall see, the classical transition of power among great states may be less of a problem than the rise of nonstate actors. In an information-based world of cyberinsecurity, power diffusion may be a greater threat than power transition.

At an even more basic level, what will it mean to wield power in the global information age of the twenty-first century? A second pitfall is to confuse power with the resources that states possess and to limit our focus solely to states. What resources will produce power? In the sixteenth century, control of colonies and gold bullion gave Spain the edge; in the seventeenth, the Netherlands profited from trade and finance; in the eighteenth, France gained from its larger population and armies; and in the nineteenth, Britain's power rested on the nation's primacy in the Industrial Revolution and on its navy. Conventional wisdom has always held that the state with the largest military prevails, but in an information age it may be the state (or nonstates) with the best story that wins.[10] As we shall see in Chapter 5, the Information Revolution and globalization are providing new power resources for nonstate actors. On September 11, 2001, a nonstate actor killed more people in New York than the state of Japan did at Pearl Harbor in 1941. This can be called the privatization of war. Today, it is far from clear how we measure a balance of power, much less how we develop successful strategies to survive in this new world. Most current projections of a shift in the global balance of power are based primarily on one factor— projections of growth in the gross national product of different countries. These projections ignore the other dimensions of power discussed in this book, not to mention the difficulties of combining the different dimensions into successful strategies.

SMART POWER

Smart power is the combination of the hard power of coercion and payment with the soft power of persuasion and attraction. Soft power is not the solution to all problems. Even though North Korean dictator Kim Jong-Il watched Hollywood movies, that had little effect on North Korea's nuclear weapons program. And soft power got nowhere in attracting the Taliban government away from its support for Al Qaeda in the 1990s. It took hard military power in 2001 to end that. To clarify that point, in my 2004 book *Soft Power: The Means to Success in World Politics* I introduced the term "smart power" to refer to the combining of hard and soft power into successful strategies. A few years later, Richard Armitage and I cochaired a bipartisan Smart Power Commission at the Center for Strategic and International Studies. It concluded that America's image and influence had declined in recent years, and that the United States had to move from exporting fear to inspiring optimism and hope.[11] The Smart Power Commission was not alone in this conclusion, and others have joined the call for smart power strategies.

The Pentagon is the best-trained and best-resourced arm of the American government, but there are limits to what military power can achieve on its own. Promoting democracy, human rights, and development of civil society are not best handled with the barrel of a gun. It is true that the American military has an impressive operational capacity, but the practice of turning to the Pentagon because it can get things done leads to an image of an overmilitarized foreign policy. Top military officials understand this. In the words of Admiral Mike Mullen, the chairman of the Joint Chiefs of Staff, "Secretaries Clinton and Gates have called for more funding and more emphasis on our soft power, and I could not agree with them more. Should we choose to exert American influence solely through our troops, we should expect to see that influence diminish in time."[12] Smart power is not simply "soft power 2.0." It refers to the ability to combine hard and soft power into effective strategies in varying contexts.

TWENTY-FIRST-CENTURY CONTEXTS

Power always depends on context. The child who dominates on the playground may become a laggard when the recess bell rings and the context changes to a well-ordered classroom. In the middle of the twentieth century, Josef Stalin scornfully asked how many divisions the pope had, but in the context of ideas five decades later the Papacy survived, whereas Stalin's empire had collapsed.

Today, power in the world is distributed in a pattern that resembles a complex three-dimensional chess game. On the top chessboard, military power is largely unipolar and the United States is likely to remain supreme for some time. But on the middle chessboard, economic power has been multipolar for more than a decade, with the United States, Europe, Japan, and China as the major players, and with others gaining in importance. Europe's economy is larger than America's. The bottom chessboard is the realm of transnational relations that cross borders outside of government control, and it includes nonstate actors as diverse as bankers electronically transferring sums larger than most national budgets at one extreme and terrorists transferring weapons or hackers threatening cybersecurity at the other. This chessboard also includes new transnational challenges such as pandemics and climate change. On this bottom board, power is widely diffused, and it makes no sense to speak here of unipolarity, multipolarity, hegemony, or any other such clichés that political leaders and pundits put in their speeches.

Two great power shifts are occurring in this century: a power transition among states and a power diffusion away from all states to nonstate actors. Even in the aftermath of the financial crisis, the giddy pace of technological change continues to drive globalization, but the political effects will be quite different for the world of nation-states and the world of nonstate actors. In interstate politics, the most important factor will be the continuing "return of Asia." In 1750, Asia had more than half of the world population and product. By 1900, after the Industrial Revolution in Europe and America, Asia's share shrank to one-fifth of the world product. By 2050, Asia will be well on its way back to its historical share. The "rise" in the power of China and India may create instability, but it is a problem with precedents, and we can learn from history about how our policies can affect the outcome. A century ago, Britain managed the rise of American power without conflict, but the world's failure to manage the rise of German power led to two devastating world wars.

In transnational politics—the bottom chessboard—the Information Revolution is dramatically reducing the costs of computing and communication. Forty years ago, instantaneous global communication was possible but costly, and it was restricted to governments and corporations. Today, this communication is virtually free to anyone with the means to enter an Internet café. The barriers to entry into world politics have been lowered, and nonstate actors now crowd the stage. Hackers and cybercriminals cause billions of dollars of damage to governments and businesses. A pandemic spread by birds or travelers on jet aircraft could kill more people than perished in World War I or II, and climate change could impose enormous costs. This is a new world politics with which we have less experience.

The problem for all states in the twenty-first century is that there are more and more things outside the control of even the most powerful states, because of the diffusion of power from states to nonstate actors. Although the United States does well on military measures, there is increasingly more going on in the world that those measures fail to capture. Under the influence of the Information Revolution and globalization, world politics is changing in a way that means Americans cannot achieve all their international goals acting alone. For example, international financial stability is vital to the prosperity of Americans, but the United States needs the cooperation of others to ensure it. Global climate change too will affect the quality of life, but the United States cannot manage the problem alone. And in a world where borders are becoming more porous than ever to everything from drugs to infectious diseases to terrorism, nations must mobilize international coalitions and build institutions to address shared threats and challenges. In this sense, power becomes a positive-sum game. It is not enough to think in terms of power *over* others. We must also think in terms of power *to* accomplish goals that involves power *with* others.[13] On many transnational issues, empowering others can help us to accomplish our own goals. In this world, networks and connectedness become an important source of relevant power.

Contextual intelligence, the ability to understand an evolving environment and capitalize on trends, will become a crucial skill in enabling leaders to convert power resources into successful strategies.[14] We will need contextual intelligence if we are to understand that the problem of American power in the twenty-first century is not one of decline, but of a failure to realize that even the largest country cannot achieve its aims without the help of others. That will require a deeper understanding of power, how it is changing, and how to construct smart power strategies. That will require a more sophisticated narrative than the classical stories of the rise and fall of great powers. America is likely to remain the strongest country of the twenty-first century, but that will not mean domination. The ability to get the outcomes we want will rest upon a new narrative of smart power. Americans will need to stop asking questions about who is number one, and entertaining narratives about dominance, and start asking questions about how the various tools of power can be combined into smart strategies for power *with* rather than merely *over* other nations. Thinking more clearly about power and stimulating that broader narrative are the purposes of this book.

I have tried to write a short book in a style that is accessible to the intelligent reader rather than aimed at an academic audience, but with a careful analytical structure disclosed in the footnotes. While I continue my exploration of the future of American power, I have tried to elaborate concepts in a way that are applicable to other countries as well. What are the problems of converting power resources into strategies that produce desired outcomes? What are the problems of "imperial overstretch" in international goals and "domestic underreach" in mobilizing resources? How can the two be brought into balance? How are the various dimensions of power changing in this century, and what does that change mean for the definition of strategic success? What will happen to American power or Chinese power or the power of nonstate actors in a cyberage? No one has the final word on the contested concept of power, but because we cannot avoid talking about it, I hope to introduce more clarity into the discussion and a larger perspective into strategic visions. That would be smart power.

PART I

TYPES OF POWER

CHAPTER 1

What Is Power in Global Affairs?

For a concept that is so widely used, "power" is surprisingly elusive and difficult to measure. But such problems do not make a concept meaningless. Few of us deny the importance of love even if we cannot say, "I love you 3.6 times more than I love something else." Like love, we experience power in our everyday lives, and it has real effects despite our inability to measure it precisely. Sometimes, analysts have been tempted to discard the concept as hopelessly vague and imprecise, but it has proven hard to replace.[1]

The great British philosopher Bertrand Russell once compared the role of power in social science to the centrality of the concept of "energy" in physics, but the comparison is misleading. Physicists can measure relations of energy and force among inanimate objects quite precisely, whereas power refers to more ephemeral human relationships that change shape under different circumstances.[2] Others have argued that power is to politics as money is to economics. Again, the metaphor misleads us. Money is a liquid or fungible resource. It can be used to buy a wide variety of goods, but the resources that produce power in one relationship or context may not produce it in another. You can use money in a housing market, at a vegetable market, or in an Internet auction, whereas military capacity, one of the most important international power resources, may produce the outcomes you want in a tank battle, but not on the Internet.

Over the years, various analysts have tried to provide formulas that can quantify power in international affairs. For example, Ray Cline was a high-ranking official in the CIA whose job was to tell political leaders about the balance of American and Soviet power during the Cold War. His views affected political decisions that involved high risks and billions of dollars. In 1977, he published a distillation of the formula he used for estimating power:

PERCEIVED POWER =
(POPULATION + TERRITORY + ECONOMY + MILITARY) × (STRATEGY + WILL)

After inserting numbers into his formula, he concluded that the Soviet Union was twice as powerful as the United States.[3] Of course, as we now know, this formula was not a very good predictor of outcomes. In a little more than a decade, the Soviet Union collapsed and pundits were proclaiming that the United States was the sole superpower in a unipolar world.

A more recent effort to create a power index included a country's resources (technology, enterprise, human, capital, physical) and national performance (external constraints, infrastructure, ideas) and how they determined military capability and combat proficiency.[4] This formulation tells us about relative military power, but not about all relevant types of power. Although effective military force remains one of the key power resources in international affairs, as we shall see in the next chapter, the world is no longer as unconstrained as in nineteenth-century Europe when historians could define a "great power" as one capable of prevailing in war.[5]

Military force and combat proficiency do not tell us much about outcomes, for example, in the world of finance or climate change.

Nor do they tell us much about the power of nonstate actors. In military terms, Al Qaeda is a midget compared to the American giant, but the impact of terrorists relies less on the size of their forces than on the theatrical effects of their actions and narratives and the overreactions they can produce. In that sense, terrorism is like the sport of jujitsu in which the weak player uses the strength of the larger against himself. This dynamic is not caught by typical indices of military power.

In certain bargaining situations, as Thomas Schelling demonstrates, weakness and the threat that a partner will collapse can be a source of bargaining power.[6] A bankrupt debtor who owes $1,000 has little power, but if it owes $1 billion, that debtor may have considerable bargaining power—witness the fate of institutions judged "too big to fail" in the 2008 financial crisis. North Korea's Kim Jong-Il "is probably the only world leader who can make Beijing look powerless. . . . Diplomats say Mr. Kim brazenly plays on Chinese fears. If the Chinese do not pump aid into his crumbling economy, he argues, they will face refugees pouring across the border and possible unrest."[7]

Any attempt to develop a single index of power is doomed to fail because power depends upon human relationships that vary in different contexts.[8] Whereas money can be used to measure purchasing power across different markets, there is no standard of value that can summarize all relationships and contexts to produce an agreed overall power total.[9]

DEFINING POWER

Like many basic ideas, power is a contested concept. No one definition is accepted by all who use the word, and people's choice of definition reflects their interests and values. Some define power as the ability to make or resist change. Others say it is the ability to get what we want.[10] This broad definition includes power over nature as well as over other people. For my interest in actions and policies, a commonsense place to start is the dictionary, which tells us that power is the capacity to do things and in social situations to affect others to get the outcomes we want.[11] Some people call this influence, and distinguish power from influence, but that is confusing because the dictionary defines the two terms as interchangeable.

There are many factors that affect our ability to get what we want. We live in a web of inherited social forces, some of which are visible and others of which are indirect and sometimes called "structural." We tend to identify and focus on some of these constraints and forces rather than others depending on our interests. For example, in his work on civilizations, political scientist Peter Katzenstein argues that the power of civilizations is different from power in civilizations. Actors in civilizations command hard and soft power. Social power operates beneath the behavioral level by shaping underlying social structures, knowledge systems and general environment.[12] Even though such structural social forces are important, for policy purposes we also want to understand what actors or agents can do within given situations.[13] Civilizations and societies are not immutable, and effective leaders can try to shape larger social forces with varying degrees of success. As the famous German theorist Max Weber puts it, we want to know the probability that an actor in a social relationship can carry out his own will.[14]

Even when we focus primarily on particular agents or actors, we cannot say that an actor "has power" without specifying power "to do what."[15] We must specify *who* is involved in the power relationship (the scope of power) as well as *what* topics are involved (the domain of power). For example, the pope has power over some Christians, but not over others (such as Protestants). And even among Catholics, he may wish to have power over all their moral decisions, but some adherents may reject his power on some issues (such as birth control or marriage outside the church). Thus, to say that the pope has power requires us to specify the context (scope and domain) of the relationship between the pope and any individual.

A psychopath may have the power to kill and destroy random strangers, but not the power to persuade them. Some actions that affect others and obtain preferred outcomes can be purely destructive and not dependent on what the victim thinks. For example, Pol Pot killed millions of Cambodian citizens. Some say such use of force is not power because there was no two-way relationship involved, but that depends on context and motive. If the actor's motive is pure sadism or terror, the use of force fits within the definition of power as affecting others to get what the actor wants. Most power relationships, however, depend very much on what the victim thinks. A dictator who wishes to punish a dissident may be misled in thinking he exercised power if the dissident really sought martyrdom to advance her cause. But if the dictator simply wanted to destroy the dissident, her intentions did not matter to his power.

Actions often have powerful unintended consequences, but from a policy point of view we are interested in the ability to produce preferred outcomes. If a North Atlantic Treaty Organization (NATO) soldier in Afghanistan kills a child by a stray bullet, he had the power to destroy but not to achieve his preferred outcome. An air strike that kills one insurgent and many civilians demonstrates a general power to destroy, but it may prove counterproductive for a counterinsurgency policy. The actions of a country with a large economy may have unintended effects that cause accidental harm (or wealth) in a small country.[16] Again, if the effects are unintended, then there is power to harm (or benefit), but it is not power to achieve preferred outcomes. Canadians often complain that living next to the United States is like sleeping with an elephant. From the Canadian point of view, intentions do not matter; it hurts if the beast rolls over. But from a policy-oriented perspective, intentions matter in terms of getting preferred outcomes.[17] A policy-oriented concept of power depends upon a specified context to tell us *who* gets *what, how, where,* and *when.*[18]

Practical politicians and ordinary people often find these questions of behavior and motivation too complicated and unpredictable.

Behavioral definitions judge power by outcomes that are determined after the action (what economists call "ex post") rather than before the action ("ex ante"). But policymakers want predictions about the future to help guide their actions. Thus, they frequently define power simply in terms of the resources that can produce outcomes. By this second definition of power as resources, a country is powerful if it has a relatively large population, territory, natural resources, economic strength, military force, and social stability. The virtue of this second definition is that it makes power appear to be concrete, measurable, and predictable—a guide to action. Power in this sense is like holding the high cards in a card game. But this definition has major problems. When people define power as synonymous with the resources that (may) produce outcomes, they often encounter the paradox that those best endowed with power do not always get the outcomes they want.

This is not to deny the importance of power resources. Power is conveyed through resources, whether tangible or intangible. People notice resources. If you show the highest cards in a poker game, others may fold their hands rather than challenge you. But power resources that win in one game may not help at all in another. Holding a strong poker hand does not win if the game is bridge. Even if the game is poker, if you play your high hand poorly, or fall victim to bluff and deception, you can still lose. Power conversion—getting from resources to behavioral outcomes—is a crucial intervening variable. Having the resources of power does not guarantee that you will always get the outcome you want. For example, in terms of resources, the United States was far more powerful than Vietnam, yet lost the war. Converting resources into realized power in the sense of obtaining desired outcomes requires well-designed strategies and skillful leadership—what I call smart power. Yet strategies are often inadequate and leaders frequently misjudge.

Nonetheless, defining power in terms of resources is a shortcut that policymakers find useful. In general, a country that is well endowed with power resources is more likely to affect a weaker country and be less dependent upon an optimal strategy than vice versa. Smaller countries may sometimes obtain preferred outcomes because they pick smaller fights or focus selectively on a few issues. On average, and in direct conflicts, we would not expect Finland to prevail over Russia.[19]

As a first step in any game, it helps to start by figuring out who is holding the high cards and how many chips that player has. Equally important, however, is that policymakers have the contextual intelligence to understand what game they are playing. Which resources provide the best basis for power behavior in a particular context? Oil was not an impressive power resource before the industrial age, nor was uranium significant before the nuclear age. In traditional realist views of international affairs, war was the ultimate game in which the cards of international politics were played. When all the cards were on the table, estimates of relative power were proven and disproven. But over the centuries, as technologies evolved, the sources of strength for war often changed. Moreover, on an increasing number of issues in the twenty-first century, war is not the ultimate arbiter.

As a result, many analysts reject the "elements of national power" approach as misleading and inferior to the behavioral or relational approach that became dominant among social science analysis in the latter half of the twentieth century. Strictly speaking, the skeptics are correct. Power resources are simply the tangible and intangible raw materials or vehicles that underlie power relationships, and whether a given set of resources produces preferred outcomes or not depends upon behavior in context. The vehicle is not the power relationship.[20] Knowing the horsepower and mileage of a vehicle does not tell us whether it will get to the preferred destination.

In practice, discussions of power in global affairs involve both definitions.[21] Many of the terms that we use daily, such as "military power" and "economic power," are hybrids that combine both resources and behaviors. So long as that is the case, we must make clear whether we are speaking of behavioral- or resource-based definitions

FIGURE 1.1 Power as Resources and Power as Behavioral Outcomes

POWER DEFINED AS RESOURCES

context   skill

Power = resources → conversion strategy → preferred outcomes

POWER DEFINED AS BEHAVIORAL OUTCOMES

Power = affect others → re: something → by means → to preferred outcomes

            (scope)   (domain)   (coercion, reward, attraction)

of power, and we must be aware of the imperfect relation between them. For example, when people speak of the rising power of China or India, they tend to point to the large populations and increased economic or military resources of those countries. But whether the capacity that those resources imply can actually be converted into preferred outcomes will depend upon the contexts and the country's skill in converting resources into strategies that will produce preferred outcomes. These different definitions are summarized in Figure 1.1. The figure also illustrates the more careful relational definition in which power is the ability to alter others' behavior to produce preferred outcomes.

This is what people are getting at when they say things like "Power doesn't necessarily lead to influence" (though for reasons already explained, that formulation is confusing).

In the end, because it is outcomes, not resources, that we care about, we must pay more attention to contexts and strategies. Power-conversion strategies turn out to be a critical variable that does not receive enough attention. Strategies relate means to ends, and those that combine hard and soft power resources successfully in different contexts are the key to smart power.

THREE ASPECTS OF RELATIONAL POWER

In addition to the distinction between resource and relational definitions of power, it is useful to distinguish three different aspects of relational power: commanding change, controlling agendas, and establishing preferences. All too often these are conflated. For example, a recent book on foreign policy defines power as "getting people or groups to do something they don't want to do."[22] But such a narrow approach can lead to mistakes.

The ability to command others to change their behavior against their initial preferences is one important dimension of relational power, but not the only one. Another dimension is the ability to affect others' preferences so that they want what you want and you need not command them to change. Former president (and general) Dwight Eisenhower referred to this as getting people to do something "not only because you tell them to do so, but because they instinctively want to do it for you."[23] This co-optive power contrasts with and complements command power. It is a mistake to think that power consists of just ordering others to change. You can affect their behavior by shaping their preferences in ways that produce what you want rather than relying on carrots and sticks to change their behavior "when push comes to shove." Sometimes you can get the outcomes you want without pushing or shoving. Ignoring this dimension by using a too narrow definition of power can lead to a poorly shaped foreign policy.

The first aspect, or "face," of power was defined by Yale political scientist Robert Dahl in studies of New Haven in the 1950s, and it is widely used today even though it covers only part of power behavior.[24] This face of power focuses on the ability to get others to act in ways that are contrary to their initial preferences and strategies. To measure or judge power, you have to know how strong another person's or nation's initial preferences were and how much they were changed by your efforts. Coercion can be quite clear in a situation in which there appears to be some degree of choice. If a man holding a gun on you says, "Your money or your life," you have some choice, but it is small and not consistent with your initial preferences (unless they included suicide or martyrdom).[25] When Czechoslovakia succumbed to German and Soviet troops entering

Prague in 1938 and again in 1968, it was not because that country wanted to.

Economic measures are somewhat more complex. Negative sanctions (taking away economic benefit) are clearly felt as coercive. Payment or economic inducement to do what you initially did not want to may seem more attractive to the subject, but any payment can easily be turned into a negative sanction by the implicit or explicit threat of its removal. A year-end bonus is a reward, but its removal is felt as a penalty. Moreover, in unequal bargaining relationships, say, between a millionaire landowner and a starving peasant, a paltry "take it or leave it" payment may give the peasant little sense of choice. The important point is that someone has the capacity to make others act against their initial preferences and strategies, and both sides feel that power.

In the 1960s, shortly after Dahl developed his widely accepted definition, political scientists Peter Bachrach and Morton Baratz pointed out that Dahl's definition missed what they called the "second face of power." Dahl ignored the dimension of framing and agenda-setting.[26] If ideas and institutions can be used to frame the agenda for action in a way that make others' preferences seem irrelevant or out of bounds, then it may never be necessary to push or shove them. In other words, it may be possible to shape others' preferences by affecting their expectations of what is legitimate or feasible. Agenda-framing focuses on the ability to keep issues off the table, or as Sherlock Holmes might put it, dogs that fail to bark.

Powerful actors can make sure that the less powerful are never invited to the table, or if they get there, the rules of the game have already been set by those who arrived first. International financial policy had this characteristic, at least before the crisis of 2008 opened things up somewhat when the Group of 8 (G-8) was supplemented by the Group of 20 (G-20). Those who are subject to this second face of power may or may not be aware of it. If they accept the legitimacy of the institutions or the social discourse that framed the agenda, they may not feel unduly constrained by the second face of power. But if the agenda of action is constrained by threats of coercion or promises of payments, then it is just an instance of the first face of power. The target's acquiescence in the legitimacy of the agenda is what makes this face of power co-optive and partly constitutive of soft power—the ability to get what you want by the co-optive means of framing the agenda, persuading, and eliciting positive attraction.

Still later, in the 1970s, sociologist Steven Lukes pointed out that ideas and beliefs also help shape others' *initial* preferences.[27] In Dahl's approach, I can exercise power over you by getting you to do what you would otherwise not want to do; in other words, by changing your situation, I can make you change your preferred strategy. But I can also exercise power over you by determining your very wants. I can shape your basic or initial preferences, not merely change the situation in a way that makes you change your strategy for achieving your preferences.

This dimension of power is missed by Dahl's definition. A teenage boy may carefully choose a fashionable shirt to wear to school to attract a girl, but the teenager may not be aware that the reason the shirt is so fashionable is that a national retailer recently launched a major advertising campaign. Both his preference and that of the other teenagers have been formed by an unseen actor who has shaped the structure of preferences. If you can get others to want the same outcomes that you want, it will not be necessary to override their initial desires. Lukes called this the "third face of power."[28]

There are critical questions of voluntarism in determining how freely people chose their preferences.[29] Not all soft power looks so soft to outside critics. In some extreme cases, it is difficult to ascertain what constitutes voluntary formation of preferences. For instance, in the "Stockholm syndrome," victims of kidnapping who suffered traumatic stress began to identify with their abductors. Captors sometimes try to "brainwash" their captives and sometimes try to win them over with kindnesses.[30] But in some situations, it is more difficult to be certain of others' interests. Are Afghan women

TABLE 1.1 Three Aspects of Relational Power

FIRST FACE: A uses threats or rewards to change B's behavior against B's initial preferences and strategies. B knows this and feels the effect of A's power.

SECOND FACE: A controls the agenda of actions in a way that limits B's choices of strategy. B may or may not know this and be aware of A's power.

THIRD FACE: A helps to create and shape B's basic beliefs, perceptions, and preferences. B is unlikely to be aware of this or to realize the effect of A's power.

---

oppressed when they choose to wear a burka? What about women who choose to wear a veil in democratic France?[31] Sometimes it is difficult to know the extent of voluntarism from mere outward appearances. Dictators such as Adolf Hitler and Stalin tried to create an aura of invincibility to attract followers, and some leaders in southeastern European countries succumbed to this effect. To the extent that force creates a sense of awe that attracts others, it can be an indirect source of co-optive power, but if the force is directly coercive, then it is simply an instance of the first face of power.

Some theorists have called these the public, hidden, and invisible faces of power, reflecting the degrees of difficulty that the target has in discovering the source of power.[32] The second and third faces embody aspects of structural power. A structure is simply an arrangement of all the parts of a whole. Humans are embedded in complex structures of culture, social relations, and power that affect and constrain them. A person's field of action is "delimited by actors with whom he has no interaction or communication, by actions distant in time and space, by actions of which he is, in no explicit sense the target."[33] Some exercises of power reflect the intentional decisions of particular actors, whereas others are the product of unintended consequences and larger social forces.

For example, why do large automobiles dominate our city streets? In part the answer reflects individual consumer choices, but these consumer preferences are themselves shaped by a social history of advertising, manufacturers' decisions, tax incentives, public transport policy, road-building subsidies, and urban planning.[34] Different choices on these issues by many visible as well as unseen past actors confront an urban resident today with a limited set of choices.

In 1993, Bill Clinton's political adviser James Carville is alleged to have joked that he wished he could be reborn as the bond market because then he would have real power.[35] When we speak of the power of markets, we are referring to a form of structural power. A wheat farmer who wants to earn more income to pay for his daughter's college tuition may decide to plant more wheat. But if other farmers plant more as well (and demand does not change), market forces may reduce his income and affect her educational prospects. In a perfect market, the agent has no pricing power. Millions of other unseen agents making independent choices create the supply and demand that determine the price. This is why poor countries that produce commodities are often subject to wide variations in their terms of trade. But if an agent can find a way to change the structure of a market by introducing an element of monopoly (a single seller) or monopsony (a single buyer), she can gain some power over price. She can do this by differentiating her product through advertising, creating brand loyalty, picking a special location, and so forth. Or in the case of oil-producing countries, agents can try to form a cartel like the Organization of Petroleum-Exporting Countries (OPEC).

Different analysts cut into the complex pattern of causation and draw the line between individual choice and larger structures at different places. For example, sociologists tend to focus less on specific actions and outcomes than political scientists do.[36] Analysts who focus only on individual agents, as the first face of power tends to do, are clearly failing to understand and describe power relationships fully. But those who focus only on broad social forces and longer historical perspective, as the second and third faces of power tend to do, pay too little attention to the individual choices and intentions that are crucial in policy. Some critics have called my approach too "agent centered," but it still allows some consideration of structural forces even if it does not include all aspects of structure.[37]

Some analysts regard these distinctions as useless abstractions that can all be collapsed into the first face of power.[38] If we succumb to this temptation, however, we are likely to limit what we see in terms of behavior, which tends to limit the strategies that policy-makers design to achieve their goals. Command power (the first face) is very visible and readily grasped. It is the basis for hard power—the ability to get desired outcomes through coercion and payment. The co-optive power of faces two and three is more subtle and therefore less visible. It contributes to soft power, the ability to get preferred outcomes through the co-optive means of agenda-setting, persuasion, and attraction. All too often policymakers have focused solely on hard command power to compel others to act against their preferences and have ignored the soft power that comes from preference formation. But when co-opting is possible, policymakers can save on carrots and sticks.[39]

In global politics, some goals that states seek are more susceptible to the second and third than to the first face of power. Arnold Wolfers once distinguished between what he called possession goals—specific and often tangible objectives—and milieu goals, which are often structural and intangible.[40] For example, access to resources or basing rights or a trade agreement is a possession goal, whereas promoting an open trade system, free markets, democracy, or human rights is a milieu goal. In the terminology used previously, we can think of states having specific goals and general or structural goals. Focusing solely on command power and the first face of power may mislead us about how to promote such goals. For example, in the promotion of democracy, military means alone are less successful than military means combined with soft power approaches—as the United States discovered in Iraq. And the soft power of attraction and persuasion can have both agentic and structural dimensions. For example, a country can try to attract others through actions such as public diplomacy, but it may also attract others through the structural effects of its example or what can be called the "shining city on the hill" effect.

Another reason not to collapse all three faces of power into the first is that doing so diminishes attention to networks, which are an important type of structural power in the twenty-first century. Networks are becoming increasingly important in an information age, and positioning in social networks can be an important power resource. For example, in a hub-and-spokes network, power can derive from being the hub of communications. If you communicate with your other friends through me, that gives me power. If the points on the rim are not directly connected to each other, their dependence on communication through the hub can shape their agenda. For example, even after independence, many communications among former French African colonies ran through Paris, and that increased French power to shape their agenda.

In other more complex network arrangements, theorists point to the importance of structural holes that prevent direct communication between certain parts of the network.[41] Those who can bridge or exploit structural holes can use their position as a source of power by controlling communication between others. Another aspect of networks that is relevant to power is their extensiveness. Even weak extensive ties can be useful in acquiring and disseminating novel and innovative information. Weak ties provide the ability to link diverse groups together in a cooperative, successful manner.[42] This increases a country's ability to gain power with, rather than over, others. The ability to create networks of trust that enable groups to work together toward common goals is what economist Kenneth Boulding calls "integrative power."[43] According to psychologists, "Years of research suggest that empathy and social intelligence are vastly more important to acquiring and exercising power than are force, deception, or terror."[44]

Political theorist Hannah Arendt once said that "power springs up among men when they act together."[45] Similarly, a state can wield global power by engaging and acting together with other states, not merely acting against them. Princeton political scientist John Ikenberry argues that American power after World War II rested on a network of institutions that constrained the United States but were open to others and thus increased America's power to act with others.[46] This is an important point in assessing the power of nations in the current international system and an important dimension for assessing the future of American and Chinese power in the twenty-first century.[47] For example, if the United States is involved in more communication networks, it has a greater opportunity to shape preferences in terms of the third face of power.

For policy purposes, it can be useful to think of the three faces of power in a reverse sequence from the order in which they were invented by social scientists. A policymaker should consider preference formation and agenda-framing as means of shaping the environment before turning to the first, or command, face of power.[48] In short, those who insist on collapsing the second and third dimensions of power into the first will miss an increasingly important aspect of power in this century.

REALISM AND THE FULL SPECTRUM OF POWER BEHAVIOR

In the United States, the tendency to focus on the first face of power is partly a reflection of American political culture and institutions. No politician wants to appear "soft," and Congress finds it easier to boost the budget of the Pentagon than that of the State Department. That bias has been reinforced by prevailing theories of international politics. For centuries, the dominant classical approach to international affairs has been called "realism," and its lineage stretches back to such great thinkers as Thucydides and Niccolò

Machiavelli. Realism assumes that in the anarchic conditions of world politics, where there is no higher international government authority above states, they must rely on their own devices to preserve their independence, and that when push comes to shove, the ultima ratio is the use of force. Realism portrays the world in terms of sovereign states aiming to preserve their security, with military force as their ultimate instrument. Thus, war has been a constant aspect of international affairs over the centuries. Realists come in many sizes and shapes, but all tend to argue that global politics is power politics. In this they are right, but some limit their understanding by conceiving of power too narrowly. A pragmatic or commonsense realist takes into account the full spectrum of power resources, including ideas, persuasion, and attraction. Many classical realists of the past understood the role of soft power better than some of their modern progeny.

Realism represents a good first cut at portraying some aspects of international relations. But as we have seen, states are no longer the only important actors in global affairs; security is not the only major outcome that they seek, and force is not the only or always the best instrument available to achieve those outcomes. Indeed, these conditions of complex interdependence are typical of relations among advanced postindustrial countries such as the United States, Canada, Europe, Australia, and Japan. Mutual democracy, liberal culture, and a deep network of transnational ties mean that anarchy has very different effects than realism predicts. In such conditions, a smart power strategy has a much higher mixture of the second and third faces of power.

It is not solely in relations among advanced countries, however, that soft power plays an important role. In an information age, communications strategies become more important, and outcomes are shaped not merely by whose army wins but also by whose story wins. In the fight against terrorism, for example, it is essential to have a narrative that appeals to the mainstream and prevents its recruitment by radicals. In the battle against insurgencies, kinetic military force must be accompanied by soft power instruments that help to win over the hearts and minds (shape the preferences) of the majority of the population.

Smart strategies must have an information and communications component. States struggle over the power to define norms, and framing of issues grows in importance. For instance, CNN and the BBC framed the issues of the First Gulf War in 1991, but by 2003 Al Jazeera was playing a large role in shaping the narrative in the Iraq War. Such framing is more than mere propaganda. In describing events in March 2003, we could say that American troops "entered Iraq" or that American troops "invaded Iraq." Both statements are true, but they have very different effects in terms of the power to shape preferences. Similarly, if we think of international institutions, it makes a difference if agendas are set in a Group of 8 with a few invited guests or in a Group of 20 equal invitees. These are just some examples of how the dimensions of the second and third faces of power are becoming more important in the global politics of an information age.

SOFT POWER BEHAVIOR AND RESOURCES

Some critics complain that the prevailing definition of soft power has become fuzzy through its expansion "to include both economic statecraft—used as both a carrot and as a stick—and even military power. . . . Soft power now seems to mean everything."[49] But these critics are mistaken because they confuse the actions of a state seeking to achieve desired outcomes with the resources used to produce them. Many types of *resources* can contribute to soft power, but that does not mean that soft power is any type of *behavior*. The use of force, payment, and some agenda-setting based on them I call hard power. Agenda-setting that is regarded as legitimate by the target, positive attraction, and persuasion are the parts of the spectrum of behaviors I include in soft power. Hard power is push; soft power is pull. Fully defined, soft power is the ability to affect others through the co-optive means of framing the agenda, persuading, and eliciting positive attraction in order to obtain preferred outcomes.[50]

Here is a representation of a spectrum of power behaviors:[51]

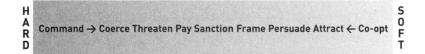

H
A   Command → Coerce Threaten Pay Sanction Frame Persuade Attract ← Co-opt
R
D

S
O
F
T

In general, the types of resources associated with hard power include tangibles such as force and money. The types of resources associated with soft power often include intangible factors such as institutions, ideas, values, culture, and the perceived legitimacy of policies. But the relationship is not perfect. Intangible resources such as patriotism, morale, and legitimacy strongly affect the military capacity to fight and win. And threats to use force are intangible, even though they are a dimension of hard power.[52]

If we remember the distinction between power resources and power behavior, we realize that the resources often associated with hard power behavior can also produce soft power behavior depending on the context and how they are used. Command power can create resources that in turn can create soft power at a later phase— for example, institutions that will provide soft power resources in the future. Similarly, co-optive behavior can be used to generate hard power resources in the form of military alliance or economic aid. A tangible hard power resource such as a military unit can produce both command behavior (by winning a battle) and co-optive behavior (by attracting) depending on how it is used. And because attraction depends upon the mind of the perceiver, the subject's perceptions play a significant role in whether given resources produce hard or soft power behavior.

For example, naval forces can be used to win battles (hard power) or win hearts and minds (soft power) depending on what the target and what the issue are. The U.S. Navy's help in providing relief to

Indonesia after the 2004 East Asian tsunami had a strong effect on increasing Indonesians' attraction to the United States, and the U.S. Navy's 2007 Maritime Strategy referred not only to war-fighting but also to "maritime forces . . . employed to build confidence and trust among nations."[53] Similarly, successful economic performance such as that of China can produce both the hard power of sanctions and restricted market access and the soft power of attraction and emulation of success.

Some analysts have misinterpreted soft power as a synonym for culture and then gone on to downgrade its importance. For example, the historian Niall Ferguson describes soft power as "nontraditional forces such as cultural and commercial goods" and then dismisses it on the grounds that "it's, well, soft."[54] Of course, eating at McDonald's or wearing a Michael Jackson shirt does not automatically indicate soft power. Militias can perpetrate atrocities or fight Americans while wearing Nikes and drinking Coca-Cola. But this criticism confuses the resources that may produce behavior with the behavior itself. Whether the possession of power resources actually produces favorable behavior depends upon the context and the skills of the agent in converting the resources into behavioral outcomes. Eating sushi, trading Pokemon cards, or hiring a Japanese pitcher (as the Boston Red Sox did) does not necessarily convey power to Japan. But this is not unique to soft power resources. Having a larger tank army may produce victory if a battle is fought in a desert, but not if it is fought in a swamp. Similarly, a nice smile can be a soft power resource, and you may be more inclined to do something for me if I smile whenever we meet, but if I smile at your mother's funeral, it may destroy soft power rather than create it.

SOFT POWER AND SMART POWER

As mentioned in the Preface, I developed the term "smart power" in 2004 to counter the misperception that soft power alone can produce effective foreign policy. I defined smart power as the ability to combine hard and soft power resources into effective strategies.[55] Unlike soft power, smart power is an evaluative as well as a descriptive concept. Soft power can be good or bad from a normative perspective, depending on how it is used. Smart power has the evaluation built into the definition. Critics who say "smart power—which can be dubbed Soft Power 2.0—has superseded Soft Power 1.0 in the U.S. foreign policy lexicon" are simply mistaken.[56] A more accurate criticism is that because the concept (unlike that of soft power) has a normative dimension, it often lends itself to slogans, though that need not be the case.

Smart power is available to all states (and nonstate actors), not just the United States. For example, as we will see in Chapter 7, small states have often developed smart power strategies. Norway, with 5 million people, has enhanced its attractiveness with legitimizing policies in peacemaking and development assistance, while also being an active and effective participant in NATO. And at the other extreme in terms of population size, China, a rising power in economic and military resources, has deliberately decided to invest in soft power resources so as to make its hard power look less threatening to its neighbors and thus develop a smart strategy.

Smart power goes to the heart of the problem of power conversion. As we saw earlier, some countries and actors may be endowed with greater power resources than others, yet not be very effective in converting the full range of their power resources into strategies that produce the outcomes they seek. Some argue that with an inefficient eighteenth-century government structure, the United States is weak in power conversion. Others respond that much of American strength is generated outside of government by the nation's open economy and civil society. And it may be that power conversion is easier when a country has a surplus of assets and can afford to absorb the costs of mistakes. But the first steps to smart power and effective power-conversion strategies are understanding the full range of power resources and recognizing the problems of combining them effectively in various contexts.

Hard and soft power sometimes reinforce and sometimes undercut each other, and good contextual intelligence is important in distinguishing how they interact in different situations. But it is a
mistake to think of information campaigns in terms that misunder-
stand the essence of soft power. If we had to choose between having
military or having soft power in world politics, we would opt for
military power. But smart power suggests it is best to have both.
"The military has to understand that soft power is more challenging
to wield in terms of the application of military force—particularly
if what that force is doing is not seen as attractive."[57] If the levers of
soft power are not pulling in the same direction, then the military
often cannot create favorable conditions on its own.

Early in 2006, Secretary of Defense Donald Rumsfeld said of the
Bush administration's global war on terror, "In this war, some of the
most critical battles may not be in the mountains of Afghanistan or
the streets of Iraq but in newsrooms in New York, London, Cairo
and elsewhere." As *The Economist* commented about Rumsfeld's
speech, "Until recently he plainly regarded such a focus on 'soft
power' as, well, soft—part of 'Old Europe's' appeasement of terrorism." Now he realized the importance of winning hearts and
minds, but "a good part of his speech was focused on how with
slicker PR America could win the propaganda war."[58] Unfortunately, Rumsfeld forgot the first rule of advertising: If you have a
poor product, not even the best advertising will sell it. He also forgot that the administration's poor power-conversion strategy was
wasting both hard and soft power assets. The first step toward developing more effective smart power strategies starts with a fuller
understanding of the types and uses of power.

CHAPTER 2

Military Power

When most people speak or write about military power, they tend to think in terms of the resources that underlie the hard power behavior of fighting and threatening to fight—soldiers, tanks, planes, ships, and so forth. In the end, if push comes to shove, such military resources matter. Napoleon famously said that "God is on the side of the big battalions."

But military power needs a closer look. There is much more to military resources than guns and battalions and more to military behavior than fighting or threatening to fight. Military power resources have long been used to provide protection to allies and assistance to friends. Even the behavior of fighting on behalf of friends can engender soft power. As we saw in the last chapter, noncoercive and benign uses of military resources can be an important source of the soft power behavior of framing of agendas, persuasion, and attraction in world politics.

Even when thinking only of fighting and threats, many people envisage interstate war between soldiers in uniforms, organized and equipped by the state in formal military units. But so far in the twenty-first century, more "wars" occur within, rather than between, states and many combatants do not wear uniforms.[1] Of course, civil war and irregular combatants are not new, as even the traditional law of war recognizes. What are new in this century are the increase in irregular conflict and the technological changes that increase vulnerabilities and put destructive power in the hands of small groups of nonstate actors that would have been priced out of the market for major destruction in earlier eras. And now technology has brought a new dimension to warfare: the prospects of cyberattacks. As we will discuss in Chapter 5, an enemy—state or non-state—can create enormous physical destruction (or threaten to do so) without an army that physically crosses another state's border.

FIGHTING AND WAR

Two and a half millennia ago, in explaining why the generals of Athens intended to capture the island of Melos and slay or enslave the inhabitants, Thucydides remarked, "The strong do as they will and the weak suffer what they must."[2] War and the use of force are endemic in human history. Indeed, political history is often told as a story of war and conquest. But as the Bible asks in Psalms 2:1–2, "Why do the nations so furiously rage together?"

One answer is human nature. Anthropologists describe chimpanzees (with whom we share nearly 99 percent of our genome) using force against each other and against other bands of chimpanzees.[3] Some classical realists stress greed as a motive. Others stress the desire for domination.[4] Great conquerors such as Genghis Khan, who swept across the Central Asian plain, or Spanish conquistadores in the Americas such as Hernán Cortés and Francisco Pizarro probably had a mixture of both motives. But ideas also play a role in organizing people for war and conquest, such as the expansion of Islam in the century after Mohammed's death, the medieval Christian Crusades, or nationalism and self-determination after the nineteenth century.

War shaped great empires as well as the state system of modern Europe, but it is important to remember that the hard coercive power generated by military resources is usually accompanied by some degree of soft power. As philosopher David Hume pointed out in the eighteenth century, no human is strong enough to dominate all others acting alone.[5] A tyrant has to have enough soft power to attract henchmen to enable him to use coercion on a large scale. Rome's long-lasting empire, for instance, reinforced its military conquests with ideology and attracted conquered barbarians by offering them opportunities to become Roman citizens.[6] One problem with military resources, including soldiers, is that they are costly and the cost of their transportation increases with distance. Locals are cheaper if they can be co-opted.

A novel technology, such as the stirrup in the case of Genghis Khan or the gun for the conquistadores, can provide leverage that allows a small number to prevail over a larger group until the technology spreads. In the nineteenth century, Sir Harry Johnson conquered Nyasaland (today's Malawi) with a handful of troops. In India, fewer than 100,000 British soldiers and administrators ruled 300 million Indians. But the secret of this success was more than technology. It included the ability to divide the targeted population and to co-opt some of them into becoming local allies. Similarly, the spread of Islam was based on the attraction of belief, not just the force of the sword. Today's military counterinsurgency doctrine stresses the importance of winning the hearts and minds of the population. In understanding military power, we must realize that explanations of success rest on more than the famous nineteenth-century aphorism "We have the Gatling gun and they have not."

A modern school of realism emphasizes not human nature, but the structure of international politics.[7] The structural approach stresses the anarchic nature of international politics and the fact that there is no higher authority above states to which they can appeal. They are in the realm of self-help, and military resources provide the most help. Motives such as greed or domination are less important than security and a simple desire to survive. States are caught in a zero-sum game where it is rational to fend for themselves because they cannot trust others. If an actor disarms and others do not, the actor is not likely to survive in anarchic conditions. Those who are benevolent and trusting tend to disappear over time. They are weeded out by the dynamics engendered by the structure of the system. The path to security and survival for the actor is to develop its own military resources through growth and to form alliances to balance the power of others. In this world, gains relative to others are more important than absolute gains.

Whether rooted in human nature as in the classic realism of Thucydides and Machiavelli or in the larger systemic forces stressed by modern structural realism, military resources that provide the ability to prevail in war are conventionally portrayed as the most important form of power in global affairs. Indeed, in the nineteenth century the definition of a great power was the ability to prevail in war, and certainly war persists today. But as we saw in the last chapter, the world has become more complex since the nineteenth century, and the realist model does not fit all parts equally.

British diplomat Robert Cooper argues that there are at least three different domains—postindustrial, industrializing, and preindustrial—of interstate relations, with war playing a different role in each. For the postindustrial world of advanced democracies, war is no longer a major instrument in their relations with each other. In this world, theorists correctly assert that it is almost impossible to find instances of advanced liberal democracies fighting each other.[8] Instead, they are locked in a politics of complex interdependence in which other tools are used in power struggles. This does not mean that advanced democracies do not go to war with other states or that fragile new democracies cannot go to war with each other.[9] And for newly industrializing states such as China and India, war remains a potential instrument, as realists would predict. Similarly, among preindustrial societies, including much of Africa and the Middle East, the realist model remains a good fit. So the twenty-first-century answer to the question "Is military power the most important form of power in world politics?" depends upon the context. In much of the world, the answer is yes, but not in all domains or on all issues.

HAS THE UTILITY OF MILITARY POWER DIMINISHED OVER TIME?

States obviously use military force today, but the past half-century has seen changes in its role. Many states, particularly large ones, find it more costly to use military force to achieve their goals than was true in earlier times. In projecting the future, the National Intelligence Council (the body that prepares estimates for the American president) argues that the utility of military force is declining in the twenty-first century.[10]

What are the reasons? One is that the ultimate means of military force—the nuclear arsenals of the major powers—are musclebound. Although once numbering more than 50,000, nuclear weapons have not been used in war since 1945. The disproportion between the vast devastation nuclear weapons can inflict and any reasonable political goals has made leaders of states understandably loath to employ them. So the ultimate form of military force is for all practical purposes too costly—in terms of both a moral taboo and risk of retaliation—for national leaders to use in war.[11]

This does not mean that nuclear weapons play no role in world politics. Indeed, terrorists may not feel bound by the nuclear taboo.[12] And even if it is difficult to use nuclear weapons to compel others, deterrence remains both credible and important. It includes the ability to extend deterrence to others, for example, by the United States to allies such as Europe and Japan. Smaller states such as North Korea and Iran seek nuclear weapons to deter the United States and to increase their regional influence and global prestige, but they are not equalizers in world politics. And under some conditions, if they trigger decisions by other countries to proliferate, they may reduce security by increasing the prospect of a nuclear weapon being released without full central control or falling into the hands of terrorists. Thus far, however, the taboo against state use of nuclear weapons has lasted for six decades. Nuclear weapons remain important in world politics, but not for war-fighting.

A second reason is that conventional force has become more costly when used to rule nationalistic and socially mobilized populations. Occupation helps to unite what under other circumstances would be disparate populations. Foreign rule is very costly in an age of broad social communication. Already in the last century, print media and mass communication allowed local peoples to broaden their awareness and identities to what have been called "imaginary communities," and the age of the Internet has extended this even further.[13] France conquered Algeria with 34,000 troops in the nineteenth century but could not hold the colony with 600,000 troops in the twentieth century.[14] The instruments, such as car bombs and improvised explosives, available to mobilized insurgents are far cheaper than those used by occupying armies. And there is a high correlation between the use of suicide bombers and occupation by foreign forces.[15]

A third reason is that the use of military force faces internal constraints. Over time there has been a growing ethic of antimilitarism, particularly in democracies. Such attitudes are stronger in Europe or Japan than in the United States, but they are present in all advanced democracies. Such views do not prevent the use of force, but they make it a politically risky choice for leaders, particularly when its use is large or prolonged. It is sometimes said that democracies will not accept casualties, but that is too simple. The United States, for example, expected some 10,000 casualties when it planned to enter the Gulf War in 1990, but it was loath to accept casualties in Somalia or Kosovo, where its national interests were less deeply involved. Moreover, the willingness to accept casualties is affected by the prospects of success.[16] And if the use of force is seen as unjust or illegitimate in the eyes of other nations, this can make it costly for political leaders in democratic polities. Force is not obsolete, and terrorist nonstate actors are less constrained than states by such moral concerns, but force is more costly and more difficult for most states to use than in the past.

Finally, a number of issues simply do not lend themselves to forceful solutions. Take, for example, economic relations between the United States and Japan. In 1853, Commodore Matthew Perry sailed into the Japanese port of Shimoda and threatened bombardment unless Japan opened its ports to trade. This would not be a very useful or politically acceptable way to solve current U.S.-Japan trade disputes. Today, China has become the leading greenhouse gas producer and is adding a new coal-burning plant each week. But the idea of threatening to use bombs or cruise missiles to destroy such plants lacks credibility, even though their output can be harmful to other countries. The scope and scale of economic globalization and complex interdependence are very different today from the nineteenth century.

Even though force remains a critical instrument in international politics, it is not the only instrument. The use of economic interdependence, communication, international institutions, and transnational actors sometimes plays a larger role than force. Military force is not obsolete as a state instrument—witness the fighting in Afghanistan, where the United States removed the Taliban government that had sheltered the terrorist network that carried out the September 2001 attacks on the United States, or the American and British use of force to overthrow Saddam Hussein in 2003. But it was easier to win the initial war against a government than to win the peace against nonstate insurgents in either instance. Moreover, military force alone is not sufficient to protect against terrorism. Before 9/11, a key Al Qaeda cell existed in Hamburg, but bombing Hamburg was not an option. Although military force remains an important instrument in international politics, changes in its cost and effectiveness make today's calculations of military power more complex than in the past.

THE CHANGING SHAPE OF WAR

War and force may be down, but they are not out. Instead, the use of force is taking new forms. Some military theorists have written about "fourth-generation warfare," which sometimes has "no definable battlefields or fronts" and in which the distinction between civilian and military may disappear.[17] According to this view, the first generation of modern warfare reflected the tactics of line and column following the French Revolution. The second generation relied on massed firepower and culminated in World War I; its slogan was that artillery conquers and then infantry occupies. The third generation of maneuver arose from tactics that the Germans developed to break the stalemate of trench warfare in 1918 and that they later perfected in the blitzkrieg tactics that allowed them to defeat larger French and British tank forces in the conquest of France in 1940. Both ideas and technology drove the changes. The same is true for today's fourth generation, which focuses on the enemy's society and political will to fight. As one theorist puts it, "Each succeeding generation reached deeper into the enemy's territory in an effort to defeat him."[18] Although dividing modern war into four generations is somewhat arbitrary and overstated, the important trend to note is the blurring of military front and civilian rear.

Taking an even longer view, Israeli theorist Martin van Creveld argues that the outstanding characteristic of war during the millennium from 1000 to 1945 was its consolidation. During the Middle Ages, hardly any territorial lords could raise more than a few thousand troops. By the eighteenth century, the numbers had grown to low hundreds of thousands. In the world wars of the twentieth century, seven states fielded more than 100 million men and engaged in battles around the globe. "Waging total war against each other, the states undertook operations so large and ferocious that in the end, forty to sixty million people were dead, and the best part of a continent lay in ruins. Then, dropping out of a clear sky on 6 August 1945, came the first atomic bomb, changing everything forever."[19]

Although there were other causes in addition to nuclear weapons,[20] and the effects were not fully understood for some time, total war soon gave way to limited wars such as the Korean War. Harry Truman, who used a nuclear weapon to end World War II, decided not to do so in Korea, and although Dwight Eisenhower hinted at the prospect of nuclear use, he also proved reluctant to do so. The age of total war seemed over.[21] Equally remarkable, even limited interstate wars "were becoming quite rare." Van Creveld counts a mere twenty in the half-century after 1945.

Armed conflict did not disappear, however. Interstate war has become less common than intrastate and transnational wars involving nonstate actors. Of 226 significant armed conflicts between 1945 and 2002, less than half were fought between states and armed groups in the 1950s, but by the 1990s that was the dominant form of armed conflict.[22] Such groups can be divided into insurgents, terrorists, militias, and criminal organizations, though the categories can overlap and blur with time.[23] For example, Revolutionary Armed Forces of Colombia guerrillas formed alliances with narcotics cartels in that country, and in Afghanistan some Taliban groups have close ties with transnational Al Qaeda terrorists, whereas others are more local in orientation. Some are supported by states, but many are not.

Such groups see conflict as a continuum of political and violent irregular operations over a long period that will provide coercive control over local populations. They benefit from the fact that scores of weak states lack the legitimacy or capacity to effectively control their own territory. The result is what General Sir Rupert Smith, former British commander in Northern Ireland and the Balkans, calls "war among the people."[24] Rarely are such conflicts decided on conventional battlefields by traditional armies. They become hybrid wars—"a fused mix of conventional weapons, irregular tactics, terrorism, and criminal behavior in the battlespace."[25] For example, in a thirty-four-day battle with Israel in Lebanon in 2006, the armed political group Hezbollah used well-trained cells that mixed propaganda, conventional military tactics, and rockets launched from densely populated civilian areas to achieve what many in the region considered a political victory. In Gaza, two years later, Hamas and Israel fought by air and land in a densely populated area. In hybrid wars, conventional and irregular forces, combatants and civilians, physical destruction and information warfare become thoroughly intertwined. Moreover, with cameras in every cell phone and Photoshop on every computer, the information contest is ever present.[26]

Some theorists have referred to this new shape of war as "asymmetrical warfare," but that characterization is less helpful than first might appear. Warfare has always been asymmetrical.[27] Leaders and commanders always seek out opponents' weak points and try to maximize their own advantages to pursue victory. After the demise of the Soviet Union, the United States held an overwhelming advantage in conventional warfare as it demonstrated in the Desert Storm operation that defeated Iraq in 1991 at the cost of only 148 American dead. Similarly, in the 1999 Kosovo war with Serbia, U.S. dominance in the air eventually led to a victory with no American casualties. Faced with such conventional asymmetry in America's favor, opponents did not give up; they instead turned to unconventional tactics to counter the American advantage. Chinese strategists, realizing that a conventional confrontation with the United States would be folly, developed a strategy of "unrestricted warfare" that combines electronic, diplomatic, cyber-, terrorist proxy, economic, and propaganda tools to deceive and exhaust American systems. As one Chinese military official puts it, "The first rule of unrestricted warfare is that there are no rules."[28] Seeking unconventional tactics to counter asymmetries is not new; it can be traced back 2,000 years to Sun Tzu. And, of course, Sun Tzu is famous for pointing out that it is best to win without having to fight.

Governments are not the only warriors that understand this age-old wisdom. Terrorists have long understood that they can never hope to compete head-on with a major government. Instead, as mentioned in Chapter 1, they follow the insights of jujitsu to leverage the strength of a powerful government against itself. Terrorist actions are designed to outrage and provoke overreactions by the strong. For example, Osama bin Laden's strategy was to provoke the United States into reactions that would destroy its credibility, weaken its allies across the Muslim world, and eventually lead to exhaustion. The United States fell into that trap with the invasion of Iraq and its concomitant failure to follow up its early success in Afghanistan. Al Qaeda follows a tactic of "inciter-in-chief" rather than "commander-in-chief."[29] This allows the organization great flexibility as local groups self-recruit to its network.

The United States was slow to adapt to these changes. With the collapse of the Soviet Union, the United States was the only military power with global capabilities, it had a military budget equal to that of all other countries combined, and it was at the forefront of an information economy that was producing a "revolution in military affairs." In the 1990s, U.S. military strategy focused on the ability to fight and win two conventional wars simultaneously (for example, against North Korea and Iraq) and the development of technologies that would maintain the "dominant battle space awareness" that had been demonstrated in Desert Storm. Other uses of military forces were considered not as war-fighting but as lesser-included cases of "military operations other than war." When Donald Rumsfeld became secretary of defense in 2001, he pursued a military transformation that relied on new technologies. A combination of high-tech airpower and limited special forces allied to Afghan fighters on the ground initially worked well in Afghanistan, and the quick success of the March 2003 invasion of Iraq, with only thirty-three casualties, showed both the strength and weakness of this approach.[30] Americans were not mistaken to invest in the revolution in military affairs; they were wrong to think it was sufficient.

Technology has always had important effects on military power, and "revolutions in military affairs" are not new. Indeed, identifying

them is somewhat arbitrary, and a variety of lists of major technological changes can be constructed.[31] Max Boot identifies four: the
gunpowder revolution in early-modern Europe, the Industrial Revolution of the nineteenth century, the Second Industrial Revolution
of the early twentieth century, and the current Information Revolution. He adds that "history is full of examples of superpowers failing to take advantage. . . . The Mongols missed the Gunpowder
Revolution; the Chinese, Turks and Indians missed the Industrial
Revolution; the French and British missed major parts of the Second
Industrial Revolution; the Soviets missed the Information Revolution."[32] The costs were clear. Less obvious are the costs of putting
too much faith in technology.

For one thing, technology is a double-edged sword. It eventually
spreads and becomes available to adversaries that may have more
primitive capabilities but also are less vulnerable to dependence on
advanced technologies. American military theorists used to argue
that even though others could eventually buy some high technology
commercially "off the shelf," the United States would be progressing
to the next generation and integrating technologies into a system of
systems. But that was round one in the chess game. American advantages in robotics and unmanned drones will eventually be available to opponents in later rounds. For example, in 2009 the
American military discovered that insurgents were hacking into the
downlinks of data from Predator unmanned aircraft using software
that cost less than $30.[33] Meanwhile, growing reliance on elaborate
satellite and computer network–controlled systems makes the
United States more vulnerable than some of its adversaries.[34]

For another thing, too much faith and focus on the advantages
of technologies can divert attention from the asymmetrical measure
available to opponents. The American campaign of "shock and awe"
relied on smart bombs for precision targeting in the early stages of
the Iraq War, but the insurgents' use of car bombs and improvised
explosive devices provided them with cheap and effective smart
bombs of their own in the insurgency phase of the war. And too

much focus on high technology can lead to failure to invest in the training, military police, linguists, and other dimensions that infantry need for dealing with insurgencies.

By 2006, the American military was rediscovering the lessons of counterinsurgency that had been almost deliberately forgotten after Vietnam, then obscured by the focus on high-tech warfare, and finally relegated primarily to the branch of special forces.[35] *The U.S. Army/Marine Corps Counterinsurgency Field Manual* supervised by General David Petraeus adopted lessons from British, French, and Vietnam experience to make securing the civilian population, rather than destroying the enemy, the top priority. The real battle became one for civilian support to deny the insurgent "fish" the cover of the civilian "sea" to swim in. Counterinsurgency, commonly called "COIN," downplayed offensive operations and emphasized winning the hearts and minds of the civilian population.

Soft power was integrated into military strategy. Hard power was used to clear an area of insurgents and to hold it, and the soft power of building roads, clinics, and schools filled in behind. As Sarah Sewall says in her introduction to the new manual, "It is a stark departure from the Weinberger-Powell doctrine of overwhelming and decisive use of offensive forces. . . . Sometimes the more force is used, the less effective it is." Instead of calculating necessary troop levels in terms of opposing fighters, the COIN manual focuses on inhabitants and recommends a minimum of 20 counterinsurgents per 1,000 residents.[36] As the chairman of the Joint Chiefs of Staff described the campaign for Marja in Afghanistan, "We did not prep the battlefield with carpet bombing or missile strikes. We simply walked in, on time. Because, frankly, the battlefield isn't necessarily a field anymore. It's in the minds of the people."[37] Nor is this trend uniquely American. The president of the Russian republic of Ingushetia says that "counterterrorism is mainly a matter of soft power. The most severe punishment, that should make up 1 percent. Ninety-nine percent should be persuasion, persuasion, persuasion."[38]

At the same time, counterinsurgency is not a solution to all military problems. Despite best efforts, civilian casualties are inevitable. In Afghanistan, "the persistence of deadly convoy and checkpoint shootings has led to growing resentment . . . a friction that has turned villages firmly against the occupation."[39] In addition, private contractors play an important role in modern operations, and their actions are often difficult to control.[40] Moreover, the numbers and time required for counterinsurgency may prove too costly in terms of both politics and budgets to be feasible in many situations. For example, the number and duration of security forces implied by the previous ratio may be unsustainable in Western public opinion, and that leads skeptics to question the effectiveness of what they call "COIN-lite."[41] As one Afghan Taliban is alleged to have said, "You have the watches, but we have the time."

Cultural conservatism, mistrust, civilian casualties, and local corruption make it difficult to win the hearts and minds that constitute the soft power part of a COIN strategy. A RAND report concludes that "the greatest weakness in the struggle with Islamic insurgency is not U.S. firepower but the ineptitude and illegitimacy of the very regimes that are meant to be the alternative to religious tyranny." Moreover, the track record of counterinsurgency campaigns is mixed. Although rough and imprecise, one estimate claims "their likelihood of success, empirically, is 50 percent."[42] Another RAND study put the rate of success at eight of the thirty cases resolved since 1979, or closer to 25 percent.[43] As one military critic puts it, the new counterinsurgency manual is "so persuasively written, so clear in its aims, that it makes the impossible seem possible."[44] And one of it proponents concludes that "counter-insurgency in general is a game we need to avoid wherever possible. . . . We should avoid such interventions wherever possible, simply because the costs are so high and the benefits so doubtful."[45]

And, of course, insurgency is not the only military threat that planners need to consider. Interstate conflict has not totally vanished, and hybrid versions of warfare remain a concern. As the undersecretary of defense for policy declared about strategic planning, "I think hybrid will be the defining character. The traditional, neat categories—those are types that really don't match reality any more."[46] In 2010, the Pentagon's *Quadrennial Defense Review Report* underscored the importance of maritime piracy, nuclear proliferation, international crime, transnational terrorism, and natural disasters as well as interstate wars as threats to national security.[47] And U.S. Army planners preparing their new capstone doctrine downplayed faith in technology, linear planning, and centralization. Instead, they stressed assumptions about uncertainty, decentralization, and a spectrum of conflicts. In the words of General H. R. McMaster, the new doctrine explicitly rejects "the belief that technological capabilities had essentially lifted the fog of war . . . and that the development of these technological capabilities would substitute for traditional elements of combat power, fighting power, especially on land."[48] That makes the task of deciding how to train forces and invest limited resources in a military budget more complex than ever.[49]

HOW MILITARY RESOURCES PRODUCE BEHAVIORAL OUTCOMES

Military planners and analysts constantly measure and compare the resources and capabilities of opposing forces. A country's population, for example, is a basic resource that can be shaped into a specific tool such as infantry, which can be subdivided into combat specialties. In general, analysts look at strategic resources such as budgets, manpower, military infrastructure and institutions, defense industries, and inventories. They then look at factors that affect conversion capability such as strategy, doctrine, training, organization, and capacity for innovation. Finally, they judge combat proficiency in detailed dimensions of ground, naval, air, and space forces. But even those planners who believe that "the ultimate yardstick of national power is military capability" admit that a capability-based methodology cannot predict combat outcomes.[50] As we have seen

earlier, we still have to specify what enables power resources to produce preferred behavioral outcomes. As military analyst Stephen
Biddle concludes, "No single, undifferentiated concept of 'military
capability' can apply to all conflicts in all places and times."[51] Force
employment is crucial. Strategy, the skill in combining resources to
accomplish goals, is the key to smart military power.

At a more basic level, we must realize that military resources are
relevant to all three aspects or faces of relational power discussed
in Chapter 1. Regarding the first face of power, force can threaten
or compel others to change their initial preferences and strategies.
Military resources also affect the agenda-framing that characterizes
the second face of power. When a small country knows that it cannot possibly defeat a stronger country, attack is less likely to be on
its agenda.[52] Mexico might wish to recover the territories that the
United States took in the nineteenth century, but military recon-
quest is not on the twenty-first-century agenda. More subtly, success in war can produce institutions that set the agenda for
subsequent periods—witness the institutions created in the aftermath of World Wars I and II. The dominance of American military
power after World War II provided the stability that allowed Europe and Japan to focus on economic agendas that stressed absolute,
rather than relative, gains and thus fostered the growth of economic
interdependence and globalization.

Force can also affect the shaping of preferences that constitutes
the third face of power. As we saw earlier, dictators such as Hitler
and Stalin tried to develop a sense of invincibility through military
might. Success attracts, and a reputation for competence in the use
of force helps to attract. In the aftermath of a competent and legitimate use of American force in the 1991 Gulf War, American standing increased in the Middle East. What this suggests is that there is
more than one way in which military resources can produce preferred outcomes. What the army calls the "kinetic" use of force is
not the only currency of military power. In a famous post–Vietnam
War dialogue, American colonel Harry Summers pointed out, "You

know, you never defeated us in a kinetic engagement on the battle-field." And his Vietnamese counterpart, Colonel Tu, accurately replied, "That may be so. But it is also irrelevant because we won the battle of strategic communication and therefore the war."[53]

Military resources can implement four types of actions that are the modalities or currencies of military power. Military resources can be used to (1) physically fight and destroy; (2) back up threats in coercive diplomacy; (3) promise protection, including peace-keeping; and (4) provide many forms of assistance. When these actions are performed well, they produce preferred behavioral changes in the targets. But whether they are effective in producing preferred outcomes depends on special qualities and skills used in the conversion strategies. Successful strategies must take into account the context of the targets of power, the conditions or environment of the action, and whether targets are likely to respond by acceptance or resistance. As Biddle concludes about military power, "Capability is not primarily a matter of material. It is chiefly a product of how states use their material resources. . . . Different military tasks are very dissimilar—the ability to do one (or several) well does not imply the ability to master others."[54]

The four major actions that constitute the modalities of military power are displayed in Table 2.1.

Fighting
Success in the first modality, fighting, depends upon a strategy that involves both competence and legitimacy. Competence in the ability to fight is obvious, but it requires a specification of "to fight what?" It involves orders of battle measured in terms of manpower, weapons, technology, organization, and budgets, as well as training and tactics exercised in war gaming and the morale of troops and the home front. Competence in the ability to fight has a broad dimension that calls for a strategic knowledge base, insight into political objectives, and a doctrinal base that covers a wide spectrum of potential conflicts. Too myopic a focus in the application of force

TABLE 2.1 Dimensions of Military Power

	COMMAND			CO-OPTIVE
TYPE OF BEHAVIOR	Physical coercion	Threat of coercion	Protection	Assistance
MODALITIES	Fighting and destruction	Coercive diplomacy	Alliance and peacekeeping	Aid and training
KEY QUALITIES FOR STRATEGIC SUCCESS	Competence	Capability and credibility	Capability and trust	Competence and benignity
SHAPED RESOURCES	Manpower, weapons, and tactics	Agile diplomacy	Troops and diplomacy	Organization and budgets

planning can undermine the effectiveness of force as an instrument of power.

God is not only on the side of the big battalions. Competence in the ability to fight can be important for small states even if they do not have a prospect of winning in a long war. For example, Switzerland historically used its geography plus conscription to make itself difficult for larger neighbors to digest quickly, and Singapore, a vulnerable city-state of 4 million, invests in impressive military capabilities to convince potential enemies that it would be as unpalatable as "a poisoned shrimp."

Legitimacy is a less obvious part of a strategy for fighting because it is intangible and variable. In the sociological sense, legitimacy refers to a widespread belief that an actor or action is right. "The concept of legitimacy allows various actors to coordinate their support . . . by appealing to their common capacity to be moved by moral reasons, as distinct from purely strategic or self-interested reasons."[55] Beliefs in legitimacy vary and are rarely universal, but the perceived legitimacy of the use of force in the eyes of the target and third parties is relevant to how the target will respond (quick surrender or prolonged fighting) and the costs that are incurred in the use of force. Legitimacy depends in part upon traditional just-war norms, such as a perceived just cause, as well as a sense of proportion and discrimination in the way the force is used.

Perceptions of legitimacy are also affected by the vagaries of political maneuvering in the United Nations, competitive interpretations of humanitarian law by nongovernmental organizations (NGOs), and the narratives created by the media, bloggers, and cell phones. The Iraq War in 2003 demonstrated great American competence in the invasion and capture of Baghdad, but suffered from a perceived lack of legitimacy in the absence of a second UN resolution. Moreover, the failure to prepare adequate forces to suppress looting, sectarian violence, and the subsequent insurgency eventually undercut the sense of competence. Some of these lessons carried forward to Afghanistan. In the words of General Stanley McChrystal, the former commander of allied forces there, "The biggest thing is convincing the Afghan people. This is all a war of perceptions. This is not a physical war in terms of how many people you kill or how much ground you capture, how many bridges you blow up. This is all in the minds of the participants."[56]

Sophisticated military men have long understood that battles are not won by kinetic effects alone. In the words of General Petraeus, "We did reaffirm in Iraq the recognition that you don't kill or capture your way out of an industrial-strength insurgency."[57] Or as McChrystal notes, when we resort to expedient measures, "we end up paying a price for it ultimately. Abu Ghraib and other situations like that are non-biodegradable. They don't go away. The enemy continues to beat you with them like a stick."[58] In Afghanistan, the Taliban has "embarked on a sophisticated information war, using modern media tools as well as some old-fashioned ones, to soften their image and win favor with local Afghans as they try to counter the Americans' new campaign to win Afghan hearts and minds."[59] As Australian COIN expert David Kilcullen notes, "This implies that America's international reputation, moral authority, diplomatic weight, persuasive ability, cultural attractiveness and strategic credibility—its 'soft power'—is not some optional adjunct to military strength. Rather, it is a critical enabler for a permissive operating environment . . . and it is also the prime political competence in countering a globalized insurgency."[60]

Similarly, in terms of fighters killed and buildings destroyed, Israel outfought Hezbollah in Lebanon in 2006, but the latter's clever use of televised civilian casualties (partly caused by its siting of missiles in close proximity to civilians) as well as it ability to persuade the population and third parties that Israel was the aggressor meant that Hezbollah was widely regarded as the victor after Israel finally withdrew.[61] In 2008, Russia had little difficulty in defeating Georgia and declaring the independence of Abkhazia and South Ossetia, but Russia had a much more difficult time in winning international recognition for its new protégés. Russian complaints that it was merely repeating what NATO did with Kosovo missed the point that even though the Kosovo war lacked UN approval, it was widely regarded as legitimate.

Legitimacy is particularly important in counterinsurgency strategies because "the essence of the challenge of modern military leadership is ethical. . . . One significant objective measure of effectiveness is the number of civilians inadvertently hurt instead of protected." The ultimate failure of the French in Algeria in the 1950s grew out of the military's use of torture and indiscriminate force.[62] An Australian military expert points out that many insurgents are "accidental guerillas" recruited to fight alongside hard-core fighters by a foreign intrusion but capable of being split from the hard core. In his view, acting in accord with international norms is "not an optional luxury or a sign of moral flaccidity. Rather it is a key strategic requirement."[63] As just-war theory reminds us, legitimacy involves both the cause of the fighting and the procedures by which the fight is carried out.

Coercive Diplomacy

The second modality of military power—coercive diplomacy— depends upon the same underlying resources as those that produce competence in kinetic fighting and destruction, but it also depends upon the credibility and cost of the threat. A threat of force can be used to compel or to deter, but the latter is often more credible. If a threat is not credible, it may fail to produce acceptance *and* it may lead to costs to the reputation of the coercing state. In general, threats are costly when they fail, not only in encouraging resistance in the target, but also in negatively influencing third parties observing the outcome.

The deployment of ships and planes is a classic example of coercive diplomacy, and naval resources benefit from the flexibility of movement in the ocean commons. In one study of 215 cases in which the United States used "force without war" in the mid-twentieth century, half involved only the movement of naval units, whereas others involved the alerting or moving of ground or air units as well.[64] Force need not be threatened explicitly. Military forces can be used to "show the flag" or "swagger." At the beginning of the twentieth century, President Theodore Roosevelt sent his newly constructed "great white fleet" on an around-the-world cruise to signal the rise of American power. Some countries stage elaborate military parades on national holidays for the same purpose.

More recently, when China destroyed one of its own satellites in low earth orbit, many observers regarded it as a coercive reminder to the United States that it could not count on uncontested control of the space commons. And in the cyberage, coercive diplomacy can be practiced indirectly with attribution left ambiguous. For instance, in 2008, when sporadic diplomatic spats over access to resources in the South China Sea became serious, what purported to be Chinese invasion plans for Vietnam were posted on major Websites in China, including the market leader, sina.com.[65] As we will see in Chapter 5, the prospect of cyberwar adds an interesting new dimension to coercion and threats.

Protection
The third modality, providing protection, is at the heart of alliance relations but can be extended to other states as well. Again, the key to a successful strategy involves credibility and whether that

produces trust in the targeted country. For example, when Russia held military exercises in the fall of 2009, an American warship toured the Baltic, six senior generals visited Latvia over the course of twelve months, and further bilateral military exercises were planned.[66] NATO military forces and personnel were used to reassure Latvia and remind Russia that Latvia's security was guaranteed by its membership in the NATO alliance.

Credibility is often costly to create but sometimes not. For example, in the wake of North Korea's 2006 nuclear explosion, the presence of American troops in Japan enhanced credibility at relatively low cost because Japan paid for their support. The ability to extend deterrence to Japan and other allies is an important factor in American power in Asia. For example, in the 1990s Japan decided not to support a Malaysian proposal for an economic bloc that would exclude the United States after the United States objected. Extended deterrence depends upon a combination of military capability and credibility. It is a gradient that varies with the degree of interest that the protector has. Costly promises to protect areas of low interest are not credible, but the stationing of American ground forces in Japan and Korea demonstrates a high degree of commitment and credibility. It means that any attack on those countries is likely to cause American casualties and thus links the fates of the countries in ways that mere words alone cannot do.

Protection can produce both hard and soft power for the state providing the protection. Alliance relations such as NATO enhance American hard power capabilities, but they also developed a web of personal ties and a climate of attraction. During the Cold War, the hard power of American military protection helped create a climate of soft power that advanced America's milieu goals of stability and economic prosperity in the Atlantic area. In contrast, American protection of Saudi Arabia (which dates back to World War II) rests upon implicit guarantees rather than formal alliance and on narrow bargains based on national interests. This protection generates limited soft power in the relationship, but it has often produced economic benefits as the Saudi government has sometimes modified its energy policies to accommodate American demands.[67]

Peacekeeping operations are another aspect of the protective modality of military resources that does not generally involve active fighting. In recent operations, peacekeepers sometimes kill or are killed, but their general purpose is deterrence and reassurance to provide stability. Here again the key to whether the military resources produce preferred outcomes depends upon a mixture of hard and soft power. Competence in this military skill can be different (and require different training) from war-fighting, yet in modern military interventions soldiers may be required to simultaneously conduct full-scale military action, peacekeeping operations, and humanitarian aid within the space of three contiguous blocks.[68] This requires that broad capabilities be built into many units if they are to have an effective force. Careful performance of these functions determines the reaction of the target as well as the effects on third parties.

Assistance

Finally, military forces can be used to provide assistance. This modality can take the form of training foreign militaries, engaging in international military education, undertaking regular exercises, or providing humanitarian assistance and disaster relief. Such assistance can enhance both hard and soft power. In training Iraqi or Afghan forces, for example, the United States is trying to enhance their capabilities for fighting insurgencies. But if the training, education, or humanitarian assistance also leads to attraction, then the military resources are producing soft power. The U.S. Navy recently developed *A Cooperative Strategy for 21st Century Seapower*, which focuses on the navy's role in partnering with other states to maintain freedom of the seas and building collective arrangements that promote mutual trust.[69] This strategy involves joint training and technical assistance, as well as capacities for delivering humanitarian assistance.

Not only neighbors such as the United States and Brazil, but also countries as distant as Israel and China sent military units to help Haiti after the devastating 2010 earthquake. Whether the currency of assistance is successfully converted into a strategy that produces preferred outcomes depends upon such qualities as competence and perceived benignity. Competence is again obvious, but benignity enhances attraction, and its absence can lead to negative reaction in the target. Aid programs that are seen as cynical, manipulative, or helping a small minority against another part of a population can actually produce negative reactions.

In short, military resources can produce both hard and soft power, and the mix varies with which of the four modalities are employed.[70] The important point is that the soft power that arises from qualities of benignity, competence, legitimacy, and trust can add leverage to the hard power of military force. Strategies that combine the two successfully represent smart military power.

THE FUTURE OF MILITARY POWER

As Barack Obama said in accepting the Nobel Peace Prize in 2009, "We must begin by acknowledging the hard truth that we will not eradicate violent conflict in our lifetimes. There will be times when nations—acting individually or in concert—will find the use of force not only necessary but morally justified."[71] Even if the prospect of the use or threat of force among states has a lower probability in the twenty-first century than in earlier eras, it will retain a high impact, and such situations lead rational actors to purchase expensive insurance. The United States is likely to be the major issuer of such insurance policies. Moreover, even if fighting among states and civil wars diminish, they are likely to continue among nonstate transnational and insurgent groups or between states and such groups. Hybrid wars and "war among the people" will persist. A capacity to fight and coerce, protect and assist, will remain important even if interstate war continues to decrease.

This leads to a larger point about the role of military force in world politics that relates to the second face of power: shaping the agenda. Military force remains important because it helps to structure world politics. Some theorists argue that military power is of such restricted utility that it is no longer "the ultimate measuring rod to which other forms of power should be compared."[72] But the fact that military power is not always sufficient to decide particular situations does not mean that it has lost all utility.[73] Even though there are more situations and contexts where it is difficult to use, military force remains a vital source of power in this century because its presence in all four modalities structures expectations and shapes the political calculations of actors.

As we shall see in the next chapter, markets and economic power rest upon political frameworks. In chaotic conditions of great uncertainty, markets fail. Political frameworks rest upon norms and institutions, but also upon the management of coercive power. A well-ordered modern state is defined in terms of a monopoly on the legitimate use of force, and that allows domestic markets to operate. Internationally, where order is more tenuous, residual concerns about the coercive use of force, even if a low probability, can have important effects. Military force provides the framework (along with norms, institutions, and relationships) that helps to provide a minimal degree of order. Metaphorically, military power provides a degree of security that is to order as oxygen is to breathing: little noticed until it begins to become scarce. Once that occurs, its absence dominates all else. In this sense, the role of military power in structuring world politics is likely to persist well into the twenty-first century. Military power will not have the same utility for states that it had in nineteenth and twentieth centuries, but it will remain a crucial component of power in world politics.

CHAPTER 3

Economic Power

At the end of the Cold War, some analysts proclaimed that "geo-economics" had replaced "geopolitics." Economic power would become the key to success in world politics. Carrots were becoming more important than sticks. As one scholar put it, "In the past it was cheaper to seize another state's territory by force than to develop the sophisticated economic and trading apparatus needed to derive benefit from commercial exchange with it."[1] Many people thought this would usher in a world dominated by Japan and Germany. Today some equate the rise in China's share of world product as a fundamental shift in the balance of global power without considering other dimensions of power.

Political observers have long debated whether economic power or military power is more fundamental. Marxist tradition casts economics as the underlying structure of power and political institutions as a parasitic superstructure. Nineteenth-century liberals believed that growing interdependence in trade and finance would make war obsolete. Realists reply that Britain and Germany were each other's leading trade partners in 1914, but that did not prevent a conflagration that set back global economic integration for a half-century. They note that markets depend upon a political structure to keep order. What was called "free trade" in the nineteenth century rested upon British naval preeminence.[2] Moreover, the workings of markets are often slower and less dramatic than the exercise of military force.

Both sides have a point, but as we saw in Chapter 1, whether one or another type of resource produces power in the sense of desired behavior depends upon the context. A carrot is more effective than a stick if you wish to lead a mule to water, but a gun may be more useful if your aim is to deprive an opponent of his mule. Military force has been called "the ultimate form of power" in world politics,[3] but a thriving economy is necessary to produce such power. Even then, as we have seen, force may not work on many crucial issues, such as financial stability or climate change. Relative importance depends on context.

Economic resources can produce soft power behavior as well as hard. A successful economic model not only produces the latent military resources for exercise of hard power, but it can also attract others to emulate its example. The soft power of the European Union (EU) at the end of the Cold War and the soft power of China today are enhanced by the success of their economic models. A large successful economy produces not only hard power resources, but also the soft power gravitational pull of attraction. The basic economic *resources* that underlie both hard and soft power are such things as the size and quality of gross domestic product (GDP), per capita income, the level of technology, natural and human resources, political and legal institutions for markets, as well as a variety of shaped resources for special domains, such as trade, finance, and competition.

Economic power *behavior* rests on the economic aspects of social life—"the production and consumption of wealth that is measurable in terms of money."[4] Some economists are skeptical about whether these activities produce anything that can be called economic power. As one puts it, "There is no politics in a purely economic exchange."[5] In the tradition of liberal market economics, if bargains are freely struck between buyers and sellers under perfect competition, there is a joint gain from the trade rather than a power relationship. But it is a mistake to focus only on the absolute gain in economic relationships. Absolute gain can enhance the capabilities of both parties, but in traditional political competition, states have often worried about relative gains more than joint gains.[6] Nineteenth-century France may have benefited from trade with a growing German economy, but it also feared the military threat that enhanced economic growth was producing across the Rhine. Moreover, few markets are perfect, and power relationships may affect the division of the joint gain. Economic growth produces a bigger pie to be divided, but relative power often determines who gets the largest slice.

Other economists accept the reality of economic power as "economic strength used so as to achieve domination or control."[7] Some see it as "the capability decisively to punish (or to reward) another party" but still remain skeptical about its utility. "Apart from its possible connection to national military power through a country's tax base, [economic power] is largely local or ephemeral or both. It is difficult to wield on a global scale. The basic reason is that the locus for most economic decision-making is households and firms, and is thus highly diffuse. . . . Firms are subject to competitive pressures which penalize them, possibly severely, if they deviate too far from what the 'market' will permit."[8] Some even argue that economic power is based on monopoly (being the only seller) or monopsony (being the only buyer), and such power is held by non-state actors such as individuals and businesses, not by states.[9] Although it is true that governments often have difficulty using potential economic power because of resistance from domestic interests, transnational corporations, linkages among issues, and international institutional constraints such as membership in the World Trade Organization (WTO), it does not follow that states lack economic power. But, again, how much power depends on the context, particularly the nature of the market.

In a perfect market, buyers and sellers are price takers who feel the structural power of market forces of supply and demand that are beyond their control. But if they can differentiate their product enough to create an imperfect market, they can gain pricing power and become price makers rather than takers. Advertising that creates a brand loyalty is a case in point. A key aspect of hard economic power behavior is efforts by actors to structure markets and thus increase their relative position. This is close to the second face of power described earlier. The other key modality of economic hard power is illustrative of the first face of power—the provision (or withdrawal) of payments that comprise positive and negative sanctions. The long list of instruments that states use to structure markets and make payments includes tariffs, quotas and rules that control access to their markets, legal sanctions, manipulation of exchange rates, creation of natural resource cartels, "checkbook diplomacy," and aid for development among others.[10] We shall look at a few of the more significant here, but an important underlying dimension of economic power behavior is to make others more dependent on you than you are on them.[11]

ECONOMIC INTERDEPENDENCE AND POWER

As states become connected by market forces, they seek to structure their interdependence both to achieve joint gains and to create asymmetries that provide a larger share of the gain and power for other purposes. "Interdependence" involves short-run sensitivity and long-term vulnerability.[12] "Sensitivity" refers to the amount and pace of the effects of mutual dependence; that is, how quickly does change in one part of the system bring about change in another part? For example, in 1998 weakness in emerging markets in Asia had a contagious effect that undercut other emerging markets as distant as Russia and Brazil. Similarly, in September 2008 the collapse of Lehman Brothers in New York quickly affected markets around the world.

A high level of sensitivity, however, is not the same as a high level of vulnerability. "Vulnerability" refers to the relative costs of changing the structure of a system of interdependence. Vulnerability produces more power in relationships than does sensitivity. The less vulnerable of two countries is not necessarily the less sensitive, but rather the one that would incur lower costs from altering the situation. In 1998, the United States was sensitive but not vulnerable to East Asian economic conditions. The financial crisis there cut 0.5 percent off the U.S. growth rate, but with a booming economy the United States could afford it. Indonesia, in contrast, was both sensitive and vulnerable to changes in global trade and investment patterns. Its economy suffered severely, and that in turn led to internal political conflict. Vulnerability involves degree. In 2008, given the bubble conditions in the country's subprime mortgage market and its growing deficits, the United States proved more vulnerable than it had been when its market was flourishing a decade earlier.

Vulnerability depends on more than aggregate measures, and this is where the earlier cautionary remarks apply to economic power. It also depends on whether a society is capable of responding quickly to change. For example, private actors, large corporations, and speculators in the market may each look at a market situation and decide to hoard supplies because they think shortages are going to grow worse. Their actions will drive the price even higher because they will make the shortages greater and put more demand on the market. Governments often find it difficult to control such market behavior.

"Symmetry" refers to situations of relatively balanced versus unbalanced dependence. Being less dependent can be a source of power. If two parties are interdependent but one is less so than the other, the less dependent party has a source of power as long as both value the interdependent relationship. Manipulating the asymmetries of interdependence is an important dimension of economic power. Perfect symmetry is quite rare, so most cases of economic interdependence also involve a potential power relationship.

In the 1980s, when President Ronald Reagan cut taxes and raised expenditures, the United States became dependent on imported Japanese capital to balance its federal government budget. Some argued that this gave Japan tremendous power over the United States. But the other side of the coin was that Japan would hurt itself as well as the United States if it stopped lending to the Americans. In addition, Japanese investors who already had large stakes in the United States would have found their investments devalued by the damage done to the American economy if Japan suddenly stopped lending to the United States. Japan's economy was little more than half the size of the American economy, and that meant the Japanese needed the American market for their exports more than vice versa, although both needed each other and both benefited from the interdependence.

A similar relationship has developed today between the United States and China. America accepts Chinese imports and pays China in dollars, and China holds American dollars and bonds, in effect making a loan to the United States. China has amassed $2.5 trillion of foreign exchange reserves, much of it held in U.S. Treasury securities. Some observers have described this as a great shift in the global balance of power because China could bring the United States to its knees by threatening to sell dollars. But in doing so, China would not only reduce the value of its reserves as the price of the dollar fell, but it also would jeopardize American willingness to continue to import cheap Chinese goods, which would mean job loss and instability in China. If it dumped its dollars, China would bring the United States to it knees, but might also bring itself to its ankles. As one Chinese economist puts it, "We live in an interdependent world, in which we will probably harm ourselves if we take unilateral action aimed at harming another side."[13]

Judging whether economic interdependence produces power requires looking at the balance of asymmetries, not just at one side of the equation. In this case, the balance of asymmetries resembles a "balance of financial terror" analogous to the Cold War military interdependence in which the United States and the Soviet Union each had the potential to destroy the other in a nuclear exchange but never did. In February 2010, angered over American arms sales to Taiwan, a group of senior Chinese military officers called for the Chinese government to sell off U.S. government bonds in retaliation, but their suggestion was not heeded.[14] Instead, Yi Gang, China's director of state administration of foreign exchange, explained that "Chinese investments in US Treasuries are market investment behavior and we don't wish to politicize them."[15] If they did, the pain would be mutual.

Nonetheless, this balance does not guarantee stability. Not only is there the danger of accidents with unintended consequences, but also both countries maneuver to change the framework and reduce their vulnerabilities. After the 2008 financial crisis, the United States pressed China to let its currency float upward as a means of reducing the American trade deficit and the dollar imbalance. At the same time, officials of China's Central Bank began making statements about America's need to increase its savings, reduce its deficits, and move toward a long-term future in which the dollar would be supplemented by International Monetary Fund (IMF)–issued special drawing rights as a reserve currency. But China's growl was louder than its bite. Despite dire predictions about the power of creditors, China's increased financial power may have increased its ability to resist American entreaties but had little effect on its ability to compel the United States to change its policies.[16] Even though China took minor measures to reduce the increase in its holdings of dollars, it was not willing to take the risks of making its currency fully convertible because of domestic political reasons. Thus, the yuan is unlikely to challenge the dollar's role as the largest component of world reserves (more than 60 percent) in the next decade. Nonetheless, as China gradually increases domestic consumption rather than relying on exports as its engine of economic growth, Chinese leaders may begin to feel less dependent than they are now on access to the American market as the source of employment that is crucial for their internal political stability. Political bargaining may then reflect perceived marginal shifts in the degree of symmetry.

Asymmetries in currency markets are a particularly important and efficient aspect of economic power because they underlie the vast systems of trade and financial markets. Monetary power can come from currency manipulation, a fostering of monetary dependence, and a capacity to disrupt the system.[17] By limiting the convertibility of its currency, China avoids discipline over domestic economic decisions that could come from international currency markets, while creating a competitive trade advantage.

When a currency is widely held as a means of exchange and a store of value, it becomes known as a world reserve currency, and this can convey a degree of power. Compare, for example, the discipline that international banks and the IMF were able to impose on Indonesia and South Korea in 1998 with the relative freedom that the United States had in adjusting during the 2008 financial crisis because American debts were denominated in the country's own currency. Rather than collapse, the dollar appreciated as investors regarded the underlying strength of the United States as a safe haven. A country whose currency represents a significant portion of world reserves can gain economic power from that position, both in easier terms for adjustment and in the ability to influence others who are in need. For example, after the British and French invasion of Egypt in the Suez Canal crisis of 1956, sterling came under attack in financial markets, and the United States conditioned its support of the pound upon a British withdrawal from Suez.[18] Britain was unhappy but could do little about it.

French president Charles de Gaulle complained that "since the dollar is the reference currency everywhere, it can cause others to suffer the effects of its poor management. This is not acceptable. This cannot last."[19] But it did. A decade later, French president Valéry Giscard d'Estaing complained that the role of the dollar gave the United States "an exorbitant privilege."[20] In the words of one economic historian, "Economic and political power tend to go hand in hand in a world that is insecure and at the same time places a high value on security and growth."[21] The military strength of the United States reinforces confidence in the dollar as a safe haven. As one observer puts it, "The combined effect of an advanced capital market and a strong military machine to defend that market, and other safety measures such as a strong tradition of property rights protection and a reputation for honoring dues, has made it possible to attract capital with great ease."[22]

We should not overestimate, however, the economic power that a country gains from having its currency held as a reserve by other countries. Seignorage (the gap between the cost of producing money and its face value) applies only to the $380 billion of banknotes held internationally, not to Treasury obligations that must pay competitive interest rates (although confidence in the dollar can allow Treasury to issue bonds at lower interest rates than would otherwise be the case). Before fiscal problems in Greece and other countries caused a loss of confidence in Europe in 2010, "simply by enhancing the size and liquidity of financial markets the euro may have helped to lower real interest rates across Europe, and not just for government borrowers."[23]

Against the ease of adjustment and financing deficits described previously, there are potential costs. For example, Treasury is constrained by international opinion about the dollar when it formulates policies. In addition, to the extent that demand for the reserve currency is raised by its international role, the currency's value rises and producers in the reserve currency country may find their products less competitive in world markets than would otherwise be the case. Many American producers would welcome a diminished role for the dollar. Because of the scale of the American economy and the comparative depth and breadth of its financial markets, the dollar is likely to remain a major international reserve currency for the next decade or longer, but the economic power that comes from being a reserve instrument in currency markets should not be ignored or, as is more often the case, exaggerated.[24]

Even though neither the United States nor China is willing to destroy the balance of asymmetries that locks them together, the United States has allowed a gradual increase in Chinese influence in international forums (as well as greater influence for other emerging economies). Thus, the G-8 forum (where four of the eight countries are European) has been effectively supplemented by a G-20 summit that includes economies representing 80 percent of world product. Such meetings have discussed the need to "rebalance" financial flows, altering the old pattern of U.S. deficits matching Chinese surpluses. Such changes would require politically difficult shifts in domestic patterns of consumption and investment, with America increasing its savings and China increasing domestic consumption. Such changes are not likely to occur quickly, but, interestingly, the G-20 has already agreed that Europe should reduce the weight of its votes in the IMF and that China and other emerging economies should gradually increase their weight.

This again shows the importance of the limitations on economic power. Although China could threaten to sell its holdings of dollars and damage the American economy, a weakened American economy would mean a smaller market for Chinese exports, and the American government might respond with tariffs against Chinese goods. Neither side is in a hurry to break the symmetry of their vulnerability interdependence, but each continues to jockey to shape the structure and institutional framework of their market relationship. Moreover, as other emerging economies such as India and Brazil find their exports hurt by an undervalued Chinese currency, they may use a multilateral forum such as the G-20 in a way that reinforces the American position.[25]

When there is asymmetry of interdependence in different issue areas, a state may try to link or unlink issues. If each issue were a separate game and all games were played simultaneously, one state might have most of the chips at one table and another state might have most of the chips at another table. Depending on a state's interests and position, it might want to keep the games separate or create linkages between the tables. Therefore, much of the political conflict over economic interdependence involves the creation or prevention of linkage. States want to manipulate interdependence in areas in which they are strong and avoid being manipulated in areas in which they are relatively weak.

By setting agendas and defining issue areas, international institutions often set the rules for the trade-offs in interdependent relationships. States try to use international institutions to set the rules that affect the transfer of chips among tables. Membership in the WTO, for example, restricts certain policy instruments that states might use and subjects others to a dispute resolution mechanism. Ironically, given the rhetoric of antiglobalization protesters, international institutions can benefit the weaker players by keeping some of the conflicts in which the poorer states are relatively better endowed separated from the tables where strong states dominate. The danger remains, however, that some players will be strong enough to overturn one or more of the tables. In 1971, for example, as the American balance of payments worsened, President Nixon abruptly announced that the United States would no longer convert dollars into gold, thus overturning the Bretton Woods monetary system that had been created by a multilateral agreement in 1944.

The largest state does not always win in the manipulation of economic interdependence. If a smaller or weaker state has a greater concern about an issue, it may do quite well. For instance, because the United States accounts for nearly three-quarters of Canada's foreign trade, whereas Canada accounts for about one-quarter of America's foreign trade, Canada is more dependent on the United States than vice versa. Nonetheless, Canada has often prevailed in a number of disputes with the United States because Canada was willing to threaten retaliatory actions, such as tariffs and restrictions, that deterred the United States.[26] The Canadians would have suffered much more than the Americans if their actions had led to a full dispute, but Canada felt it was better to risk occasional retaliation than to agree to rules that would *always* make Canada lose.

Deterrence via manipulation of economic interdependence is some-what like nuclear deterrence in that it rests on a capability for effective damage and credible intentions. Small states can often use their greater intensity, greater focus, and greater credibility to overcome their relative vulnerability in asymmetrical interdependence. In terms of the concepts discussed in Chapter 1, they may develop a greater power-conversion capability. The asymmetry in resources is sometimes balanced by an opposite asymmetry in attention and will.

NATURAL RESOURCES

Sometimes people equate a rich endowment in natural resources with economic power, but the relationship is complicated. Japan, for example, became the second richest country in the world in the twentieth century without significant natural resources, and some well-endowed countries have not been able to turn their natural resources into national wealth or power. For example, some oil-producing countries remain weak, and because of oil's some-times perverse social and economic effects, observers refer to an "oil curse." To the extent that oil wealth leads to corrupt institutions and an unbalanced economy that discourages broader entrepreneurship and investment in human capital, it may inhibit the development of national power.[27]

States struggle to shape the structure of markets to their advantage by manipulating market access with tariffs, quotas, and licenses; diversifying supply chains; pursuing equity shares in companies; and using aid to gain special concessions. Success varies with the asymmetries in particular markets. For example, for decades the annual price-setting negotiations between big suppliers of iron ore and leading steelmakers were dull as prices rose only gradually. But after China emerged as a buyer of more than half of all iron ore exports, prices quadrupled between 2002 and 2008. The Chinese government was nervous about its dependence because just three firms (BHP, Rio Tinto, and Vale) dominated trade in iron ore. So China's government, acting through state-controlled companies, tried to overturn the oligopoly "by encouraging Chinese customers to negotiate purchases in unison, by hunting for alternate supplies and even by buying a stake in Rio, all to little effect."[28] In this case, buoyant demand and limited supply restricted Chinese government power to restructure the market, though China later brought bribery charges against officials of Rio Tinto.[29] In other cases, which depend upon direct investment or access to the internal Chinese market, the situation is reversed, and the government has wielded its economic power. And in September 2010, after a maritime dispute, China curtailed its export of rare earth minerals to Japan.

Even where natural resources are scarce within a nation's borders, their absence is not an index of low economic power. Much depends on a country's vulnerability, and that depends on whether substitutes are available and whether there are diverse sources of supply. For example, in the 1970s some analysts expressed alarm about the increasing dependence of the United States on imported raw materials and therefore its vulnerability. Of thirteen basic industrial raw materials, the United States was dependent on imports for nearly 90 percent of aluminum, chromium, manganese, and nickel. The ability of oil producers to form a cartel (OPEC) was taken as a harbinger for other commodities. Power was seen as shifting to the producers of natural resources. But over the next decade, raw materials prices went down, not up. What happened to the prediction? In judging vulnerability, the analysts failed to consider the alternative sources of raw materials and the diversity of sources of supply that prevented producers from jacking up prices artificially. Moreover, technology improves over time. Projections of U.S. vulnerability to shortages of raw materials were inaccurate because they failed to adequately consider technology and alternatives.

OIL, GAS, AND ECONOMIC POWER

Mao Zedong once said that power comes out of the barrel of a gun, but many people today believe that power comes out of a barrel of oil. It turns out that oil is the exception, not the rule, in judgments about economic power derived from natural resources, and thus it is worth a more detailed analysis. Oil is the most important raw material in the world, in both economic and political terms, and it is likely to remain a key source of energy well into this century. The United States consumes 20 percent of the world's oil (compared to 8 percent for China, though Chinese consumption is growing more rapidly). Even with high Chinese growth, the world is not running out of oil anytime soon. More than 1 trillion barrels of reserves have been proven, and more is likely to be found. But more than 66 percent of the proven reserves are in the Persian Gulf and are therefore vulnerable to political disruption, which could have devastating effects on the world economy.

The framework of rules, norms, and institutions that affect oil markets has changed dramatically over the decades.[30] In 1960, the oil regime was a private oligopoly with close ties to the governments of the major consuming countries. Seven large transnational oil companies, primarily British and American in origin and sometimes called the "seven sisters," determined the amount of oil that would be produced. The price of oil depended on how much the large companies produced and on the demand in the rich countries where most of the oil was sold. Transnational companies set the rate of production, and prices were determined by conditions in rich countries. The strongest powers in the international system in traditional military terms occasionally intervened to maintain the unequal structure of oil markets. For example, in 1953 when a nationalist movement tried to overthrow the shah of Iran, Britain and the United States covertly intervened to return the shah to his throne.

After the 1973 oil crisis, there was a major change in the international regime governing oil markets. There was an enormous shift of power and wealth from rich to relatively weak countries. The producing countries began to set the rate of production and therefore had a strong effect on price, rather than price being determined solely by the market in the rich countries. A frequently offered explanation is that the oil-producing countries banded together and formed OPEC, but OPEC was formed in 1960 and the dramatic change did not occur until more than a decade later in 1973. In 1960, half the OPEC countries were colonies of Europe; by 1973, they were all independent. Accompanying the rise in nationalism was a rise in the costs of military intervention. It is much more expensive to use force against a nationalistically awakened and decolonized people. When the British and Americans intervened in Iran in 1953, it was not very costly in the short term, but if the Americans had tried to keep the shah on his throne in 1979 in the face of the Iranian Revolution, the costs would have been prohibitive.

The relative symmetry of economic power in oil markets also changed. During the two Middle East wars of 1956 and 1967, the Arab countries tried an oil embargo, but their efforts were easily defeated because the United States was producing enough oil to supply Europe when it was cut off by the Arab countries. Once American production peaked in 1971 and the United States began to import oil, the power to balance the oil market switched to such countries as Saudi Arabia and Iran. The United States was no longer the supplier of last resort that could make up any missing oil.

The "seven sisters" gradually lost power over this period. One reason was their "obsolescing bargains" with the producer countries.[31] When a transnational corporation goes into a resource-rich country with a new investment, it can strike a bargain in which the multinational gets a large part of the joint gains. From the point of view of the poor country, having a multinational come in to develop its resources will make the country better off. At the early stages when the multinational has a monopoly on capital, technology, and access to international markets, it strikes a bargain with the poor country in which the multinational gets the lion's share. But over time, the multinational inadvertently transfers resources to the poor country and trains locals, not out of charity but out of the normal process of doing business. Eventually, the poor country wants a better division of the profits. The multinational could threaten to pull out, but now the poor country can threaten to run the operation by itself. So over time, the power of the transnational company to structure a market, particularly in raw materials, diminishes in terms of its bargaining with the host country. The seven sisters were joined by "little cousins" when new transnational corporations entered the oil market. Although they were not as large as the seven sisters, they were still big, and they began to strike their own deals with the oil-producing countries. That competition further reduced the power of the largest transnational corporations to structure the market. Today, the six largest transnational corporations control only 5 percent of world oil reserves; state-owned companies control the rest.[32]

There was also a modest increase in the effectiveness of OPEC as a cartel. Cartels restricting supply had long been typical in the oil industry, but in the past they had been private arrangements of the seven sisters. Cartels generally have a problem because there is a tendency to cheat on production quotas when markets are soft and the price drops. With time, market forces tend to erode cartels. OPEC was unable to enforce price discipline from the year it was founded, 1960, until the early 1970s. But after oil supplies tightened, OPEC's role in coordinating the bargaining power of the producers increased.

The Middle East war of 1973 gave OPEC a boost, a signal that now it could use its power. The Arab countries cut off access to oil during the 1973 war for political reasons, but that created a situation in which OPEC could become effective. Iran, which is not an Arab country, was supposed to be the American instrument for policing the Persian Gulf, but the shah moved to quadruple oil prices, and the other OPEC countries followed suit. Over the long term, OPEC could not maintain permanently high prices because of market forces, but there was a stickiness on the downside that was an effect of the OPEC coalition.

At one point in the crisis, Secretary of State Henry Kissinger said that if the United States faced "strangulation," military force might have to be used. Fifteen percent of traded oil had been cut, and the

Arab embargo reduced oil exports to the United States by 25 percent. However, oil companies made sure that no one country suffered much more than any other. They redistributed the world's traded oil. When the United States lost 25 percent of its Arab oil imports, the companies shipped it more Venezuelan or Indonesian oil. They smoothed the pain of the embargo so that the rich countries all lost about 7–9 percent of their oil, well below the strangulation point. The companies, acting primarily out of their own interest in maintaining stability, helped prevent the economic conflict from becoming a military conflict.[33]

How powerful was oil as an economic weapon at the turning point of 1973? By cutting production and embargoing sales to countries friendly to Israel, Arab states were able to bring their issues to the forefront of the U.S. agenda. The oil weapon encouraged the United States to play a more conciliatory role in arranging the settlement of the Arab-Israeli dispute in the aftermath of the Yom Kippur War. However, the oil weapon did not change the basic policy of the United States in the Middle East.

Why was the oil weapon not more effective, and what are the lessons for today? Part of the answer is symmetry in overall interdependence. Saudi Arabia, which became the key country in oil markets, had large investments in the United States. If the Saudis damaged the U.S. economy too much, they would also hurt their own economic interests. In addition, Saudi Arabia depended on the United States in the security area. In the long run, the United States was the only country able to keep a stable balance of power in the Persian Gulf region. The Saudis knew this, and they were careful about how far they pushed the oil weapon. At one point, they quietly made sure that the American Sixth Fleet in the region was supplied with oil.[34] The Saudis were benefiting from the long-run security guarantee provided by the United States. There was an indirect linkage between the security interdependence and the oil interdependence. Force was too costly to use overtly, but it played a role as a power resource in the background. In other words, the outcome of the crisis involved asymmetries caused by changes in the structure of the market, but

FIGURE 3.1 Real Domestic Crude Oil Prices (1946–2008)*

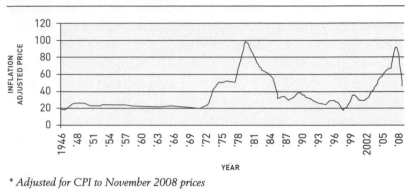

YEAR

Adjusted for CPI to November 2008 prices

Source: Data from Illinois Oil and Gas Association and U.S. Bureau of Labor Statistics.

the outcome was not determined by economic power alone. This complex set of factors persists today in creating and limiting the power that comes from possessing oil resources.

By the late 1990s, oil prices had plummeted. Efficiency gains stimulated by high prices cut demand, and on the supply side the emergence of new non-OPEC oil sources meant that OPEC faced more competition on the world market. Advances in technology led geologists to gain access to oil that had previously been impossible to reach. After 2005, however, oil prices spiked again, partly in response to disruptions from war, hurricanes, and terrorist threats, but largely because of projections of rising demand accompanying rapid economic growth in Asia. The two most populous nations on earth, China and India, are experiencing rapid increases in demand for energy as they modernize and industrialize. Both countries are making mercantilist efforts to buy and control foreign oil supplies, though the lessons of the 1970s crisis suggest that oil is a fungible commodity and markets tend to spread supplies and even out the pain no matter who owns the oil. In any event, the rapid economic growth of these two countries will contribute significantly to the global demand for oil, and this means that the biggest global oil-producing regions, such as the Persian Gulf, will still play an important role in world politics. Because Saudi Arabia is the world's number one producer and source of reserves, any major changes in its political stability could have widespread consequences.

It is interesting to compare the markets in oil and natural gas. Russia is a major producer of both, but Russia's efforts to gain power by structuring market asymmetries is more obvious in the area of natural gas than in oil. As we have seen, oil is a relatively fungible commodity with multiple sources of supply and relative ease of transport, whereas until recently gas has been regarded as scarce and more dependent upon fixed pipelines for supply. Although this may change in the future because of liquefied natural gas shipments and new technologies for producing gas from plentiful fields of shale rock, until now Russia has been a major supplier of natural gas to Europe. The Russian government has consolidated ownership of gas fields and pipelines in one company, Gazprom, and used it to structure markets in Russia's favor. When Russia had disputes with neighbors such as Ukraine over gas prices, it did not hesitate to cut off gas supplies as a form of economic power. Later, when a more sympathetic government came to power in Ukraine, Russia used the lure of heavily discounted gas prices to obtain the extension of its lease of a naval base in Ukraine, thus complicating the prospect that Ukraine might one day join NATO.[35]

Germany depends on Russia for a third of its natural gas, but the German government claims not to be overly concerned because it regards the interdependence as symmetrical.[36] In German eyes, German customers are such a large group that Russian income depends on the security of German demand just as much as German customers depend on the security of Russian supply. Thus, when the European Union has tried to stimulate interest in a pipeline to route Caspian gas to Europe without crossing Russian territory, Germany has expressed less interest. Instead, Germany supported a pipeline under the Baltic Sea that will increase its dependence on Russian supply and allow Russia to bypass Ukraine and Poland.

This will increase the vulnerability of Ukraine and Poland. In the past, those states had bargaining power based on their ability to stop gas flowing through pipelines that crossed their territory. The pain this caused in Germany added to Ukraine and Poland's bargaining power with Russia. In short, Russia has used its pipeline diplomacy to increase its economic power. It has an incentive to keep its promise to be a reliable supplier to large customers such as Germany, but Russia can wield its asymmetrical advantage over smaller customers such as the Baltics, Georgia, Belarus, and Ukraine in what Russia sees as its sphere of influence. Similarly, Russia has tried to contract for gas from the Central Asian republics to be routed to Europe through Russian pipelines, but this market structuring is being countered by Chinese efforts to construct pipelines eastward from Central Asia. Even more important were the recent discovery and exploitation of technologies to unlock the massive amounts of gas trapped in shale rock in the United States and elsewhere. Projects designed to liquefy natural gas and ship it to the United States were no longer competitive in American markets. As this gas began to be shipped instead to European markets, it reduced the power that Russia could develop through its pipeline diplomacy.[37]

What these oil and gas examples show is that even though raw materials are less crucial in the so-called lightweight economies of the information age than they were in the industrial age, oil and gas still matter when it comes to generating economic power. But even the power that comes from the control of energy resources waxes and wanes. Economic power is highly contingent on the particular market context.

SANCTIONS: NEGATIVE AND POSITIVE

Just as many people think of fighting as the heart of military power, they often think of sanctions as the most visible instrument of economic power. Imposing sanctions is less subtle than structuring markets (though sanctions sometimes involve manipulating control over market access). "Sanctions" are defined as measures of encouragement or punishment designed to reinforce a decision or make a policy authoritative. They can be both negative and positive. As Thomas Schelling once pointed out, "The difference between a threat and a promise, between coercion and compensation, sometimes depends on where the baseline is located. We originally offered our children a weekly allowance on condition they make their own beds and do a few other simple chores. . . . But once it became standard practice and expectation that the weekly allowance would be paid, withholding it for nonperformance became in the children's eyes a punishment."[38] Perceptions affect how sanctions are experienced.

David Baldwin lists eleven examples of negative trade sanctions ranging from embargos to preclusive buying and seven capital sanctions that include freezing of assets, unfavorable taxation, and suspension of aid. Among a dozen positive sanctions, he includes tariff reductions, favorable market access, provision of aid, and investment guarantees.[39] Other recent examples of sanctions include travel bans and arms embargoes. Sanctions can be applied by and against both state and nonstate actors. What sanctions all have in common is the manipulation of economic transactions for political purposes.

States restrict access to their markets for protectionist purposes in a competition to secure a greater share of the gains from trade or to favor a politically important domestic group, but many protectionist measures are also designed to generate power. For example, when the European Union granted preferential trade access to its market for its ex-colonies, it could be seen as righting a historical injustice (and thereby seeking to generate soft power) or as exercising a means of neocolonial control (hard power), but the purposes were political.

States with large markets often use threats of restructuring market access to extend their regulatory power beyond their territory. In the area of privacy regulations, for example, Brussels has taken the lead in establishing global standards because no firm wishes to be excluded from the European market. Similarly, because of the importance of the American and European markets, transnational firms adhere to the strictest set of antitrust regulations. Even when the American Justice Department approved GE's acquisition of Honeywell (both American companies), GE abandoned the deal after the European Union objected. And companies that want access to China's market find they have to agree to minority ownership rules, transfer of proprietary technology, and restrictive rules on communication. As its market size increases, China has been making stricter demands that in effect force suppliers to share their technology and adopt Chinese technical standards "as a conscious strategy to use China's economic girth to shift technology standards by making it too costly for the industry not to adapt."[40] Foreign investors have warned China about policies that undercut the climate of confidence of investment, but to little avail. During a visit to Brussels in 2009, Chinese vice premier Wang Qishan asked the European Union to keep its markets open, lift its arms embargo, and grant more visas to Chinese citizens. When the Europeans demurred, "Mr. Wang's response was dismissive: whatever you tell me doesn't really make a difference. You are going to invest in China anyway."[41] Not surprisingly, states with larger markets are better placed to control market access and to apply sanctions.

As the world's largest economy, the United States has often taken the lead in applying sanctions. The United States alone applied eighty-five new sanctions on foreign states between 1996 and 2001,[42] and some wags complained that the country had sanctions against half of humankind. Yet the conventional wisdom of most pundits is that "sanctions don't work." This judgment is reinforced by famous cases such as the failure of League of Nations sanctions to stop Italian aggression in Ethiopia, the failure of the American trade embargo to topple Fidel Castro for half a century, or the failure of sanctions to remove Saddam Hussein from power in Iraq. Why, then, are sanctions so often used?

The answer may be in part that the judgment of failure is overstated. A careful study of 115 uses of economic sanctions by major countries from 1950 to 1990 concluded that in about a third of the cases, sanctions made at least a modest contribution to obtaining the goals of those using them. The study found that sanctions were most likely to be successful when the objective was modest and clear, the target was in a weakened position to begin with, economic relations were great, sanctions were heavy, and the duration was limited.[43] Others have challenged these results, with one scholar claiming that sanctions were effective in only 5 of the 115 cases, but the successes included significant instances such as South Africa and Libya.[44]

Baldwin points out that judgments about effectiveness relate only to outputs, unlike judgments about efficiency or utility, which relate instruments and outputs. The important question in any situation is, What is the alternative to sanctions? Even if the probability of reaching a desired end through economic sanctions is low, the relevant issue is whether it is higher than for alternative policy options. Military power is sometimes more effective, but its costs may be so high that it is less efficient. Take the case of sanctions against the Castro regime in Cuba. As the Cuban Missile Crisis showed, the costs of using military means to remove Castro were potentially enormous, including the risks of nuclear war. At the same time, given the bipolar Cold War, doing nothing would have been costly for America's political competition with the Soviet Union. Although it is true that sanctions were not effective in removing Castro, they were an efficient means of imposing costs and containing Castro. Military action might (or might not—witness the Bay of Pigs failure) have removed Castro, but given the potential military costs, sanctions might have been the most efficient policy choice available.[45]

Like all forms of power, efforts to wield economic sanctions depend upon the context, purposes, and skill in converting resources into desired behavior. Judging success requires clarity about goals, and both actors and observers sometimes mix the goals together. The major goals of sanctions include behavioral change, containment, and regime change in another country.[46] Alternatively, the goals can be described as coercing, constraining, and signaling. Coercion is an effort to make the target do something, prevention means making it costly for a target to do something, and signaling indicates commitment—to the target, to domestic audiences, or to third parties.[47] One study concluded that trade sanctions rarely force compliance or subvert the target government and have limited deterrent value, but they often succeed as international and domestic symbols.[48]

To go back to the famous Cuban "failure," although sanctions did not remove Castro and only somewhat inhibited his international capabilities (because he received countervailing Soviet aid), they did allow American policymakers to signal to a domestic audience and to other countries that alliance with the Soviet Union could be costly. (Whether the sanctions outlived their purpose and became counterproductive when the end of the Cold War changed their context is a different question.) Similarly, after the Soviet Union invaded Afghanistan in 1979, President Jimmy Carter curtailed grain sales and boycotted the Moscow Olympics rather than use a threat of force, which would not have looked credible. Threats are cheap to make but costly to credibility when they fail. The fact that these sanctions were costly to the United States helped to establish some credibility in the American reaction to the Soviet invasion.

General sanctions are a blunt instrument in which the suffering may be borne by the poor and powerless rather than the elites that make decisions in autocratic countries. Moreover, as in the case of Iraq, Hussein was able to construct dramatic narratives about their brutal effects as a way to delegitimize UN sanctions and seek concessions that undercut their effect. The prevalence of sanctions with limited results in the 1990s led to efforts to construct "smart sanctions" that would be targeted at elites rather than at the general public. Specific members of the elite were banned from travel and had overseas financial assets frozen. In 2007, the effectiveness of the American Treasury Department's freezing of North Korean assets in a Macao bank is credited with helping to bring Pyongyang back to the bargaining table. In addition, policymakers began to realize that sanctions should be regarded as one tool among many, rather than an all-or-nothing condition, and used flexibly in a bargaining relationship. For example, as America began to repair its relations with Vietnam in the 1990s, a gradual relaxation of sanctions was part of the process, along with other diplomatic tools. More recently, in relation to Burma, Secretary of State Hillary Rodham Clinton announced that "engagement versus sanctions is a false choice . . . so going forward, we will be employing both these tools."[49]

The signaling role of sanctions has often been dismissed as "merely symbolic." But if we consider legitimacy and soft power, we see clearly that signaling can impose real costs upon a target. Naming and shaming campaigns are important ways in which nongovernmental actors try to affect the policies of transnational corporations by attacking the equity they have built up in their brands. NGOs also try to shame states into action by attack on national reputation, and states themselves compete to create narratives that increase their soft power and reduce that of their opponents. Sometimes the campaigns fail and sometimes they succeed, but legitimacy is a power reality, and struggles over legitimacy involve real costs. Some observers believe that the main effect of antiapartheid sanctions that eventually led to majority rule in South Africa in 1994 lay not in the economic effects, but in the sense of isolation and doubts about legitimacy that developed in the ruling white minority. Similarly, the success of UN sanctions in helping to bring about a reversal in Libyan policies of support for terrorism and development of nuclear weapons were related to Libyan concerns about legitimacy as much as economic effects.[50] Because of their value in signaling and soft power, and because they are often the only relatively inexpensive policy option, sanctions are likely to remain a major instrument of power in the twenty-first century despite their mixed record.

Payments, aid, and other positive sanctions also have both a hard and a soft power dimension. As noted earlier, providing a payment and removing a payment are two sides of the same coin. Providing aid and cutting off aid are the positive and negative aspects of a similar sanction. Providing payments to secure the support of other countries has a long history in cabinet diplomacy, and it persists in today's democratic age. Indeed, the score of small countries that continue to recognize the Republic of China government in Taipei rather than Beijing receive significant economic aid from Taiwan. Similarly, if we try to understand why some nonwhaling countries vote with Japan in international forums on issues related to whaling, we must note that they receive aid from Japan.

After 2005, the rise in oil and gas prices boosted the political leverage of energy-producing countries such as Russia, Venezuela, and Iran that had suffered from the low oil prices of the 1990s. Although they did not have Saudi Arabia's economic power to structure markets, their extra cash provided money for payments and aid to advance their foreign policy objectives. President Hugo Chávez of Venezuela used his country's oil wealth to gain soft power in Latin America and even offered cheap oil to consumers in Massachusetts as a soft power propaganda ploy. Iran used its oil wealth to reinforce its influence in Lebanon and elsewhere. Russia used oil money to buy influence: It allegedly paid $50 million to the tiny Pacific island of Nauru to recognize Georgia's breakaway provinces of Abkhazia and South Ossetia—although non-oil-producing China allegedly paid only $5 million a year to Nauru to recognize Beijing rather than Taipei.[51]

Large states give foreign aid for a variety of purposes. The largest recipients of American aid (after the war-torn states of Afghanistan and Pakistan) are Israel and Egypt, and the payments are designed to influence both states with regard to security in the area. Chinese aid is often used to gain access to raw materials. A raw material concession is often accompanied by a Chinese offer to build a new stadium or airport terminal. According to some experts, "China, which is not a member of the OECD [Organization for Economic Cooperation and Development], is operating under rules that the West has largely abandoned. It mixes aid and business in secret government-to-government agreements."[52] The Chinese approach, which avoids good governance or human rights conditions, is often welcomed by authoritarian states. Rwandan president Paul Kagame compares it favorably to the Western approach.[53] Nor is China alone. India and Brazil are other emerging economies that both receive and give aid at the same time. "None of the new donors (all of which except Russia, still get aid themselves) publishes comprehensive, or even comprehensible, figures."[54]

Russian aid is designed to increase Russian influence in what Russia calls "the near abroad" of former Soviet states. Some countries, such as Great Britain, devote a large portion of their aid to development and separate its administration in a special bureaucracy—in Britain, the Department for International Development rather than the Foreign Office. When we look at American assistance programs, less than half are administered by the Agency for International Development (AID) and devoted to development.[55] As a superpower, the United States has many objectives for assistance that are not directly related to development. A quarter of American aid is administered by the Pentagon.

Even when aid is designated for development only, it can still be used to create hard economic power, for example, by building up the economic and administrative capabilities of an allied country. "Nation-building" can develop the hard power of an ally. The Marshall Plan, in which the United States contributed 2 percent of its gross domestic product to restore the economies of Europe that had

TABLE 3.1 U.S. Aid Program Composition (2008)[1]

CATEGORY	PERCENTAGE OF TOTAL AID
Bilateral development	35.5
Economic, political, security	27.1
Military	17.5
Humanitarian	14.4
Multilateral	5.5

Source: U.S. Department of State, "Summary and Highlights, International Affairs, Function 150, FY2009"; House and Senate Appropriations Committees; and CRS calculations.
1. Curt Tarnoff and Marian Lawson, "Foreign Aid: An Introduction to U.S. Programs and Policy" (Washington, DC: Congressional Research Service Report, April 2009), www.fas.org/sgp/crs/row/R40213.pdf.

been devastated by World War II, is an important case in point. By restoring growth and prosperity to Western Europe, the United States succeeded in strengthening resistance to communism and the Soviet Union—a major foreign policy goal. The Marshall Plan also helped to develop a sense of gratitude in Europe and enhanced American soft power among the recipient countries.

Occasionally, people have called for similar Marshall Plans for development in many less-developed regions, but two of the problems with such proposals are the scale of the original plan and the fact that the European economies were already developed and needed only to be restored. Moreover, they administered much of the aid effectively. Today, economists do not agree that there is a clear formula for development or if there is, that aid is always productive. Indeed, some go so far as to argue that aid can be counterproductive by creating a culture of dependency and corruption. For example, Jeffrey Sachs thinks that extreme poverty can be eliminated by 2025 through carefully planned development aid, whereas former World Bank economist William Easterly is very skeptical of foreign aid in general, and believes that it creates perverse incentives.[56] Sachs has developed pilot projects in Kenya villages that work, but "Easterly and others have criticized Mr. Sachs as not paying enough attention to bigger-picure issues like governance and corruption, which have stymied some of the best-intentioned and best-fiananced aid projects."[57] Even if we do not determine the merits of the arguments among economists, we can recognize that the degree of uncertainty about development and nation-building sets limits on the way that aid can be used to generate economic power by building up allies. This does not mean that aid is always ineffective, only that we exercise caution in taking at face value overly optimistic estimates about development-oriented aid as a source of hard economic power. Indeed, when donors have strategic goals, they may lose the leverage to impose growth-promoting reforms.[58]

Aid programs may also be used for humanitarian purposes, and if properly administered, they can generate soft power. But such soft power effects are not guaranteed. Although assistance may curry favor among elites, if it leads to corruption and disruption of existing power balances among social groups, it can also engender resentment, rather than attraction, among the general populace. Moreover, conditionality designed to restrict local elites can backfire. For example, when the United States unveiled its $7.5 billion aid budget for Pakistan in 2009, it set conditions that restricted some parts for civilian development purposes, but the restrictions raised a nationalist furor in the Pakistan press.[59] Similarly, a study of aid projects in Afghanistan found that sometimes aid was not merely ineffectual but was counterproductive in terms of soft power. By disturbing local political balances and stimulating corruption, large aid projects often generated jealousy, conflict, and resentment among local groups. As one observer concluded, "If there are lessons to be drawn from the still tentative successes here, they are that small projects often work best, that the consent and participation of local people are essential and that even baby steps take years."[60] Like negative sanctions, positive sanctions of payment and assistance have a mixed record as generators of both hard and soft power.

THE FUTURE OF ECONOMIC POWER

Bargaining and power struggles occur among states, private corporations, and hybrids of the two. "Wherever you look you can see the proliferation of hybrid organizations that blur the line between the public and private sector. These are neither old-fashioned nationalized companies, designed to manage chunks of the economy, nor classic private-sector firms that sink or swim according to their own strength. Instead they are confusing entities that seem to flit between one world and another to suit their own purposes."[61] Russian firms like Gazprom, Chinese state-owned enterprises, and sovereign wealth funds like Dubai World complicate market behavior and increase the opportunities for political manipulation.

A robust and growing economy provides the basis for all instruments of power. In addition, economic tools like sanctions and aid will be crucial in this century because they are often the most efficient instruments in terms of relative costs. But it is a mistake to argue that the twenty-first century will be the age of geoeconomics. The diffusion of power to nonstate actors, including transnational corporations, sets limits on state strategies to use economic instruments. States will often find economic power difficult to wield both because market actors are difficult to control and because market conditions are variable. But even as it is a mistake to make generalizations about the dominance of economic power over military power in the twenty-first century, it is equally important to understand the full range of economic policy instruments. Structuring markets is more important than imposing sanctions and providing aid. Very often, policies that promote open market structures and diversification of sources of supply will turn out to be more effective in denying economic power to suppliers than mercantilist efforts to lock up supplies through ownership. Economic power will be one of the most important implements in the toolbox of smart power policies, but policy answers will often depend on the context of each market and its asymmetries of vulnerability.

CHAPTER 4

Soft Power

Soft power is an academic concept that has migrated to the front pages of newspapers and been used by top leaders in China, Indonesia, Europe, and elsewhere. However, wide usage has sometimes meant misuse of the concept as a synonym for anything other than military force.[1] Moreover, because soft power has appeared to be an alternative to raw power politics, it is often embraced by ethically minded scholars and policymakers. But soft power is a descriptive, rather than a normative, concept. Like any form of power, it can be wielded for good or bad purposes. Hitler, Stalin, and Mao all possessed a great deal of soft power in the eyes of their acolytes, but that did not make it good. It is not necessarily better to twist minds than to twist arms.[2]

Skeptics have dismissed soft power as "one of those beautiful academic ideas that failed a lot of foreign policy tests" and argued that "armies weren't stopped by even the deepest cultural affinity."[3] Though the concept of soft power is recent, the behavior it denotes is as old as human history. It is implicit in Lao-tzu's comment that a leader is best not when people obey his commands, but when they barely know he exists. In eighteenth-century Europe, the spread of French language and culture enhanced French power. In 1762, when Frederick the Great of Prussia was on the brink of defeat, he was saved by his personal soft power when "Czarina Elizabeth died and was succeeded by her son Peter, who idolized the soldier-king . . . and ordered home the Russian armies."[4] During the American Civil War, some British statesmen considered supporting the South, but despite their obvious commercial and strategic interests, British elites were constrained by popular opposition to slavery and attraction to the cause of the North. Before World War I, when the United States wrestled with the choice of going to war with Germany or Britain, "Germany's primary disadvantage in 1914 was not its record in American opinion, but the absence of a record. So little existed to counteract the natural pull toward Britain . . . which dominated the channels of transatlantic communication."[5] Contrary to the skeptics, soft power has often had very real effects in history, including on the movement of armies.

Because it is a form of power, only a truncated and impoverished version of realism ignores soft power.[6] Traditional realists did not. In 1939, noted British realist E. H. Carr described international power in three categories: military power, economic power, and power over opinion. As we have seen, much of this subtlety was lost by contemporary neorealists in their desire to make power measurable for their structural judgments.[7] They committed what might be called "the concrete fallacy."[8] Power was reduced to measurable, tangible resources. It was something that could be dropped on your foot or on cities, rather than something that might change your mind about wanting to drop anything in the first place.

As Machiavelli, the ultimate realist, described five centuries ago, it may be better for a prince to be feared than loved, but the prince is in greatest danger when he is hated. There is no contradiction between realism and soft power. Soft power is not a form of idealism or liberalism. It is simply a form of power, one way of getting desired outcomes. Legitimacy is a power reality. Competitive struggles over legitimacy are part of enhancing or depriving actors of soft power, and this is particularly true in the information age of the twenty-first century.

Not just states are involved. Corporations, institutions, NGOs, and transnational terrorist networks often have soft power of their own. Even individual celebrities are able to use their soft power "by making ideas, palatable, acceptable, colorful. Or as the singer Bono put it . . . his function is to bring applause when people get it right, and make their lives a misery when they don't."[9] In 2007, in the run-up to the Beijing Olympics, Steven Spielberg sent an open letter to President Hu Jintao asking China to use its influence to push Sudan to accept a UN peacekeeping force in Darfur. "China soon dispatched Mr. Zhai to Darfur, a turnaround that served as a classic study of how a pressure campaign, aimed to strike Beijing in a vulnerable spot at a vulnerable time, could accomplish what years of diplomacy could not."[10]

Incorporating soft power into a government strategy is more difficult than may first appear. For one thing, success in terms of outcomes is more in the control of the target than is often the case with hard power. A second problem is that the results often take a long time, and most politicians and publics are impatient to see a prompt return on their investments. Third, the instruments of soft power are not fully under the control of governments. Although governments control policy, culture and values are embedded in civil societies. Soft power may appear less risky than economic or military power, but it is often hard to use, easy to lose, and costly to reestablish.

Soft power depends upon credibility, and when governments are perceived as manipulative and information is seen as propaganda, credibility is destroyed. One critic argues that if governments eschew imposition or manipulation, they are not really exercising soft power, but mere dialogue.[11] Even though governments face a difficult task in maintaining credibility, this criticism underestimates the importance of pull, rather than push, in soft power interactions. The best propaganda is not propaganda.

Of course, it is important not to exaggerate the impact of soft (or any other form of) power. There are some situations where soft power provides very little leverage. It is difficult, for example, to

see how soft power would solve the dispute over North Korea's nuclear weapons. Some critics make the mistake of assuming that because soft power is often insufficient, it is not a form of power. But
that problem is true of all forms of power. Nevertheless, when a
government is concerned about structural milieu goals or general
value objectives, such as promotion of democracy, human rights,
and freedom, it is often the case that soft power turns out to be superior to hard power. And in a century marked by global information and a diffusion of power to nonstate actors, soft power will
become an increasingly important part of smart power strategies.

SOURCES OF SOFT POWER

The soft power of a country rests heavily on three basic resources:
its culture (in places where it is attractive to others), its political
values (when it lives up to them at home and abroad), and its foreign policies (when others see them as legitimate and having moral
authority). The parenthetical conditions are the key in determining
whether potential soft power resources translate into the behavior
of attraction that can influence others toward favorable outcomes.
With soft power, what the target thinks is particularly important,
and the targets matter as much as the agents. Attraction and persuasion are socially constructed. Soft power is a dance that requires
partners.

In some contexts, culture can be an important power resource.
"Culture" is the pattern of social behaviors by which groups transmit
knowledge and values, and it exists at multiple levels.[12] Some aspects of human culture are universal, some are national, and others
are particular to social classes or small groups. Culture is never
static, and different cultures interact in different ways. More research needs to be done on the connection between culture and
power behavior. For example, can Western cultural attraction reduce current extremist appeals in some Muslim societies today?
Some see an unbridgeable cultural divide. But consider the Islamic

state of Iran. Western music and videos are anathema to the ruling mullahs, but attractive to many of the younger generation.

Sometimes, a third party helps with cultural intermediation. In China, many American and Japanese cultural ideas are proving more attractive when they arrive via South Korea. As a university student puts it in discussing television shows, "American dramas also show the same kind of lifestyle. We know that South Korea and America have similar political systems and economies. But it is easier to accept the lifestyle from South Koreans because they are culturally closer to us. We feel we can live like them in a few years."[13]

But direct cultural contacts can also be important. As the son of China's foreign minister described Chinese students in the United States: "Our experiences made us see that there are alternative ways for China to develop and for us to lead our personal lives. Being in the United States made us realize that things in China can be different."[14] Over time, cultures influence each other. For example, the American University in Beirut originally enhanced American soft power in Lebanon, but studies show that it later enhanced Lebanon's soft power in America.[15]

Culture, values, and policies are not the only resources that produce soft power. As we saw in the last chapter, economic resources can also produce soft as well as hard power behavior. They can be used to attract as well as coerce. Sometimes in real-world situations, it is difficult to distinguish what part of an economic relationship is composed of hard power and what is made up of soft power. European leaders describe the desire by other countries to accede to the European Union as a sign of Europe's soft power.[16] It is impressive, for example, that former communist countries in Central Europe oriented their expectations and revised their laws to comply with Brussels's framework. Turkey has made changes in its human rights policies and laws on similar grounds. But how much are the changes the result of the economic inducement of market access, and how much is the result of attraction to Europe's successful economic and political system? The situation is one of mixed motives, and different actors in a country may see the mix in different ways. Journalists and historians must trace particular processes in detail to disentangle causation.

A number of observers see China's soft power increasing in Asia and other parts of the developing world, particularly after the 2008 global financial crisis that started in the United States.[17] According to the *People's Daily*, "Soft power has become a key word. . . . There is great potential for the development of China's soft power."[18] In parts of the developing world, the so-called Beijing Consensus on authoritarian government plus a successful market economy has become more popular than the previously dominant Washington Consensus of liberal market economics with democratic government. But to what extent are Venezuelans and Zimbabweans attracted to the Beijing Consensus, admire China's doubling of its gross domestic product over a decade, or are induced by the prospect of access to a large and growing market? Moreover, even if the authoritarian growth model produces soft power for China in authoritarian countries, it does not produce attraction in democratic countries. What attracts in Caracas may repel in Paris.[19]

We also saw that military resources can sometimes contribute to soft power. Dictators often cultivate myths of invincibility to structure expectations and attract others to join their bandwagon. Some people are generally attracted to strength. As Osama bin Laden has said, people are attracted to a strong horse rather than a weak horse. A well-run military can be a source of attraction, and military-to-military cooperation and training programs can establish transnational networks that enhance a country's soft power. At the same time, misuse of military resources can undercut soft power. Indifference to just-war principles of discrimination and proportionality can destroy legitimacy. The efficiency of the initial American military invasion of Iraq in 2003 may have created admiration in the eyes of some Iraqis and others, but that soft power was undercut by the subsequent inefficiency of the occupation and the scenes of mistreatment of prisoners. In contrast, the United States, China,

Brazil, and others all increased their soft power by using military resources for earthquake relief in Haiti in 2010.

SOFT POWER AND AMERICAN HEGEMONY

Some analysts see soft power in the twenty-first century as a form of cultural imperialism and argue that American culture has created a hegemonic liberal dialogue.[20] Global politics involves "verbal fighting" among competing narratives, and these analysts argue that the ability of the United States to frame global politics after 9/11 as a "global war on terror" channeled arguments and actions into an American framework.[21] But to describe American dominance over contemporary communications as coercive is an odd use of the word "coercion." As Steven Lukes argues, there are rational and nonrational modes by which the third face of power operates and empowering and disempowering ways by which agents influence targets' formulation of their preferences and self-interest. Although not always easy, we can distinguish indoctrination from free choice in most instances.[22]

American values are not universal in some absolute sense, but many are similar to the values of others in an information age where more people want participation and freedom of expression. When values are widely shared, they can provide a basis for soft power that works in multiple directions, both to and from the United States. Americans may benefit but simultaneously find themselves constrained to live up to values shared by others if the United States wishes to remain attractive. Given the political diversity and institutional fragmentation of global relations, those who believe in an American hegemony over discourse have a difficult case to make. Many countries and groups have different values. Otherwise, there would be far more uniformity of views than now exists in global affairs. Local cultures continue to command loyalty because "people are involved in networks of status and caste, and they pursue religious and communal markers of identity."[23]

To put the question of American soft power hegemony in perspective, it helps to look at China. There is no lack of Chinese interest in the idea of "soft power." A Singaporean analyst argues that "soft power is central to China's strategic vision and underlines its sensitivity to external perceptions."[24] Since the early 1990s, hundreds of essays and scholarly articles have been published in the People's Republic of China on soft power. The term has also entered China's official language. In his keynote speech to the Seventeenth National Congress of the Communist Party of China (CPC) on October 15, 2007, President Hu Jintao stated that the CPC must "enhance culture as part of the soft power of our country . . . a factor of growing significance in the competition in overall national strength."[25]

China has always had an attractive traditional culture, but now it is entering the realm of global popular culture as well. A total of 1.4 million Chinese students studied abroad between 1978 and 2008, and in 2009, 220,000 foreign students enrolled in Chinese universities. Chinese officials expect the number to increase to 500,000 by 2020.[26] China has created several hundred Confucius Institutes around the world to teach its language and culture, and while the Voice of America was cutting its Chinese broadcasts from nineteen to fourteen hours a day, China Radio International was increasing its broadcasts in English to twenty-four hours a day.[27] In 2009–2010, China invested $8.9 billion in "external publicity work," including a twenty-four-hour Xinhua cable news channel designed to imitate Al Jazeera.[28]

China has also adjusted its diplomacy. In the early 1990s, it was wary of multilateral arrangements and was at cross-purposes with many of its neighbors. Subsequently, it joined the World Trade Organization, contributed more than 3,000 troops to serve in UN peacekeeping operations, became more helpful on nonproliferation diplomacy (including hosting the six-power talks on North Korea), settled territorial disputes with neighbors, and joined a variety of regional organizations of which the East Asian summit is only the latest example. This new diplomacy helped to alleviate fears and reduce the likelihood of other countries allying to balance a rising power.[29] According to one study, "The Chinese style emphasized symbolic relationships, high-profile gestures, such as rebuilding the Cambodian Parliament or Mozambique Foreign Affairs Ministry."[30] But there are limits to Chinese as well as American soft power.

In 2006, China used the anniversary of the naval explorations of its great Ming Dynasty admiral Zheng He to create a narrative that justified its modern naval expansion into the Indian Ocean, but that did not produce soft power in India, where suspicions of Chinese naval ambitions led to a climate of mistrust.[31] Similarly, China tried to enhance its soft power by the successful staging of the 2008 Olympics, but shortly afterward its domestic crackdown in Tibet, in Xianjiang, and on activists like Liu Xiaobo (who later received the Nobel Peace Prize) undercut the country's soft power gains. In 2009, Beijing announced plans to spend billions of dollars to develop global media giants to compete with Bloomberg, Time Warner, and Viacom "to use soft power rather than military might to win friends abroad."[32] But China's efforts were hindered by its domestic political censorship. For all the efforts to turn Xinhua and China Central Television into competitors for CNN and the BBC, "there is no international audience for the brittle propaganda." India's Bollywood films command far greater international audiences than do Chinese films. "When Zhang Yimou, the acclaimed director, was asked recently why his films were always set in the past, he said that films about contemporary China would be neutered by the censors."[33]

Thus, it is not surprising that a poll taken in Asia late in 2008 found China's soft power less than that of the United States, and concluded that "China's charm offensive has thus far been ineffective."[34] This was confirmed by a 2010 BBC poll of twenty-eight countries that showed a net positive image of China only in Pakistan and Africa, whereas in Asia, the Americas, and Europe the modal opinion was neutral to poor.[35] Great powers try to use culture and narrative to create soft power that promotes their advantage, but it is not always an easy sell if the words and symbols are inconsistent with domestic realities.

Soft power can be used for both zero-sum and positive-sum interactions. As we have seen, it is a mistake to think of power—the ability to affect others to obtain preferred outcomes—simply as "power over" rather than "power with" others. Some observers have expressed alarm over the potential increase in Chinese soft power. Whether this will be a problem for other countries or not will depend on the way the power is used. If China uses its soft power to manipulate the politics of Asia to exclude the United States, its strategy will cause friction, but to the extent that China adopts the attitude of a rising "responsible stakeholder" in international affairs, its combination of hard and soft power can make a positive contribution.

China is far from America's or Europe's equal in soft power, but it would be foolish to ignore the gains China is making. Fortunately, these gains can be good for China and also good for the rest of the world. Soft power need not be a zero-sum game in which one country's gain is necessarily another country's loss. If China and the United States, for example, both become more attractive in each other's eyes, the prospects of damaging conflicts will be reduced. If the rise of China's soft power reduces the likelihood of conflict, it can be part of a positive-sum relationship.

SOFT POWER BEHAVIORS: AGENDA-SETTING, ATTRACTION, AND PERSUASION

Thus far we have focused on soft power resources, but soft power fits with all three faces or aspects of power behavior discussed in Chapter 1.

For example, suppose a school principal does not want a teenager to smoke. Under the first face of power, the principal could threaten the student with fines or expulsion to change her desire to smoke (hard power) or spend hours persuading her to change her existing

TABLE 4.1 Three Faces of Power Behavior

FIRST FACE
(DAHL: INDUCING OTHERS TO DO
WHAT THEY OTHERWISE WOULD NOT DO)
Hard: A uses force/payment to change B's existing strategies.
Soft: A uses attraction/persuasion to change B's existing preferences.

SECOND FACE
(BACHRACH AND BARATZ: FRAMING AND SETTING AGENDA)
Hard: A uses force/pay to truncate B's agenda (whether B likes it or not).
Soft: A uses attraction or institutions so that B sees the agenda as legitimate.

THIRD FACE
(LUKES: SHAPING OTHERS' PREFERENCES)
Hard: A uses force/pay to shape B's preferences ("Stockholm syndrome").
Soft: A uses attraction and/or institutions to shape B's initial preferences.

preference about smoking (soft power). Under the second dimension, the principal could ban cigarette vending machines (a hard aspect of agenda-setting) or use public service advertisements about cancer and yellow teeth to create a climate in which smoking becomes unpopular and unthinkable (soft power). Under the third dimension of power behavior, the principal could hold a school assembly in which students discuss smoking and vow not to smoke (soft power) or go further and threaten to ostracize the minority who smoke (hard power). In other words, the principal can use her hard power to stop students from smoking or use the soft power of framing, persuasion, and attraction. The success of her soft power efforts will depend upon her ability to attract and create credibility and trust.

Attraction is more complex than it first appears. It can refer to drawing attention—whether positive or negative—as well as creating alluring or positive magnetic effects. Like magnetism or gravitational pull, attention may be welcome or unwelcome, depending on the context. Lawyers refer to some things as an "attractive nuisance." If attraction is asymmetrical and leads to a hard power response, it produces vulnerability rather than power. For example, India was attractive to Britain in the nineteenth century, and that led to colonial subjugation, rather than soft power, for India.[36] Moreover, attention is often asymmetrical. The bigger the problem is, the more attention it is likely to attract. A smaller or weaker party can gain tactically from its greater focus compared to the larger or stronger party—witness the United States and Canada or China and Vietnam. But this type of attraction is not soft power. Soft power relies on positive attraction in the sense of "alluring."

What generates positive attraction? Psychologists tell us we like those who are similar to us or with whom we share group membership, and we are also attracted by physical characteristics as well as shared attitudes.[37] At the level of states, Alexander Vuving usefully suggests three clusters of qualities of the agent and action that are central to attraction: benignity, competence, and beauty (charisma). "Benignity" is an aspect of how an agent relates to others. Being perceived as benign tends to generate sympathy, trust, credibility, and acquiescence. "Brilliance" or "competence" refers to how an agent does things, and it produces admiration, respect, and emulation. "Beauty" or "charisma" is an aspect of an agent's relation to ideals, values, and vision, and it tends to produce inspiration and adherence.[38] These clusters of qualities are crucial for converting resources (such as culture, values, and policies) into power behavior.

Without such perceived qualities, a given resource may produce indifference or even revulsion—the opposite of soft power. The production of soft power by attraction depends upon both the qualities of the agent and how they are perceived by the target. What produces attraction for one target may produce revulsion for another. When an actor or action is perceived as malign, manipulative, incompetent, or ugly, it is likely to produce revulsion. Thus, a given cultural artifact, such as a Hollywood movie that portrays liberated women acting independently, may produce positive attraction in Rio but revulsion in Riyadh. An aid program that is seen as manipulative may undercut soft power, and a slick television production that is perceived as pure propaganda may produce revulsion.

Persuasion is closely related to attraction. It is the use of argument to influence the beliefs and actions of others without the threat of force or promise of payment. Persuasion almost always involves some degree of manipulation, with some points being emphasized and others neglected. Dishonest persuasion may go so far as to involve fraud. In persuasion, rational argument appealing to facts, beliefs about causality, and normative premises are mixed with the framing of issues in attractive ways and the use of emotional appeals.[39] That is why attraction, trust, and persuasion are closely related. Some rational arguments are self-executing. An elegant proof in pure math can convince on its own internal merit even if propounded by an enemy. But most arguments involve assertions about facts, values, and framing that depend upon some degree of attraction and trust that the source is credible. Take, for instance, the anecdote about the French nuclear sale to Pakistan at the beginning of this book. The American argument appealed to common interests in nonproliferation shared by France and the United States, but without some attraction between the French and American governments and trust that the Americans were not lying and that the intelligence was accurate, the effort at persuasion would have failed.

In turn, framing of an agenda is closely related to persuasion.[40] An attractively framed argument seen as legitimate by the target is more likely to be persuasive. Moreover, much persuasion is indirect, mediated through mass audiences rather than elites. Perceptions of legitimacy can also involve third-party audiences. Indirect attempts at persuasion often involve efforts to persuade third parties with emotional appeals and narratives rather than pure logic. Narratives are particularly important in framing issues in persuasive ways so that some "facts" become important and others fall by the wayside. Yet if a narrative is too transparently manipulative and discounted as propaganda, it loses persuasive power. Again, it is not just the influence effort by the agent, but also the perceptions by the targets that are critical for the creation of soft power.

HOW SOFT POWER WORKS

Sometimes attraction and the resulting soft power it engenders require little effort. As we saw earlier, the effects of an actor's values can be like the light shining from "a city on the hill." This attraction by example is the passive approach to soft power. At other times, an actor makes active efforts to create attraction and soft power by a variety of programs, such as public diplomacy, broadcasting, exchanges, and assistance. There are, then, two models of how soft power affects its targets: direct and indirect. In the direct form, leaders may be attracted and persuaded by the benignity, competence, or charisma of other leaders—witness the example of Czar Peter and Frederick the Great cited previously or an account of the persuasive effect of President Obama's arguments leading to an increase in donations at a G-20 meeting.[41] Elite relations and networks often play an important role. More common, however, is a two-step model in which publics and third parties are influenced, and they in turn affect the leaders of other countries. In this case, soft power has an important indirect effect by creating an enabling environment for decisions. Alternatively, if an actor or action is perceived as repulsive, it creates a disabling environment.

Judging the causal effects of soft power varies with each model. In the first model, judging direct causation requires careful process-tracing of the sort that good historians or journalists do, with all the difficulties of sorting out multiple causes. In the second model, judging indirect causation also requires careful process-tracing because multiple causal factors are involved, but here public opinion polls and careful content analysis can help provide a first estimate

FIGURE 4.1 Soft Power: Direct and Indirect Causal Models

MODEL 1
DIRECT EFFECTS
Resources → government elites → attraction →
elite decision and outcome

MODEL 2
INDIRECT EFFECTS
Resources → publics → attract/repel →
enabling or disabling environment → elite decision

of the existence of an enabling or a disabling environment. Even though polls can measure the existence and trends in potential soft power resources, they are only a first approximation for behavioral change in terms of outcomes. Correlations, such as a study of 143 pairs of countries that found a greater incidence of terrorism where polls showed people of one country disapproving of the leadership of another country, are suggestive but do not prove causation.[42] Where opinion is strong and consistent over time, it can have an effect, but the impact of public opinion in comparison to other variables can be determined only by careful process-tracing. This is often difficult to catch in the short term and is sometimes best judged by historians able to sort causes well after the events.

Some skeptics discount polls completely. They argue that "the fact that the state controls public opinion rather than being controlled by it in the realm of foreign policy is a fact that undermines the logic of soft power."[43] This argument is wrong, however, because it ignores direct effects, matters of degree, types of goals, and interactions with other causes. Moreover, public opinion sometimes acts as a constraint on authoritarian leaders, and in many authoritarian states where internal dissent is muted, international opprobrium has an effect. Even if it is true that many governments in many contexts are only weakly constrained by public opinion, it does not follow that soft power is irrelevant.

Regarding specific goals, sometimes there is a one-step model with direct effects on policymakers that does not go through public opinion. Student and leadership exchanges are a good example. Forty-six current and 165 former heads of government are products of U.S. higher education. Not all of the nearly 750,000 foreign students who come to the United States annually are attracted to the country, but a large majority are. "Research has consistently shown that exchange students return home with a more positive view of the country in which they studied and the people with whom they interacted," and foreign-educated students are more likely to promote democracy in their home country if they are educated in democratic countries.[44] Moreover, such programs can have beneficial "ripple effects" on indirect participants.[45] The results can be dramatic. For example, Mikhail Gorbachev's embrace of perestroika and glasnost was influenced by ideas learned in the United States by Alexander Yakovlev decades earlier. And even though the end of the Cold War involved multiple causes, there is ample testimony by former Soviet elites about how ideas interacted with their economic decline. As former Soviet official Georgi Shaknazarov puts it, "Gorbachev, me, all of us were double thinkers."[46]

Even with the two-step model, public opinion often affects elites by creating an enabling or a disabling environment for specific policy initiatives. For example, in regard to Iraq in 2003, Turkish officials were constrained by public and parliamentary opinion and unable to allow the American Fourth Infantry Division to cross their country. The Bush administration's lack of soft power hurt its hard power. Similarly, Mexican president Vicente Fox wished to accommodate George W. Bush by supporting a second UN resolution authorizing invasion, but he was constrained by public opinion. When being pro-American is a political kiss of death, public opinion has an effect on policy that the skeptics' simple proposition does not capture. Even Britain, a close ally, when reacting to Bush administration intelligence standards decided that "we still have to work with them, but we work with them in a rather different fashion."[47]

It is often easier to see causation in these negative cases where a "veto" is relatively easy to identify. In positive cases, the impact of soft power among multiple variables is more difficult to isolate and prove. One study suggests three necessary conditions for effective state use of soft power via the second model of public opinion: communicating to an intended target in a functioning marketplace of ideas, persuading the target to change its attitude on a political issue, and ensuring the new attitude influences political outcomes.[48] Analyzing each of these steps is helpful in addressing the efforts of a government to change another government's policy through soft power. However, it misses not only the first model of direct effect but also another dimension of the second model: creating an enabling environment through long-term attraction. Such a climate may be the product of civil society and nonstate actors, often seen as more credible, rather than direct governmental efforts. Instead of focusing solely on government agents and targeted efforts to change specific policies, we must also consider the city on a hill effect and attraction by example. To the extent that one society is attractive to another, it can create an enabling environment for general milieu goals as well as specific elite decisions.

Here the target of soft power *is* broad public opinion and cultural attitudes. Most historians who have studied the period agree that in addition to troops and money, American power to promote such goals in postwar Europe was strongly affected by culture and ideas. Even though governmental programs such as the Marshall Plan were important, historians of the period stress the impact of nonstate actors as well. "American corporate and advertising executives, as well as the heads of Hollywood studios, were selling not only their products but also America's culture and values, the secrets of its success, to the rest of the world."[49] As one Norwegian scholar argues, "Federalism, democracy, and open markets represented core American values. This is what America exported." That made it much easier to maintain what he calls an "empire by invitation."[50]

Such general goals remain important today. For example, many acts of terrorism are less designed to overthrow a particular government than to create a climate of polarization in which an extremist narrative can spread to wider parts of the Muslim world. An interesting study of the impact of the American University in Beirut and the American University in Cairo, both nongovernmental, found that they were successful in promoting their own (and indirectly American government) milieu goals of liberal, secular, private education despite perilous times in their host societies, but they did not contribute to acceptance of the specific goals of unpopular American foreign policies.[51]

The passive city on the hill effect of soft power should not be exaggerated, however, particularly in its impact on specific short-term goals. European soft power had an important impact on achieving the long-term milieu goals of democratization of Central Europe after the Cold War, but when Europeans went to the 2009 Copenhagen climate summit, the soft power of their superior domestic example on climate was not effective. "Europe's strategy was to press others to match its own concessions on carbon emissions. But the EU barely existed at the talks" because its lofty aspirations were too far from the limited bargains being struck by other countries.[52]

An interesting "natural experiment" can be seen in the 2008 election of Barack Obama, which helped to dispel negative stereotypes of a closed American political system based solely on money and family dynasties. In 2009, polls showed an impressive "revival of America's global image in many parts of the world reflecting confidence in the new president."[53] One poll-based assessment of brand values even suggested the Obama effect was worth $2 trillion in brand equity.[54] By 2010, the popularity of the United States had risen in Europe, Russia, and China but had declined in Egypt,[55] and in areas such as Pakistan and the Palestinian territories where American policies were unpopular, "ratings of Obama were only marginally better than the abysmal ratings accorded to Bush."[56] And on particular policy requests made by Obama in his first year, such as more allied troops for Afghanistan or the willingness of other countries to accept detainees released from the Guantánamo prison, the results were better, but only modestly so, than those that had been achieved by Bush. In other words, the Obama effect was positive, but of limited magnitude in the short term.

Not only do actors try to influence each other directly and indirectly through soft power; they also compete to deprive each other of attractiveness and legitimacy, thus creating a disabling environment either in public opinion in the other country and/or in the eyes of relevant third parties. For example, after the U.S. Senate passed a $30 million bill to document and publicize human rights violations in Iran, the Iranian parliament created a $20 million fund to expose human rights violations in the United States.[57] Sometimes leaders are prepared to ignore the opinion of third parties (somewhat misleadingly labeled "world public opinion"), but at other times their concerns about diplomatic isolation can inhibit their actions.

In 2008, after invading Georgia, Russia carefully controlled its domestic media, but seemed ill prepared to press its case internationally. Georgian president Mikhail Saakasvili used his fluency in English to dominate coverage in the rest of the world. "The Kremlin's reluctance to muster support for its position with the same intensity that it sent tanks into Georgia offers an insight into its worldview."[58] Russian military power dominated, but Russia was not as adept in wielding soft power to consolidate its military victory.

As we have seen, there are a wide variety of basic resources that can be converted into soft power by skillful conversion strategies. Basic resources include culture, values, legitimate policies, a positive domestic model, a successful economy, and a competent military. Sometimes these resources are specially shaped for soft power purposes. Such shaped resources include national intelligence services, information agencies, diplomacy, public diplomacy, exchange programs, assistance programs, training programs, and various other measures. Shaped resources provide a wide variety of policy tools, but whether they produce positive or negative responses in the targets (and thus preferred outcomes) depends upon the context, the

FIGURE 4.2 Conversion of Soft Power Resources to Behavior (outcomes)

Resources (CULTURE, etc.)
↓
Policy tools (QUALITIES)
↓
Conversion skills
↓
Target response (POS./NEG.)
↓
Outcome (SPECIFIC OR GENERAL)

target, and the qualities of the power-conversion strategies. This conversion process is illustrated in Figure 4.2.

To convert soft power resources and tools into outcomes requires the critical ability to create in the target perceptions of such qualities as benignity, competence, and charisma. The perception may be false (as in the effect of some propaganda), but what matters is whether the target believes it and responds positively or negatively.

WIELDING SOFT POWER
THROUGH PUBLIC DIPLOMACY

As we have seen, soft power is difficult for governments to wield. Sustained attraction—being a city on a hill—requires consistency of practice with values. Going further to project attraction, frame agendas, and persuade others is even more difficult. As we have seen, the causal paths are often indirect, the effects often take time to ripen, some of the general goals to which soft power is directed are diffuse, and governments are rarely in full control of all the instruments. In Chapters 2 and 3, we saw some of the potential but also the difficulties of using military and economic resources to create soft power. That is equally true of efforts to create soft power through the instruments of public diplomacy. The policy difficulty is compounded by the plethora of available information, the importance of networks, and changing leadership styles in democratic societies. But the fact that creating soft power through public diplomacy is often difficult does not mean that it is unimportant.

To be credible in a century where power is diffusing from states to nonstate actors, government efforts to project soft power will have to accept that power is less hierarchical in an information age and that social networks have become more important. To succeed in a networked world requires leaders to think in terms of attraction and co-option rather than command. Leaders need to think of themselves as being in a circle rather than atop a mountain. That means that two-way communications are more effective than commands. As a young Czech participant at a Salzburg seminar observed, "This is the best propaganda because it's not propaganda."[59]

Soft power is generated only in part by what the government does through its policies and public diplomacy. The generation of soft power is also affected in positive (and negative) ways by a host of nonstate actors within and outside a country. Those actors affect both the general public and governing elites in other countries and create an enabling or a disabling environment for government policies. As mentioned earlier, in some cases, soft power will enhance the probability of other elites adopting policies that allow us to achieve our preferred outcomes. In other cases, where being seen as friendly to the U.S. administration is seen as a local political kiss of death, the decline or absence of soft power will prevent Americans from obtaining particular goals. But even in such instances, the interactions of civil societies and nonstate actors may help to further general milieu goals such as democracy, liberty, and development.

Classical diplomacy, sometimes called "cabinet diplomacy," involved messages sent from one ruler to another, often in confidential communications. In terms of the first model in Figure 4.3, government A communicated directly with government B. But governments also found it useful to communicate with the publics of other countries in an effort to influence other governments through the indirect model in Figure 4.3. That indirect form of

FIGURE 4.3 Two Models of Diplomacy

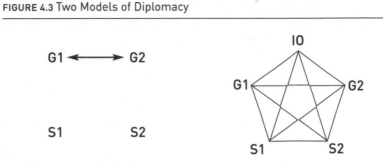

Key: G = government; S = society; IO = international organization.

diplomacy became known as public diplomacy. Efforts to affect the publics of other countries have long roots. After the French Revolution, the new French government sent agents to America to try to directly affect public opinion. In the late nineteenth century, after France's defeat in the Franco-Prussian War, the French government created the Alliance Française to popularize its culture and restore national prestige. During World War I, the American government organized tours and persuaded Hollywood to make films that portrayed the United States in a positive light.[60]

With the new technology of radio, broadcasting became the dominant model of public diplomacy in the 1920s. The BBC was founded in 1922, and the totalitarian governments perfected the form of propaganda broadcasts and films in the 1930s. Broadcasting remains important to this day, but in the age of the Internet and inexpensive air travel, and with the development of intergovernmental and transnational organizations, the diffusion of power away from states has made public diplomacy more complex. The lines of communication are no longer a straight bar between two governments, but more like a star that includes lines among governments, publics, societies, and nongovernmental organizations.

In such a world, actors other than governments are well placed to use soft power. Government A will try to influence the public in society B, but transnational organizations in society B will also wage information campaigns to influence government A as well as government B. They use campaigns of naming and shaming to influence other governments as well as to put pressure on other nongovernmental actors such as large corporations. Sometimes they will also work through intergovernmental organizations. The result is a new set of mixed coalitions of governmental, intergovernmental, and nongovernmental actors each using public diplomacy for its own goals. For example, the International Campaign to Ban Landmines allied smaller governments, such as Canada and Norway, along with networks created by an activist in Vermont, and the public fame of Princess Diana to defeat the strongest bureaucracy (the Pentagon) in the world's only superpower.

Governments trying to utilize public diplomacy to wield soft power face new problems. Promoting attractive images of one's country is not new, but the conditions for trying to create soft power have changed dramatically in recent years. For one thing, nearly half the countries in the world are now democracies. In such circumstances, diplomacy aimed at public opinion can become as important to outcomes as the traditional classified diplomatic communications among leaders. Information creates power, and today a much larger part of the world's population has access to that power. Technological advances have led to a dramatic reduction in the cost of processing and transmitting information. The result is an explosion of information, and that has produced a "paradox of plenty."[61] Plentiful information leads to scarcity of attention. When people are overwhelmed with the volume of information confronting them, they have difficulty knowing what to focus on. Attention, rather than information, becomes the scarce resource, and those who can distinguish valuable information from background clutter gain power. Cue-givers become more in demand, and this is a source of power for those who can tell us where to focus our attention.

Among editors and cue-givers, credibility is the crucial resource and an important source of soft power. Reputation becomes even more important than in the past, and political struggles occur over the creation and destruction of credibility. Governments compete for credibility not only with other governments, but also with a broad range of alternatives, including news media, corporations, NGOs, intergovernmental organizations, and networks of scientific communities.

Politics has become a contest of competitive credibility. The world of traditional power politics is typically about whose military or economy wins. As noted earlier, politics in an information age "may ultimately be about whose story wins."[62] Narratives become the currency of soft power. Governments compete with each other and with other organizations to enhance their own credibility and weaken that of their opponents. Witness the struggle between Serbia and NATO to frame the interpretation of events in 2000 in which broadcasts and the Internet played a key role, or consider the contest between the government and protesters after the Iranian elections in 2009 in which the Internet and Twitter played important roles in transnational communication.

Information that appears to be propaganda may not only be scorned, but it may also turn out to be counterproductive if it undermines a country's reputation for credibility. Exaggerated claims about Saddam Hussein's weapons of mass destruction and ties to Al Qaeda may have helped mobilize domestic support for the Iraq War, but the subsequent disclosure of the exaggeration dealt a costly blow to British and American credibility. Under the new conditions more than ever, a soft sell may prove more effective than a hard sell. The relative independence of the BBC, sometimes to the consternation of British governments, has paid dividends in credibility as indicated by an account of how President Jakaya Kikwete of Tanzania spends his day: "He rises at dawn, listens to the BBC World Service, than scans the Tanzanian press."[63]

Skeptics who treat the term "public diplomacy" as a mere euphemism for propaganda miss this point. Simple propaganda is counterproductive as public diplomacy. Nor is public diplomacy merely public relations campaigns. Conveying information and selling a positive image are part of it, but public diplomacy also involves building long-term relationships that create an enabling environment for government policies.[64]

The mix of direct government information to long-term cultural relationships varies with three concentric circles or stages of public diplomacy, and all three are important.[65] The first and most immediate circle is daily communications, which involves explaining the context of domestic and foreign policy decisions. The first stage must also involve preparation for dealing with crises. In today's information age, many actors will rush in to fill any vacuum in information that might occur after an event. A rapid response capability in public diplomacy means that false charges or misleading information can be answered immediately. This circle is measured in terms of hours, days, and weeks.

The second stage or concentric circle is strategic communication, which develops a set of simple themes much as a political or advertising campaign does. Whereas the first dimension is measured in hours and days, the second occurs over weeks, months, and even years. Special events such as the Shanghai Exposition of 2010 or the World Cup in South Africa fit this description. President Jacob Zuma justified the expenditures on the World Cup as "the greatest marketing opportunity of our time."[66] A public diplomacy campaign plans symbolic events and communications to reinforce central themes or to advance a particular government policy. Special themes focus on particular policy initiatives. For example, when the Reagan administration decided to implement NATO's two-track decision of deploying missiles while negotiating to remove existing Soviet intermediate range missiles, the Soviet Union responded with a concerted campaign to influence European opinion and make the deployment impossible. As former secretary of state George Shultz later concluded, "I don't think we could have pulled it off if it hadn't been for a very active program of public diplomacy. Because the Soviets were very active all through 1983 . . . with peace movements and all kinds of efforts to dissuade our friends in Europe from deploying."[67]

The third and broadest circle or stage of public diplomacy is the development of lasting relationships with key individuals over many years or even decades through scholarships, exchanges, training, seminars, conferences, and access to media channels. Over time, about 700,000 people have participated in American cultural and academic exchanges, and these exchanges helped to educate such world leaders as Anwar Sadat, Helmut Schmidt, and Margaret Thatcher. Other countries have similar programs. For example, Japan has developed an exchange program bringing 6,000 young foreigners each year from forty countries to teach their languages in Japanese schools, with an alumni association to maintain the bonds of friendship that are developed.[68] These programs develop what Edward R. Murrow once called the crucial "last three feet"— face-to-face communications that are a two-way process characterized by the enhanced credibility that reciprocity creates.

Each of these three stages of public diplomacy plays an important role in helping governments to create an attractive image of a country that can improve its prospects for obtaining its desired outcomes. But even the best advertising cannot sell an unpopular product. A communications strategy cannot work if it cuts against the grain of policy. Actions speak louder than words, and public diplomacy that appears to be mere window dressing for hard power projection is unlikely to succeed. The treatment of prisoners at Abu Ghraib and Guantánamo in a manner inconsistent with American values led to perceptions of hypocrisy that could not be reversed by broadcasting pictures of Muslims living well in America. In fact, the slick production values of the American satellite television station Al Hurrah did not make it competitive in the Middle East, where it was widely regarded as an instrument of government propaganda. All too often, policymakers treat public diplomacy as a bandage that can be applied after damage is done by other instruments. For example, when one advocate of bombing Iran was asked whether attacking Iran might cause the opposition there to coalesce around the regime, he said that wouldn't be a problem because all that would be needed to avoid such an outcome was an accompanying public diplomacy campaign.[69]

Under the new conditions of the information age, more than ever the soft sell proves more effective than the hard sell. Without underlying national credibility, the instruments of public diplomacy cannot translate cultural resources into the soft power of attraction. The effectiveness of public diplomacy is measured by minds changed (as shown in interviews or polls), not dollars spent or slick production packages produced. When the U.S. Congress asked Secretary of Defense Gates about the 2010 budget for strategic communications, "no one could say because there was no central communication. The first answer came back at $1 billion, but that was later changed to $626 million." Many of these operations "in the past had been in the purview of the State Department's public diplomacy section."[70]

Critics worry that the overmilitarization of foreign policy undercuts credibility. One complains that "tasking the military with strategic communications . . . is somewhat akin to asking an aid worker to direct an air strike, or a diplomat to run a field hospital." Others argue that what is needed is a new public diplomacy "on steroids" staffed by diplomats trained in new media, cross-cultural communications, granular local knowledge, and networks of contacts with underrepresented groups.[71]

The centralized mass media approach to public diplomacy still plays an important role. Governments need to correct daily misrepresentations of their policies as well as try to convey a longer-term strategic message. The main strength of the mass media approach is its audience reach and ability to generate public awareness and set the agenda. But the inability to influence how the message is perceived in different cultural settings is its weak point. The sender knows what she says, but not always what the target(s) hears. Cultural barriers are apt to distort what is heard.

Networked communications, in contrast, can take advantage of two-way communications and peer-to-peer relations to overcome cultural differences. Rather than a central design and broadcast of a message across cultural boundaries, "networks *first* establish the structure and dynamics for effective communications channels, *then* members collaborate to craft the message. Because the message or story is co-created across cultures, it is not culture-bound. . . . Rather than being a barrier or impediment, culture is incorporated into network dynamics."[72] This type of decentralization and flexibility is difficult for governments to accomplish, given their central accountability structures.

The greater flexibility of NGOs in using networks has given rise to what some call "the new public diplomacy," which is "no longer confined to messaging, promotion campaigns, or even direct governmental contacts with foreign publics serving foreign policy purposes. It is also about building relationships with civil society actors in other countries and about facilitating networks between non-governmental parties at home and abroad."[73] In this approach to public diplomacy, government policy is aimed at promoting and participating in, rather than controlling, such networks across borders. Indeed, too much government control or even the appearance thereof can undercut the credibility that such networks are designed to engender. The evolution of public diplomacy from one-way communications to a two-way dialogue model treats publics as peer-to-peer cocreators of meaning and communication.[74]

For governments to succeed in the networked world of the new public diplomacy, they are going to have to learn to relinquish a good deal of their control, and this runs the risk that nongovernmental civil society actors are often not aligned in their goals with government policies or even objectives. Governments can take advantage of new technologies of social networking with employees licensed to use Facebook and Twitter.[75] They may even use a loose rein, but they rarely are willing to allow free rein when one node of a network has an official label. In democracies, for example, it is too easy for opposition parliamentarians to score points about disloyal or ineffective foreign ministry employees failing to protect the national message and national interest. The same criticisms are leveled at home-domiciled nongovernmental actors, particularly if they have access to government facilities or support.

The domestic political problem of the new public diplomacy is real, but the international effects can be beneficial. The presence of dissent and self-criticism is likely to enhance the credibility of messages, as well as create a degree of attraction to the society that is willing to tolerate dissent. Criticism of government policies can be awkward for a government, but it can also cast a society in a more attractive light and thus help to create soft power. The paradox of using public diplomacy to generate soft power in a global information age is that decentralization and diminished control may be central to the creation of soft power.

As public diplomacy is done more *by* publics, governments find themselves caught in a dilemma about control. Unruly citizens like the Florida pastor who threatened to burn the Koran in 2010 can destroy soft power. But difficult though the new public diplomacy may be for democracies, it is likely to be even more difficult for the international relations of autocracies such as China. As one observer notes, if "real soft power comes from a society, not from government, China's government continues to muzzle many of its most creative and diverse elements, while China's human rights record, its political system, economic strength, and growing military power all continue to negatively afflict its image abroad."[76] Wielding soft power is important, but it is not always easy, particularly in a cyberage.

PART II

POWER SHIFTS: DIFFUSION AND TRANSITIONS

CHAPTER 5

Diffusion and Cyberpower

Two types of power shifts are occurring in this century: power transition and power diffusion. Power transition from one dominant state to another is a familiar historical event, but power diffusion is a more novel process. The problem for all states in today's global information age is that more things are happening outside the control of even the most powerful states. In the words of a former State Department director of policy planning, "The proliferation of information is as much a cause of nonpolarity as is the proliferation of weaponry."[1] Or as one British analyst puts it, "We face more and more risks, threats and challenges that affect people in one country but originate mainly or entirely in the other countries . . . financial crisis, organized crime, mass migration, global warming, pandemics and international terrorism, to name but a few. . . . One of the main reasons for the difficulty is that power has been diffused both vertically and horizontally. We have not so much a multi-polar world as a no-polar world."[2]

Some observers welcome this trend as marking the decline of the sovereign state that has been the dominant global institutions since the Peace of Westphalia in 1648. They predict that the Information Revolution will flatten bureaucratic hierarchies and replace them with network organizations. More governmental functions will be handled by private markets as well as by nonprofit entities. As virtual communities develop on the Internet, they will cut across territorial jurisdictions and develop their own patterns of governance. States will become much less central to people's lives. People will live by multiple voluntary contracts and drop in and out of communities at the click of a mouse. The new pattern of crosscutting communities and governance will become a modern and more civilized analog to the feudal world that existed before the rise of the modern state.[3]

INFORMATION REVOLUTION

Such extreme cybertransformations are still fanciful, but a new information revolution is changing the nature of power and increasing its diffusion. States will remain the dominant actor on the world stage, but they will find the stage far more crowded and difficult to control. A much larger part of the population both within and among countries has access to the power that comes from information—witness the Middle East today. Governments have always worried about the flow and control of information, and the current period is not the first to be strongly affected by dramatic changes.

The current Information Revolution, sometimes called "the Third Industrial Revolution," is based on rapid technological advances in computers, communications, and software that in turn have led to dramatic decreases in the cost of creating, processing and transmitting, and searching for information. Computing power doubled every eighteen months for thirty years, and by the beginning of the twenty-first century it cost one-thousandth of what it had in the early 1970s. If the price of automobiles had fallen as quickly as the price of semiconductors, a car would cost $5.

In 1993, there were about 50 Websites in the world; by 2000, that number had surpassed 5 million. A decade later, China alone had over 400 million Internet users and the social network Facebook has some half a trillion users. Communications bandwidths are expanding rapidly, and communications costs continue to fall even more rapidly than computing power. As recently as 1980, phone calls over copper wire could carry only 1 page of information per second; today a thin strand of optical fiber can transmit 90,000 *volumes* in a second. In 1980, 1 gigabyte of storage occupied a room; now 200 gigabytes of storage fit in your shirt pocket. The amount of digital information increases tenfold every five years.[4]

The key characteristic of this Information Revolution is not the *speed* of communications between the wealthy and powerful: For more than 130 years, instantaneous communication by telegraph has been possible between Europe and North America. The crucial change is the enormous reduction in the *cost* of transmitting information. For all practical purposes, the actual transmission costs have become negligible; hence, the amount of information that can be transmitted worldwide is virtually infinite. The result is an explosion of information, of which documents are a tiny fraction. By one estimate, 161 billion gigabytes of digital information were created and captured in the year 2006 alone (that is about 3 million times the information in all the books ever written). In 2010, the annual growth in digital information is expected to increase more than sixfold to 988 billion gigabytes. At the beginning of the twenty-first century, computer users sent roughly 25 trillion e-mail messages per year. By 2010, 70 percent of all information generated every year in the world came from e-mails, online videos, and the World Wide Web. This dramatic change in the linked technologies of computing and communications is changing the nature of government and accelerating a diffusion of power.

In the middle of the twentieth century, people feared that the computers and communications of the current Information Revolution would create the central government control dramatized in George Orwell's dystopian novel *1984*. Mainframe computers seemed set to enhance central planning and increase the surveillance powers of those at the top of a pyramid of control. Government television would dominate the news. Through central databases, computers could make government identification and surveillance easier.

Instead, as computing power has decreased in cost and computers have shrunk to the size of smart phones and other portable devices, their decentralizing effects have outweighed their centralizing effects. Power over information is much more widely distributed today than even a few decades ago. Compared with radio, television, and newspapers controlled by editors and broadcasters, the Internet creates unlimited communication one to one (via e-mail), one to many (via a personal homepage, blog, or Twitter), many to one (such as Wikipedia), and, perhaps most importantly, many to many (as in online chat rooms or social networking sites such as Facebook or LinkedIn). Comparing these new methods to previous advances in communication, we can see the difference is that "internet messages have the capacity to flow farther, faster, and with fewer intermediaries."[5] Information can often provide a key power resource, and more people have access to more information than ever before.

What this means is that world politics will not be the sole province of governments. As the cost of computing and communication comes down, the barriers to entry decline. Both individuals and private organizations, ranging from corporations to NGOs to terrorists, are empowered to play direct roles in world politics. The spread of information means that power will be more widely distributed and informal networks will undercut the monopoly of traditional bureaucracy. The speed of Internet time means all governments have less control of their agendas. Political leaders will enjoy fewer degrees of freedom before they must respond to events, and then they will have to share the stage with more actors.

In principle, as costs and barriers of entry into markets diminish, the Information Revolution should reduce the power of large states and enhance the power of small states and nonstate actors. But in practice, international relations are more complex than such technological determinism implies. Some aspects of the Information Revolution help the small; but some help the already large and powerful. Size still matters. What economists call economies of scale remain in some of the aspects of power that are related to information. Although a hacker and a government can both create information and exploit the Internet, it matters for many purposes that large governments can deploy tens of thousands of trained people and have vast computing power to crack codes or intrude into other organizations. In the case of soft power, large established entertainment industries like Hollywood and Bollywood enjoy considerable economies of scale in content production and distribution. Moreover, in the information economy, there are "network effects" with increasing returns to scale. As we know, one telephone is useless. The next adds value and so forth as the network grows.

In addition, even though the dissemination of existing information doesn't cost much, the collection and production of new information often require major investment. In many competitive situations, *new* information matters most. In some situations, information is a nonrival public good: One person's consumption does not diminish that of another. Thomas Jefferson used the analogy of a candle: If I give you a light, it does not diminish my light. But in a competitive situation, it may make a big difference if I have the light first and see things before you do. Intelligence collection is a good example. America, Russia, Britain, China, and France have capabilities for collection and production of intelligence that dwarf those of most states.

As we saw in Chapter 2, military power remains important in critical domains of global politics. Information technology has some effects on the use of force that benefit the small and some that favor the already powerful. It is a double-edged sword. Off-the-shelf commercial availability of formerly costly military technologies benefits small states and nongovernmental actors and increases the vulnerability of large states. For example, today anyone can order satellite images from commercial companies or simply use Google

Earth software to see what goes on in other countries at little or no cost. Global positioning devices that provide precise locations, once the property of the military alone, are readily available in stores. What's more, information systems create vulnerabilities for rich states by adding lucrative and easily disrupted targets for terrorist groups. And nongovernmental actors such as Wikileaks collect and disseminate sensitive information that complicates military campaigns. It's conceivable that a sophisticated adversary (such as a small country with cyberwarfare resources) will decide it can blackmail large states. There is also the prospect of state-sponsored "freelance" or "privateer" cyberattacks.

Other trends, however, benefit already powerful states. Space-based sensors, direct broadcasting, high-speed computers, and complex software provide the ability to gather, sort, process, transfer, and disseminate information about complex events that occur over wide geographic areas. This networking of military systems produces a powerful advantage (as well as a potential vulnerability). The key is not possession of fancy hardware or advanced systems, but the ability to integrate a system of systems. In this dimension, even a small edge makes a difference. The Information Revolution is leading to a diffusion of power, but larger states still have larger resources.

GOVERNMENTS AND TRANSNATIONAL ACTORS

The debate about the diffusion of power and the fate of the sovereign state is often oversimplified.[6] People sometimes think of long-term challenges to the system of states "only in terms of entities that are institutionally substitutable for the state."[7] A better historical analogy is the development of markets and town life in the early feudal period. Medieval trade fairs were not substitutes for the institutions of feudal authority. They did not tear down the castle walls or remove the local lord, but they did create new wealth, new coalitions, and new attitudes.

Medieval merchants developed the *Lex Mercatoria* ("Merchant Law"), which governed their relations largely as a private set of rules for conducting business. Similarly today, everyone from hackers to large corporations is developing the code and norms of the Internet partly outside the control of formal political institutions. These private systems, such as corporate Intranets or worldwide newsgroups devoted to specific issues such as the environment, do not frontally challenge the governments of sovereign states; they simply add a layer of relations that sovereign states do not fully control. People will participate in transnational Internet communities without ceasing to be loyal citizens, but their perspectives will be different.

The real issue related to the diffusion of power is not the continued existence of the state, but how it functions. Contradictory movements can occur simultaneously. State-owned enterprises co-exist and compete with multinational corporations that span hundreds of boundaries. IBM, for example, derives two-thirds of its revenue from overseas, and only one-quarter of its 400,000-person workforce is located in the United States.[8] The United Nations estimates there are 214 million migrants across the globe, and many diasporas stay connected through modern communications.[9] Politics becomes more volatile and less self-contained within national shells. In a world of global interdependence, the agenda of international politics is broader, and everyone seems to get into the act.

Some of this transnational activity is not new. Multinational corporations have a long lineage, transnational religious organizations go back centuries, and the nineteenth century saw the founding of the Socialist International, the Red Cross, peace movements, women's suffrage organizations, and the International Law Association, among others. Before World War I, there were already 176 international nongovernmental organizations. More recently, however, there has been an explosion in the number of NGOs, increasing from 6,000 to approximately 26,000 in the last decade of the twentieth century. A few decades ago, rapid communication to diverse parts of the globe was technically possible but very expensive.

Now it is available to anyone with the price of entry to an Internet café. And with Skype, it is free. The cost of creating a transnational organization or network has become trivial.

Many of these new transnational actors claim to act as a "global conscience" representing broad public interests beyond the purview of individual states. Though they are not democratically elected, these actors sometimes help develop new norms by directly pressing governments and business leaders to change policies and by indirectly altering public perceptions of legitimacy and what governments and firms should be doing. In terms of power resources, these groups rarely possess much hard power, but the Information Revolution has greatly enhanced their soft power. They can mount "naming and shaming" campaigns against corporate brands or governments relatively easily.

Not only is there a great increase in the number of transnational actors, but there has also been a change in type. Earlier transnational flows were heavily controlled by large formally organized structures, such as multinational corporations or the Catholic Church, that could profit from economies of scale. Such organizations remain important, but the lower costs of communication in the Internet era have opened the field to loosely structured network organizations with little headquarters staff and even to individuals. Terrorist groups have often had a transnational dimension, but now the Information Revolution has made Al Qaeda into a loose network that spans the globe with its franchise.

Terrorism is a method of violence with roots stretching far back in history. In the nineteenth century, terrorism was used by anarchists and other transnational revolutionaries who killed half a dozen heads of state, and in the twentieth century, World War I was triggered in part by such a terrorist-turned-assassin. What is new today is that technology is putting into the hands of deviant individuals and groups destructive powers that were once reserved primarily to governments. That is why some observers refer to terrorism as the privatization of war. Moreover, technology has made the complex systems of modern societies more vulnerable to large-scale attack. "This trend toward increased vulnerability was occurring even before the Internet sped it along."[10]

The current generation of violent Islamist extremists may extol a seventh-century ideal for Islam, but they are very adept at using the twenty-first-century Internet. Terrorism, like theater, is a competition for audience. Shocking events are designed to capture attention, polarize, and provoke overreactions from their targets. In 2004, a shocking video of Al Qaeda operative Abu Musab al Zarqawi decapitating an American in Iraq was downloaded millions of times on the Internet and stimulated copycat beheadings by other groups.

One of the hardest things for terrorists to do is to organize trustworthy cells across borders that cannot be taken down by intelligence and police agencies. By moving from the physical sanctuaries of the 1990s to the virtual sanctuaries of the Internet, the terrorists reduce their risk. No longer does recruiting occur only in physical locations such as mosques and jails. Instead, alienated individuals in isolated national niches can also make contact with a new virtual community of fellow believers around the world. Such Websites not only recruit; they also train. They include detailed instructions on how to make bombs, how to cross borders, how to plant and explode devices to kill soldiers and civilians. And experts use chat rooms and message boards to answer trainees' questions. Plans and instructions are then sent through coded messages. Of course, such Websites can be monitored by governments. Some sites are shut down, whereas others are left open so that they can be monitored.[11] But the cat-and-mouse game between state agencies and transnational terrorists is a close one.

Terrorists are only the most dramatic of the many new transnational actors. Even large countries with impressive hard power, such as the United States, find themselves sharing the stage with new actors and having more trouble controlling their borders. Cyberspace will not replace geographical space and will not abolish state sovereignty, but like the town markets in feudal times, it will coexist and greatly complicate what it means to be a sovereign state or a powerful country in the twenty-first century.

CYBERPOWER

Power based on information resources is not new; cyberpower is. There are dozens of definitions of cyberspace but generally "cyber" is a prefix standing for electronic and computer-related activities. By one definition, "cyberspace is an operational domain framed by use of electronics to . . . exploit information via interconnected systems and their associated infrastructure."[12]

We sometimes forget how new cyberspace is. In 1969, the Defense Department started a modest connection of a few computers called ARPANET, and in 1972, the codes for exchanging data (TCP/IP) were created to constitute a rudimentary Internet capable of exchanging packets of digital information. The domain name system of Internet addresses started in 1983, and the first computer viruses were created about that time. The World Wide Web began in 1989; Google, the most popular search engine, was founded in 1998; and the open source encyclopedia Wikipedia began in 2001. In the late 1990s, businesses begin to use the new technology to shift production and procurement in complex global supply chains. Only recently have there been the bandwidth and server farms needed to support "cloud computing," in which companies and individuals can store their data and software on the Web. ICANN (the Internet Corporation for Assigned Names and Numbers) was created in 1998, and the U.S. government began to develop serious national plans for cybersecurity only since the turn of the century. In 1992, there were only 1 million users on the Internet; within fifteen years that had grown to 1 billion.[13] In the Internet's early days, libertarians proclaimed that "information wants to be free" and portrayed the Internet as the end of government controls and the "death of distance." In practice, governments and geographical jurisdictions continue to play a major role, but the domain is also marked by power diffusion.[14]

We can conceptualize cyberspace in terms of many layers of activities, but a simple first approximation portrays it as a unique hybrid regime of physical and virtual properties.[15] The physical infrastructure layer follows the economic laws of rival resources and increasing marginal costs and the political laws of sovereign jurisdiction and control. The virtual, or informational, layer has economic network characteristics of increasing returns to scale and political practices that make jurisdictional control difficult.[16] Attacks from the informational realm, where costs are low, can be launched against the physical domain, where resources are scarce and expensive. But conversely, control of the physical layer can have both territorial and extraterritorial effects on the informational layer.

Cyberpower can be defined in terms of a set of resources that relate to the creation, control, and communication of electronic and computer-based information—infrastructure, networks, software, human skills. This includes not only the Internet of networked computers, but also Intranets, cellular technologies, and space-based communications. Defined behaviorally, cyberpower is the ability to obtain preferred outcomes through use of the electronically interconnected information resources of the cyberdomain. Cyberpower can be used to produce preferred outcomes *within* cyberspace, or it can use cyberinstruments to produce preferred outcomes in other domains *outside* cyberspace.

By analogy, seapower refers to the use of resources in the oceans domain to win naval battles on the ocean, to control shipping chokepoints such as straits, and to demonstrate an offshore presence, but it also includes the ability to use the oceans to influence battles, commerce, and opinions on land. In 1890, Alfred Thayer Mahan popularized the importance of seapower in the context of new technologies of steam propulsion, armor, and long-range guns. President Theodore Roosevelt responded by greatly expanding America's blue water navy and sending it around the world in 1907.

After the introduction of aircraft in World War I, military men began to theorize about the domain of airpower and the ability to strike directly at an enemy's urban center of gravity without armies having to first cross borders. Franklin Roosevelt's investments in airpower were vital in World War II. After the development of intercontinental missiles and surveillance and communications satellites in the 1960s, writers began to theorize about the particular domain of space power, and John F. Kennedy launched a program to ensure an American lead in space and to put a man on the moon. Similarly, in 2009, President Barack Obama called for a major new initiative in cyberpower, and other governments followed suit.[17] As technological change reshapes power domains, political leaders soon follow.

The cyberdomain is unique in that it is human-made, recent, and subject to even more rapid technological changes than other domains. As one observer puts it, "The geography of cyberspace is much more mutable than other environments. Mountains and oceans are hard to move, but portions of cyberspace can be turned on and off with the click of a switch."[18] Low barriers to entry contribute to the diffusion of power in the cyberdomain. It is cheaper and quicker to move electrons across the globe than to move large ships long distances through the friction of saltwater. The costs of developing multiple-carrier task forces and submarine fleets create enormous barriers to entry and make it still possible to speak of American naval dominance. Although piracy remains a local option for nonstate actors in areas such as Somalia or the Malacca Straits, sea control remains out of the reach of nonstate actors. Similarly, even though there are many private and government actors in the air domain, a country can still seek to achieve air superiority through costly investments in fifth-generation fighters and satellite support systems.

The barriers to entry in the cyberdomain, however, are so low that nonstate actors and small states can play significant roles at low levels of cost. In contrast to sea, air, and space, "cyber shares three characteristics with land warfare—though in even greater dimensions: the number of players, ease of entry, and opportunity for concealment. . . . On land, dominance is not a readily achievable criterion."[19] Even though a few states, such as the United States, Russia, Britain, France, and China, are reputed to have greater capacity than others, it makes little sense to speak of dominance in cyberspace as in seapower or airpower. If anything, dependence on complex cybersystems for support of military and economic activities creates new vulnerabilities in large states that can be exploited by nonstate actors.

Extreme conflict in the cyberdomain, or "cyberwar," is also different. In the physical world, governments have a near monopoly on large-scale use of force, the defender has an intimate knowledge of the terrain, and attacks end because of attrition or exhaustion. Both resources and mobility are costly. In the virtual world, actors are diverse, sometimes anonymous; physical distance is immaterial; and a "single virtual offense is almost cost free."[20] Because the Internet was designed for ease of use rather than security, the offense currently has the advantage over the defense. This might not remain the case in the long term as technology evolves, including efforts at "reengineering" some systems for greater security, but it remains the case at this stage. The larger party has limited ability to disarm or destroy the enemy, occupy territory, or effectively use counterforce strategies. As we shall see later in the chapter, deterrence is not impossible, but it differs because of problems of attribution of the source of an attack. Ambiguity is ubiquitous and reinforces the normal fog of war. Redundancy, resilience, and quick reconstitution become crucial components of defense. As one expert summarizes the situation, "Attempts to transfer policy constructs from other forms of warfare will not only fail but also hinder policy and planning."[21]

Cyberpower affects many other domains from war to commerce. We can distinguish "intra-cyberspace power" from "extra-cyberspace power," just as with seapower we can distinguish naval power on the oceans from naval power projection onto land. For example,

carrier-based aircraft can participate in land battles, trade and commerce may grow because of the efficiency of a new generation of
container ships, and the soft power of a country may be increased
by the visit of naval hospital ships in humanitarian missions.

As Table 5.1 illustrates, *inside* the cyberdomain, information instruments can be used to produce soft power in cyberspace through
agenda-framing, attraction, or persuasion. For example, attracting
the open source software community of programmers to adhere to
a new standard is an example of soft power targeted within cyberspace. Cyberresources can also produce hard power inside cyberspace. For example, states or nonstate actors can organize a
distributed denial of service attack by using "Botnets" of hundreds
of thousands (or more)[22] of corrupted computers that swamp a
company or country's Internet system and prevent it functioning,
as occurred, for example, to Georgia in 2008. Organizing a Botnet
by infiltrating a virus into unguarded computers is relatively inexpensive, and Botnets can be illegally rented on the Internet for a
few hundred dollars. Sometimes individual criminals do this for
purposes of extortion.

Other cases may involve "hacktivists," or ideologically motivated
intruders. For example, Taiwanese and Chinese hackers regularly
deface each other's Websites with electronic graffiti. In 2007, Estonia suffered a distributed denial of service attack that was widely
attributed to "patriotic hackers" in Russia who were offended by
Estonia's movement of a World War II monument to Soviet soldiers. In 2008, shortly before Russian troops invaded, Georgia suffered a denial of service attack that shut down its Internet access.
(In both instances, however, the Russian government seems to have
abetted the hackers while maintaining plausible deniability.) Other
forms of hard power within cyberspace include insertions of malicious code to disrupt systems or to steal intellectual property. Criminal groups do this for profit, and governments may do it as a way of
increasing economic resources. China, for example, has been accused
of such activities by a number of other countries. Proof of the origin

TABLE 5.1 Physical and Virtual Dimensions of Cyberpower

TARGETS OF CYBERPOWER		
	INTRA-CYBERSPACE	EXTRA-CYBERSPACE
INFORMATION INSTRUMENTS	Hard: denial of service attacks Soft: setting of norms and standards	Hard: attack on SCADA systems Soft: public diplomacy campaign to sway opinion
PHYSICAL INSTRUMENTS	Hard: government control of companies Soft: software to help human rights activists	Hard: bomb routers or cutting of cables Soft: protests to name and shame cyberproviders

or motive of such attacks is often very difficult, however, as attackers can route their intrusions through servers in other countries to make attribution difficult. For example, many of the attacks on Estonian and Georgian targets were routed through American servers.[23]

Cyberinformation can travel through cyberspace to create soft power by attracting citizens in another country. A public diplomacy campaign over the Internet such as described in Chapter 4 is an example. But cyberinformation can also become a hard power resource that can do damage to physical targets in another country. For example, many modern industries and utilities have processes that are controlled by computers linked in SCADA (supervisory control and data acquisition) systems. Malicious software inserted into these systems could be instructed to shut down a process, such as the Stuxnet worm did to Iranian nuclear facilities in 2010. If a hacker or a government shut down the provision of electricity in a northern city like Chicago or Moscow in the middle of February, the devastation could be more costly than if bombs had been dropped. In some facilities such as hospitals, backup generators can provide resilience in the case of a disruptive attack, but widespread regional blackouts would be more difficult to cope with.

As Table 5.1 indicates, physical instruments can provide power resources that can be brought to bear on the cyberworld. For instance, the physical routers and servers and the fiber-optic cables that carry the electrons of the Internet have geographical locations within government jurisdictions, and companies running and using the Internet are subject to those governments' laws. Governments can bring physical coercion to bear against companies and individuals—what has been called "the hallmark of traditional legal systems." Legal prosecution made Yahoo restrict what it distributed in France to fit French laws, and Google removed hate speech from searches in Germany. Even though the messages were protected free speech in the companies' "home country," the United States, the alternative to compliance was jail time, fines, and loss of access to those important markets. Governments control behavior on the Internet through their traditional physical threats to such intermediaries as Internet service providers, browsers, search engines, and financial intermediaries.[24]

As for investment in physical resources that create soft power, governments can set up special servers and software designed to help human rights activists propagate their messages despite the efforts of their own governments to create information firewalls to block such messages. For example, in the aftermath of the Iranian government's repression of protests following the election of 2009, the American State Department invested in software and hardware that would enable the protesters to disseminate their messages.

Finally, as Table 5.1 illustrates, physical instruments can provide both hard and soft power resources that can be used against the Internet. The cyberinformation layer rests upon a physical infrastructure that is vulnerable to direct military attack or sabotage by both governments and nonstate actors such as terrorists or criminals. Servers can be blown up, and cables can be cut. And in the domain of soft power, nonstate actors and NGOs can organize physical demonstrations to name and shame companies (and governments) that they regard as abusing the Internet. For example, in 2006 protesters in Washington marched and demonstrated against Yahoo and other Internet companies that had provided the names of Chinese activists that led to their arrest by the Chinese government.

Another way of looking at power in the cyberdomain is to consider the three faces or aspects of relational power described in Chapter 1. We can find evidence of hard and soft power behavior in all three aspects as applied to cyberspace. The first face of power is the ability of an actor to make others do something contrary to their initial preferences or strategies. Examples related to hard power could include the denial of services attacks described previously, as well as the arrest or prevention of dissident bloggers from sending their messages. For example, in December 2009, China sentenced Liu Xiaobo, a veteran human rights activist and blogger, to eleven years in prison for "inciting subversion of state power" and introduced new restrictions on registration and operation of Websites by individuals. As one Chinese Web hosting service provider comments, "For nine years I have run a successful and legal business, and now I have suddenly been told that what I do makes me a criminal."[25]

In terms of soft power, an individual or organization might attempt to persuade others to change their behavior. The Chinese government sometimes used the Internet to mobilize Chinese students to demonstrate against Japan when its officials took positions that offended Chinese views of the 1930s relationship. Al Qaeda videos on the Internet designed to recruit people to their cause are another case of soft power being used to change people from their original preferences or strategies.

The second face of power is agenda-setting or agenda-framing in which an actor precludes the choices of others by exclusion of their strategies. If this agenda-setting is against their will, it is an aspect of hard power; if it is accepted as legitimate, it is an instance of soft power. For example, on the February 2010 anniversary of the Iranian Revolution, the Iranian government slowed the Internet to prevent protesters sending films of protests to be seen on YouTube as

TABLE 5.2 Three Faces of Power in the Cyberdomain

FIRST FACE
(A INDUCING B TO DO WHAT B WOULD INITIALLY OTHERWISE NOT DO)
Hard: denial of service attacks, insertion of malware, SCADA
    disruptions, arrests of bloggers
Soft: information campaign to change initial preferences of hackers,
    recruitment of members of terrorist organizations

SECOND FACE
(A PRECLUDING B'S CHOICE BY EXCLUDING B'S STRATEGIES)
Hard: firewalls, filters, and pressure on companies to exclude some
    ideas
Soft: self-monitoring of ISPs and search engines, ICANN rules on
    domain names, widely accepted software standards

THIRD FACE
(A SHAPING B'S PREFERENCES SO THAT SOME STRATEGIES ARE NEVER
EVEN CONSIDERED)
Hard: threats to punish bloggers who disseminate censored material
Soft: information to create preferences (such as stimulation of
    nationalism and patriotic hackers), development of norms of
    revulsion (such as for child pornography)

they had successfully done six months earlier. As one Iranian exile comments, "It was the day the Greens grew up and learned that fighting a government as determined as the Islamic Republic of Iran will require much more than Facebook fan pages, Twitter clouds, and emotional YouTube clips."[26] In a game of cat and mouse, technologies can be used to promote both freedom and repression.

According to the Open Net Initiative, at least forty countries use highly restrictive filters and firewalls to prevent the discussion of suspect materials. Eighteen countries engage in political censorship, which the initiative describes as "pervasive" in China, Vietnam, and Iran and "substantial" in Libya, Ethiopia, and Saudi Arabia. More than thirty states filter for social reasons, blocking content related to topics such as sex, gambling, and drugs. Even the United States and many European states do this "selectively."[27] Sometimes this blocking is accepted and sometimes not. If the filtering is secretive, it is hard for citizens to know what they do not know. First-generation filtering technologies are installed at key Internet chokepoints and work by preventing requests for a predetermined list of Websites and addresses. These technologies are often known to users, but they have been supplemented by more sophisticated technologies that are more stealthy, dynamic, and targeted on opponents "just in time."[28] In some instances, what looks like hard power to one group looks attractive to another. After riots in Xinjiang in 2009, China closed thousands of Websites and censored text messages, which made communication more difficult for residents of that region, but it also cultivated homegrown alternatives to foreign-based Websites, such as YouTube, Facebook, and Twitter, that were attractive in the eyes of nationalistic "patriotic hackers."[29] Among American corporations, when the music industry sued more than 12,000 Americans for intellectual property theft in downloading music illegally, the threat was felt as hard power by those sued and by many who were not sued as well. But when a transnational corporation such as Apple decides not to allow certain applications to be downloaded to its I-phones, many consumers are not even aware of the truncations of their potential agendas, and few understand the algorithms that guide their searches for information.[30]

The third face of power involves one actor shaping another's initial preferences so that some strategies are not even considered. When companies choose to design one code, rather than another, into their software products, few consumers notice.[31] Governments may carry out campaigns to delegitimize certain ideas, such as the Falun Gong religion in China, and restrict dissemination of those ideas on the Internet and thus make it difficult for citizens to know about them. Saudi Arabia makes certain infidel Websites unavailable to its citizens. The U.S. government has taken measures against credit card companies to make Internet gambling unavailable to citizens. France and Germany prevent discussion of Nazi ideology on the Internet. Occasionally, as with child pornography, there is broad cross-cultural consensus on keeping certain ideas and pictures from being available.

ACTORS AND THEIR RELATIVE
POWER RESOURCES

The diffusion of power in the cyberdomain is represented by the vast number of actors therein and the relative reduction of power differentials among them. Anyone from a teenage hacker to a major modern government can do damage in cyberspace, and as the famous *New Yorker* cartoon once put it, "On the internet, no one knows you are a dog." The infamous "Love Bug" virus unleashed by a hacker in the Philippines is estimated to have caused $15 billion in damage.[32] The Pentagon has 7 million computers in 15,000 networks, and those networks are approached by outsiders "hundreds of thousands of times every day."[33] Cybercriminal groups were said to have stolen more than $1 trillion in data and intellectual property in 2008.[34] One cyberespionage network—GhostNet—was found to be infecting 1,295 computers in 103 countries, of which 30 percent were high-value governmental targets.[35] Terrorist groups use the Web to recruit new members and plan campaigns. Political and environmental activists disrupt Websites of companies and governments.

What is distinctive about power in the cyberdomain is not that governments are out of the picture, as the early cyberlibertarians predicted, but that different actors possess different power resources and that the gap between state and nonstate actors is narrowing in many instances. But relative reduction of power differentials is not the same as equalization. Large governments still have more resources. On the Internet, all dogs are not equal.

As a rough approximation, we can divide actors in cyberspace into three categories: governments, organizations with highly structured networks, and individuals and lightly structured networks. (Of

TABLE 5.3 Relative Power Resources of Actors in the Cyberdomain

---

MAJOR GOVERNMENTS

1. development and support of infrastructure, education, intellectual property
2. legal and physical coercion of individuals and intermediaries located within borders
3. size of market and control of access—e.g., EU, China, U.S.
4. resources for cyberattack and cyberdefense: bureaucracy, budgets, intelligence agencies
5. provision of public goods, such as regulations necessary for commerce
6. reputation for the legitimacy, benignity, and competence that produce soft power
   Key vulnerabilities: high dependence on easily disrupted complex systems, political instability, possible reputation loss

ORGANIZATIONS AND HIGHLY STRUCTURED NETWORKS

1. large budgets and human resources, economies of scale
2. transnational flexibility
3. control of code and product development, generativity of applications
4. brands and reputation
   Key vulnerabilities: legal prosecution, intellectual property theft, systems disruption, possible reputation loss (name and shame)

INDIVIDUALS AND LIGHTLY STRUCTURED NETWORKS

1. low cost of investment for entry
2. virtual anonymity and ease of exit
3. asymmetrical vulnerability compared to governments and large organizations
   Key vulnerabilities: legal and illegal coercion by governments and organizations if caught

---

course, there are many subcategories, and some governments have much more capacity than others, but this is a first approximation.)

Government Actors

Because the physical infrastructure of the Internet remains tied to geography and governments are sovereign over geographical spaces, location still matters as a resource in the cyberdomain. Governments can take steps to subsidize infrastructure, computer education, and protection of intellectual property that will encourage (or discourage) the development of capabilities within their borders. The provision of public goods, including a legal and regulatory environment, can stimulate commercial growth of cybercapabilities. South Korea, for example, has taken a lead on public development of broadband capabilities. A reputation that is seen as legitimate, benign, and competent can enhance (or conversely undercut) a government's soft power with other actors in the cyberdomain.

Geography also serves as a basis for governments to exercise legal coercion and control. For example, after the Xinjiang riots in 2009, the Chinese government was able to deprive 19 million residents in an area twice as big as Texas of text messaging, international phone calls, and Internet access to all but a few government-controlled Websites. The damage to business and tourism was significant, but the Chinese government was more concerned about political stability.[36] In 2010, when SWIFT, a private company that coordinates and logs money transfers among banks, moved key computer servers from the United States to Europe, it needed EU permission to hand over data voluntarily to the U.S. Treasury for antiterrorist purposes. When the European Parliament balked at approval of a Europe-wide agreement, SWIFT announced that "there is no legal basis for us to hand over data from our European centers to the Treasury." In a subsequent compromise, the European Parliament imposed new privacy restrictions on the data transfers.[37]

If a market is large, a government can exert its power extraterritorially. Europe's tight privacy standards have had a global effect. When companies such as Yahoo or Dow Jones faced legal claims based on Internet activity in France or Australia, they decided to comply rather than walk away from those markets. Obviously, this is a power resource available to governments with jurisdiction over large markets, but not necessarily to all governments.

Governments also have the capacity to carry out offensive cyber-attacks.[38] For example, America's Tenth Fleet and Twenty-fourth Air Force have no ships or planes. Their battlefield is cyberspace.[39] Their troops use computers and the Internet rather than ships or planes. Unfortunately, news accounts of "millions of attacks" use the word "attack" loosely to refer to everything from computer port scanning to hacking (illegal computer trespassing) or defacing Websites to full-scale operations designed to wreak physical destruction. We should distinguish simple attacks, which use inexpensive tool kits that anyone can download from the Internet, from advanced attacks that identify new vulnerabilities that have not yet been patched, involve new viruses, and involve "zero-day attacks" (first-time use.) These attacks require more skill than simple hacking does. Experts also distinguish cyberexploitation for spying purposes from cyberattack for destructive or disruptive purposes. Governments carry out activities of both types. Little is publicly confirmed about cyberespionage, but most reports describe intrusions into computer systems as ubiquitous and not limited to governments.

There are reports of attacks related to warfare in the cases of Iraq in 2003 or Georgia in 2008 and sabotage of electronic equipment in covert actions.[40] Israel is alleged to have used cybermeans to defeat Syrian air defenses before bombing a secret nuclear reactor in September 2007.[41] Most experts see cyberattack as an important adjunct, rather than an overwhelming weapon (unlike nuclear), in interstate wars. States intrude into each other's cyber-systems in "preparation of the battlefield" for what could be future conflicts. Both American and Chinese military theorists have discussed such steps (as we saw in Chapter 2), but little is publicly stated about offensive cyberdoctrines. A National Research Council Report concluded in 2009 that "today's policy and legal framework for guiding and regulating the U.S. use of cyber attack is ill-formed, undeveloped, and highly uncertain."[42] Presumably, many large governments engage in such activity, though the success of such attacks would depend upon the target's vulnerabilities, and thus premature exercise or disclosure would undercut their value. Zero-day attacks without prior warning are likely to be the most effective, and even their effects may depend on measures the target has taken to develop resiliency, some of which may not be fully known to the attacker.

Nongovernment Actors with Highly Structured Networks

Cyberattacks that deny service or disrupt systems are also carried out by nonstate actors whether for ideological or criminal purposes, but such groups do not have the same capacities as large governments. Sophisticated attacks against high-value targets such as defense communications systems involve large intelligence agencies that intrude physically (through supply chains or spies) and/or crack highly encrypted codes. A teenage hacker and a large government can both do considerable damage over the Internet, but that does not make them equally powerful in the cyberdomain. Power diffusion is not the same as power equalization. Some government experts believe that concerted technological improvements in encryption and identity management could greatly reduce threats at the low end of the spectrum within the next five to ten years.[43] In the words of Mike McConnell, former director of national intelligence, "The technologies are already available from public and private sources and can be further developed if we have the will to build them into our systems."[44]

Some transnational corporations have huge budgets, skilled human resources, and control of proprietary code that give them power resources larger than those of many governments. In 2009, Microsoft, Apple, and Google had annual revenues of $58, $35, and $22 billion, respectively, and together employed more than 150,000 people.[45] Amazon, Google, Microsoft, and others are competing in the development of cloud computing and have server farms with more then 50,000 servers. Their transnational structure allows them to exploit markets and resources around the globe. At the same time, to preserve their legal status as well as their brand equity, transnational corporations have strong incentives to stay compliant with local legal structures.

No such legal niceties constrain the power of criminal organizations. Some are small "strike-and-exit" operations, which make their gains quickly before governments and regulators can catch up.[46] Others have impressive transnational scale and presumably buy protection from weak governments. Before being dismantled by law enforcement, the Darkmarket online network had more than 2,500 members across the world buying and selling stolen financial information, passwords, and credit cards.[47] Up to one-quarter of network-connected computers may be part of a Botnet, and some Botnets include millions of computers. Although estimates vary, cybercrime may cost companies more than $1 trillion a year.[48] Some criminal groups, such as the so-called Russian Business Network (RBN), may have inherited some capabilities of the Soviet state after its dissolution and are alleged to retain informal connections with the Russian government. According to a British official, "There were strong indications RBN had the local police, local judiciary and local government in St. Petersburg in its pocket. Our investigation hit significant hurdles."[49] Moreover, "the hacking skills of criminal groups may make them natural allies for nation-states looking for a way to augment their capabilities while denying involvement in cyber attacks."[50] The scale of some criminal operations is expensive and costly but apparently profitable. In 2006, the U.S. Government Accountability Office estimated that only 5 percent of cybercriminals were ever arrested or convicted.[51]

Terrorist groups make active use of cybertools, as we saw earlier, though cyberterrorism narrowly defined as the direct use of virtual tools to wreak destruction (see the top row in Table 5.1) has thus far been rare. Although there is nothing stopping terrorist groups from recruiting able computer specialists or purchasing malware from criminal groups on the Internet, "cyber attacks appear much less useful than physical attacks: they do not fill potential victims with terror, they are not photogenic, and they are not perceived by most people as highly emotional events."[52] Of twenty-two plots disrupted since 9/11, all involved explosives or small arms, and "while the United States' critical infrastructure from the electrical grid to the financial sector is vulnerable to attack through cyberspace, al-Qaeda lacks the capability and motivation to exploit these vulnerabilities."[53] Others are not so sanguine. For example, McConnell believes that the vulnerabilities of financial and electrical systems present a huge target for any group that wishes to wreak destruction, and that such groups will develop the capabilities to become a greater threat than other nation-states. In his words, "When terrorist groups have the sophistication, they'll use it."[54]

So far, terrorists seem to have decided that for their purposes explosives provide a tool with more bang for the buck. But that does not mean that terrorist groups do not use the Internet for promoting terrorism. As we saw earlier, it has become a crucial tool that allows them to operate as networks of decentralized franchises, create a brand image, recruit adherents, raise funds, provide training manuals, and manage operations. It is far safer to send electrons than agents through customs and immigration controls. Thanks to cybertools, Al Qaeda has been able to move from a hierarchical organization restricted to geographically organized cells to a horizontal global network to which local volunteers can self-recruit. As one expert on terrorism remarks, the key place for radicalization is "neither Pakistan nor Yemen nor Afghanistan . . . but in a solitary experience of a virtual community: the ummah on the Web."[55]

Individuals with Lightly Structured Networks
This is an example of how cybertools begin to blur the lines between organizations with highly structured networks and individuals with lightly structured networks. As a number of previous examples have shown, individuals can easily play in the cyberdomain because of the low cost of investment for entry, virtual ano-

nymity, and ease of exit. Sometimes they act with government approval and sometimes against them. For example, before the 2008 Russian attack on Georgia, "any civilian, Russian born or otherwise, aspiring to be a cyber warrior was able to visit pro-Russia websites to download the software and instructions necessary to launch denial of service attacks on Georgia."[56] During student protests in Iran in 2009, Twitter and social networking sites were crucial for organizing and reporting demonstrations. "The U.S. government asked Twitter executives not to take the site down for scheduled maintenance. They were worried that might interfere with how Twitter was being used to organize demonstrations." Six months later, however, an unknown group called the Iranian Cyber Army successfully redirected Twitter traffic to a Website with an anti-American message, and in February 2010 the Iranian government blocked most access to Twitter and other sites.[57]

In light of our discussion in Chapter 3 of the ways in which asymmetrical interdependence helps to produce power, it is worth noting that individual actors in the cyberdomain benefit from asymmetrical vulnerability compared to governments and large organizations. They have very low investment and little to lose from exit and reentry. Their major vulnerability is to legal and illegal coercion by governments and organizations if they are apprehended, but only a small percent are actually caught. In contrast, corporations have important vulnerabilities because of large fixed investments in complex operating systems, intellectual property, and reputation. Similarly, large governments depend on easily disrupted complex systems, political stability, and reputational soft power. Although hit-and-run cyberstrikes by individuals are unlikely to bring governments or corporations to their knees, they can impose serious costs of disruption to operations and to reputations with a miniscule investment. Governments are top dogs on the Internet, but smaller dogs still bite, and dealing with those bites can lead to a complex politics.

GOOGLE AND CHINA

This complex interaction of public and private actors is illustrated by the case of Google, an American company, and the government of China.[58] Early in 2010, Google announced that it was withdrawing from business in China and thus inflicted a noticeable cost upon Chinese soft power. The case involved three issues that were technically different but became linked politically: alleged efforts by the Chinese government to steal Google's source code (intellectual property), intrusion into the G-mail accounts of Chinese activists (human rights), and, in response, Google's decision to stop complying with censorship of searches by Google.cn (although Google had been complying for four years). Technically, pulling out of China did nothing to solve the first two issues, which did not depend on servers located in China. But Google aspired to be the cloud provider of choice (in competition with rivals such as Microsoft), and it may have decided that its reputation related to security and human rights was more valuable than capturing the search market in China, where Baidu, a Chinese company, was ahead in market share. Moreover, search in China was not a big source of revenue for Google.

Attacks designed to steal the intellectual property of foreign companies were not uncommon in China, but after July 2009 experts detected a new level of audacity against multiple companies now subjected to sophisticated new (zero-day) attacks. China seemed to be upping the ante, and unlike low-tech companies with little choice if they wanted to stay in the China market, Google needed to preserve the soft power of its reputation for supporting freedom of expression to recruit and nurture creative personnel and to maintain the security reputation of its G-mail brand.

At this point, the American government became involved. Google alerted the White House before its announcement. Secretary of State Clinton had already been planning a speech on Internet freedom, and adding the Google example raised the issue to the intergovernmental level. The Chinese government initially dismissed the issue as a commercial dispute, but the American government involvement led to political statements about the need to obey Chinese laws and complaints about American cyberimperialism.[59] Other officials referred to American efforts to maintain hegemony over the Internet. At the same time, other Chinese views were expressed. Some citizens deposited flowers on Google's logo, and others worried that Google's exit would hurt China if Baidu became a monopoly. "When the Chinese companies go outside of China, they will find that they fail to understand their competitors as well as they did when they were competing in China."[60] Initially, Google automatically redirected users in mainland China to its Hong Kong site, but China rejected this ploy and threatened not to renew Google's Internet provider license. Google then created a landing page that offered visitors an optional, rather than automatic, link to Hong Kong. Google remained in China, but the Chinese government reasserted the supremacy of Chinese laws.[61]

The American government, however, had used the case to ask for new norms on the Internet. At the same time, it failed to say what the United States would stop doing. For example, would the American government try to halt private intrusions into Chinese systems? Many intrusions into Chinese and American computer systems are reciprocal. "Simply put, the United States is in a big way doing the very things that Secretary Clinton criticized. The U.S. is not, like the Chinese, stealing intellectual property from U.S. firms or breaking into the accounts of democracy advocates. But it aggressively uses the same or similar computer techniques for ends it deems worthy."[62] One survey of cyberexperts found that the United States was perceived to present the greatest threat of intrusions, followed closely by China.[63] Some intrusions originating from the United States were undoubtedly by the government, but others were by private hacktivists trying to advance human rights and Internet freedom in China and elsewhere in the world. Would the United States be able or willing to control such hacktivists? It seems unlikely in human rights cases, yet China's government sees Tibetan exiles and Falun Gong hackers as national security threats. In principle, we could imagine some areas in which Chinese and American goals overlap in reality and in perception, but a private company's initiative linking intellectual property theft and human rights hacking certainly led to a more complex political situation. Companies, governments, and individual hackers all used various instruments available to them to struggle for their preferred outcomes in this aspect of the cyberdomain.

GOVERNMENTS AND GOVERNANCE

Some see cyberspace as analogous to the ungoverned and lawless Wild West, but in practice there are many areas of private and public governance. Certain technical standards related to Internet protocol are set (or not) by consensus among engineers involved in the nongovernmental Internet Engineering Task Force. Whether such standards are broadly applied often depends upon private corporate decisions about their inclusion in commercial products. The nongovernmental World Wide Web Consortium develops standards for the Web. ICANN has the legal status of a nonprofit corporation under American law, though its procedures have evolved to include government voices (though not votes). In any event, ICANN's mandate is limited to domain names and routing management, not the full panoply of cyberspace governance. National governments control copyright and intellectual property laws, though they are subject to negotiation and litigation, sometimes within the frameworks of the World Intellectual Property Organization and the World Trade Organization. Governments also determine national spectrum allocation within an international framework negotiated at the International Telecommunications Union. Above all, national governments try to manage problems of security, espionage, and crime within national legal frameworks, though the technological volatility of the cyberdomain means that laws and regulations are always chasing a moving target. Although there is no single regime for the governance of cyberspace, there is a set of loosely coupled norms and institutions that ranks somewhere between an integrated institution that imposes regulation through hierarchical rules and highly fragmented practices and institutions with no identifiable core and nonexistent linkages.[64]

The cyberspace domain is often described as a public good or a global commons, but these terms are an imperfect fit. A public good is one from which all can benefit and none can be excluded, and even though this may describe some of the information protocols of the Internet, it does not describe its physical infrastructure, which is a scarce proprietary resource located within the boundaries of sovereign states. And cyberspace is not a commons like the high seas because parts of it are under sovereign control. At best, it is an "imperfect commons" or a condominium of joint ownership without well-developed rules.[65]

Cyberspace can be categorized as what Nobel Laureate Elinor Ostrom terms a "common pool resource" from which exclusion is difficult and exploitation by one party can subtract value for other parties.[66] Government is not the sole solution to such common pool resource problems. Ostrom shows that community self-organization is possible under certain conditions. However, the conditions that she associates with successful self-governance are weak in the cyberdomain because of the large size of the resource, the large number of users, and the poor understanding of how the system will evolve (among others). In its earliest days, the Internet was like a small village of known users, and an authentication layer of code was not necessary, and development of norms was simple. All that changed with burgeoning growth. Even though the openness and accessibility of cyberspace as a medium of communication provide valuable benefits to all, free-riding behavior in the form of crime, attacks, and threats creates insecurity. The result is a demand for protection that can lead to fragmentation, "walled gardens," private networks, and cyberequivalents of the seventeenth-century enclosures that were used to solve that era's "tragedy of the commons."[67]

Providing security is a classic function of government, and some observers believe that increasing insecurity will lead to an increased role for governments in cyberspace. Many states desire to extend their sovereignty in cyberspace and seek technological means to do so. As two experts put it, "Securing cyberspace has definitely entailed a 'return of the state' but not in ways that suggest a return to the traditional Westphalian paradigm of state sovereignty." Efforts to secure the network help to facilitate its use by burgeoning nonstate actors and often entail devolution of responsibilities and authority to private actors.[68] For example, banking and financial firms have developed their own elaborate systems of security and punishment through networks of connectedness, such as depriving repeat offenders of their trading rights and slowing speeds and raising transactions costs for addresses associated with suspect behavior. Companies that provide Web-hosting services or social media platforms have strong incentives to remove troublesome or unpopular users who generate little revenue but are costly to defend if they come under attack from other users.[69] Governments want to protect the Internet so that their societies can continue to benefit, but at the same time, they want to protect their societies from what comes through the Internet. China, for example, is described as developing its own companies behind its firewall and planning to disconnect from the Internet if it is attacked.[70] Nonetheless, China—and other governments—still seeks the economic benefits of connectivity. The resulting tension leads to imperfect compromises.[71]

If we treat most hacktivism as merely a nuisance, there are four major cyberthreats to national security, each with a different time horizon and with different (in principle) solutions: economic espionage, crime, cyberwar, and cyberterrorism. For the United States at the present time, the highest costs come from the first two categories, but over the next decade the order may be reversed, and as alliances and tactics evolve among different actors, the categories may increasingly overlap. As described by the former director of national intelligence, "Terrorist groups today are ranked near the bottom of cyberwar capability. Criminal organizations are more sophisticated. There is a hierarchy. You go from nation states, who can destroy things, to criminals, who can steal things, to aggravating but sophisticated hackers. . . . Sooner or later, terror groups will achieve cyber-sophistication. It's like nuclear proliferation, only far easier."[72]

According to President Obama's 2009 cyberreview, theft of intellectual property by other states (and corporations) was the highest immediate cost. Not only did it result in current economic losses, but by destroying competitive advantage, it also jeopardized future hard power.[73] Every year, an amount of intellectual property many times larger than all the intellectual property in the Library of Congress is stolen from business, government, and university networks, threatening American military effectiveness and America's competitiveness in the global economy.[74] As we have already seen, cybercriminals are also a significant burden on the economy. And as we look further ahead, as other states develop their capacities for cyberattack on critical infrastructures and are able to deprive American military forces of their information advantages, the costs to American hard power could be significant. And as terrorist groups that wish to wreak destruction develop their capacity to do so, they could impose dramatic costs. The remedies for each threat are quite different.

Cyberwar is the most dramatic of the potential threats. It can be managed through a form of interstate deterrence (though different from classical nuclear deterrence), offensive capabilities, and designs for network and infrastructure resilience if deterrence fails. At some point in the future, it may be possible to reinforce these steps with certain rudimentary norms.[75] In the case of war, fighting would be subject to the classic norms of discrimination and proportionality that are central to the existing laws of armed conflict, but cyberwar raises new and difficult problems of how to distinguish civilian from military targets and how to be sure about the extent of collateral damage. For example, an American general is quoted as saying that American planners did not use one particular cybertechnique to disable the French-made Iraqi air defense network because we "were afraid we were going to take down all the automated banking machines in Paris." Moreover, because cyberdefense is sometimes analogous to shooting the gun out of an outlaw's hand before he can shoot, and it must be handled by machines working at "netspeed" when an attack is first detected, offense and defense blur and rules of engagement that maintain civilian control become difficult to establish.[76]

Some observers argue that because of the difficulty of attribution of the source of an attack, deterrence does not work in cyberspace. However, this common view is too simple. Even though interstate deterrence is more difficult in the cyberdomain, it is not impossible. Too often people think of deterrence in terms of the nuclear model that prevailed for the past half-century, in which the threat of punitive retaliation is so catastrophic that it deters attack. But nuclear deterrence was never this simple. Although a second-strike capability and mutual assured destruction may have worked to prevent attacks on the homeland, they were never credible for issues at the low end of the spectrum of interests. Lying somewhere in between these extremes were extended deterrence of attacks against allies and defense of vulnerable positions such as Berlin in the Cold War. Nuclear deterrence was supplemented by other measures (such as forward basing of conventional forces), a variety of signaling devices in the movement of forces, and a learning process that occurred over the decades and led to areas of agreements ranging from nonproliferation to management of incidents at sea.

Cyberattacks lack the catastrophic dimensions of nuclear weapons attacks, and attribution is more difficult, but interstate deterrence through entanglement and denial still exists. Even when the source of an attack can be successfully disguised under a "false flag," other governments may find themselves sufficiently entangled in interdependent relationships that a major attack would be counterproductive. Unlike the single strand of military interdependence that linked the United States and the Soviet Union in the Cold War, the United States, China, and other countries are entangled in multiple networks. China, for example, would itself lose from an attack that severely damaged the American economy, and vice versa.

In addition, an unknown attacker may be deterred by denial. If firewalls are strong, or the prospect of a self-enforcing response seems possible ("an electric fence"), attack becomes less attractive. Offensive capabilities for immediate response can create an active defense that can serve as a deterrent even when the identity of the attacker is not fully known. Futility can also help deter an unknown attacker. If the target is well protected, or redundancy and resilience allow quick recovery, the risk-to-benefit ratio in attack is diminished. Finally, to the extent that false flags are imperfect and rumors of the source of an attack are widely deemed credible (though not probative in a court of law), reputational damage to an attacker's soft power may contribute to deterrence.

Cyberterrorism and nonstate actors are harder to deter. As we have seen, cyberattacks are not the most attractive route for terrorists today, but as groups develop their capacity to inflict great damage against infrastructure over the coming years, the temptation will grow. Because attribution will be difficult, improved defenses such as preemption and human intelligence become important. At a more fundamental level, many experts believe that the long-term solution is a program to reengineer the Internet to make such attacks more difficult than under today's structure, which emphasizes ease of use rather than security. One approach is to reduce the vulnerability of some sensitive aspects of the national infrastructure by reducing their connectivity to the Internet. Some suggest special "opt-in" incentives for private owners of critical infrastructure (e.g., finance and electricity) to join secure systems rather than rely on the open Internet (which would continue to exist for those with lower stakes and a willingness to tolerate greater risks).

Cybercrime can also be reduced by similar approaches that make access to some systems more difficult than they are today. In addition, it may be possible to develop degrees of international cooperation to limit cybercrime that are analogous to efforts to discourage piracy in an earlier era. At one time, many governments found it convenient to tolerate some pirates and even charter privateers (until the Declaration of Paris in 1856), and today some governments have similar attitudes toward crime on the Internet. Russia and China, for example, have refused to sign the Council of Europe Convention on Cyber Crime, which has been signed by more than thirty countries. But their attitudes may change over time if costs exceed benefits. For example, "Russian cyber-criminals no longer follow hands-off rules when it comes to motherland targets, and Russian authorities are beginning to drop the laisser faire policy."[77] Although the immediate prospects for the convention are not promising, it is possible to imagine coalitions of the willing that set a higher standard and work together to raise the costs for those who violate an emergent norm, much as occurs with financial money-laundering regulations or the proliferation security initiative.

Internet espionage is likely to continue unabated unless there are new state approaches. Spying is as old as human history and does not violate any explicit provisions of international law. Nonetheless, at times governments have established rules of the road for limiting espionage and engaged in patterns of tit-for-tat retaliation to create an incentive for cooperation. Experiments have shown that partners in prisoner's dilemma and public goods games can develop cooperation in repeated play over extended periods.[78] Even though it is difficult to envisage enforceable treaties in which governments agree not to engage in espionage, it is plausible to imagine a process of iterations (tit for tat) that develops rules of the road that could limit damage in practical terms. In the words of Howard Schmidt, the American cybersecurity chief, "One of the key things has been going back to the countries that it appears it's coming from and saying: if it's not you, you need to investigate this."[79] Failure to respond can be followed by measured retaliation. Under international legal doctrine, proportionate countermeasures can be taken in response to harm originating from a state even if the government is not behind that harm. Although less than perfect, efforts can be made to deal with nonstate actors by holding states responsible for actions that originate within their sovereign boundaries. To avoid escalation or "defection lock-in," it helps to offer assistance and to engage in discussions that can develop common perceptions, if not fully agreed norms. Such "learning" is still at an early stage in the cyberdomain, analogous to what took place in the nuclear era in the early 1950s.[80]

At this stage, large-scale arms control treaties do not seem promising without a capacity for verification, though more limited agreements may be possible.[81] During the 2000s, the UN General Assembly passed a series of resolutions condemning criminal activity and drawing attention to defensive measures that governments can take. During that same period, Russia sought a treaty for broader international oversight of the Internet, banning deception or the embedding of malicious code or circuitry that could be activated in the event of war. But Americans have argued that measures banning offense can damage defense against current attacks and would be impossible to verify or enforce. Moreover, the United States has resisted agreements that could legitimize authoritarian governments' censorship of the Internet. Nonetheless, the United States has begun informal discussions with Russia.[82] Even advocates for an international law for information operations are skeptical of a multilateral treaty akin to the Geneva Conventions that could contain precise and detailed rules given future technological volatility, but they argue that like-minded states could announce self-governing rules that could form norms for the future.[83]

Normative differences present a difficulty in reaching any broad agreements on regulating content on the Internet. As we saw earlier, the United States has called for the creation of "norms of behavior among states" that "encourage respect for the global networked commons," but as Jack Goldsmith argues, "even if we could stop all cyber attacks from our soil, we wouldn't want to. On the private side, hacktivism can be a tool of liberation. On the public side, the best defense of critical computer systems is sometimes a good offense."[84] From the American point of view, Twitter and YouTube are matters of personal freedom; seen from Beijing or Tehran, they are instruments of attack. Even on the issue of child pornography, where norms of condemnation are broadly shared, governments are more likely to unilaterally institute national filtering technologies rather than issuing a take-down notice to the service provider and relying on legal prosecution by the hosting state. For example, Australia has imposed some of the toughest Internet filters regarding crime that have been proposed by any established democracy.[85] Self-help remains the dominant norm.

The cyberdomain is both a new and a volatile human-made environment. The characteristics of cyberspace reduce some of the power differentials among actors and thus provide a good example of the diffusion of power that typifies global politics in this century. The largest powers are unlikely to be able to dominate this domain as much as they have others, such as sea or air. But cyberspace also demonstrates that diffusion of power does not mean equality of power or the replacement of governments as the most powerful actors in world politics. Even the small United Arab Emirates was able to force the maker of the BlackBerry to compromise. "Research in Motion is learning a lesson that other companies have learned before. As we saw in 2000 with Yahoo's failed attempt to maintain a forum to sell Nazi memorabilia in France, and with Google's repeated attempts in recent years to deliver uncensored search results in China, no provider of information services is exempt from the power of the state. The stakes are simply too high for governments to cede the field to private interests alone."[86] But although companies have an incentive to obey laws, other nonstate actors such as criminals and terrorists are not similarly constrained.

Although cyberspace may create some power shifts among states by opening limited opportunities for leapfrogging by small states using asymmetrical warfare, it is unlikely to be a game changer in the power transitions that we will turn to in the next chapter. However, while leaving governments the strongest actors, the cyberdomain is likely to see an increase in the diffusion of power to nonstate actors and network centrality as a key dimension of power in the twenty-first century.

CHAPTER 6

Power Transition

The Question of American Decline

No matter how power is measured, an equal distribution of power among states is relatively rare. More often the processes of uneven growth mean that some states will be rising and others declining. When one state is preponderant in resources, observers often refer to the situation as "hegemony," and as far back as ancient Greece, historians have explained the origin of major wars in terms of hegemonic transition. Thucydides ascribed the cause of the Peloponnesian War (which tore apart the Greek city-state system in the fifth century BCE) to the rise in the power of Athens and the fear it created in Sparta. Similarly, many historians attribute the underlying cause of World War I, which destroyed Europe's centrality in the world, to the rise in the power of Germany and the fear it created in Britain. As one political scientist puts it, "The outbreaks of hegemonic struggles have most frequently been triggered by fears of ultimate decline and the perceived erosion of power."[1]

Some expect that the rise of China will have similar effects on the United States in the twenty-first century. One Sinologist argues that "sooner or later, if present trends continue, war is probable in Asia. . . . China today is actively seeking to scare the United States away from East Asia rather as Germany sought to frighten Britain before World War I." Similarly, columnist Robert Kagan claims, "The Chinese leadership views the world in much the same way Kaiser Wilhelm II did a century ago. . . . Chinese leaders chafe at the constraints on them and worry that they must change the rules of the international system before the international system changes them."[2] University of Chicago political scientist John Mearsheimer asserts, "To put it bluntly, China cannot rise peacefully."[3] Two more cautious analysts argue, "It is hardly inevitable that China will be a threat to American interests, but the United States is much more likely to go to war with China than it is with any other major power."[4]

HEGEMONIC TRANSITIONS

There is nothing inevitable, however, about war between a state with preponderant resources and a rising power. In the 1890s, Britain successfully accommodated the rise of American power despite opportunities for war,[5] and of the nine general or "world wars" since 1500, not all were hegemonic.[6] Moreover, the word "hegemony" is used in diverse and confused ways. There is no general agreement on how much inequality and what types of power resources constitute hegemony. Some writers use the word interchangeably with "imperial" and refer to nineteenth-century Britain as hegemonic even though Britain ranked third (behind the United States and Russia) in GDP and third (behind Russia and France) in military expenditures even at the height of its power in 1870.

After World War II, when the United States represented more than one-third of world product and had an overwhelming preponderance in nuclear weapons, many considered it a global hegemon, but nonetheless the United States was unable to prevent the "loss" of China, roll back communism in Eastern Europe, prevent stalemate in the Korean War, stop the "loss" of North Vietnam, or dislodge the Castro regime in Cuba. Even in the era of alleged

American hegemony, only one-fifth of its efforts to compel change in other countries through military threats and one-half through economic sanctions were successful.[7] As we saw in Chapter 1, power measured in resources does not mean power measured in preferred outcomes. Context, scope, and domain must be specified, and there is the danger of allowing the golden glow of the past to color the appraisal of history. Vague definitions and arbitrary history should cause us to be wary of grand theories of hegemony and decline.

Many believe that America's current preponderance in power resources is hegemonic and will decline like that of Britain before it. Some Americans react emotionally to the idea of decline because it touches a raw nerve in politics, but it would be counterintuitive and ahistorical to believe that the United States will have a preponderant share of power resources forever. However, the word "decline" mixes up two different dimensions: absolute decline in the sense of decay or the loss of ability to use one's resources effectively and relative decline in which the power resources of other states grow greater or are used more effectively. For instance, seventeenth-century Netherlands flourished domestically but declined in relative power as other states grew in strength. Conversely, the Western Roman Empire did not succumb to the rise of another state but rather to internal decay and swarms of barbarians. As one British historian warns, "Doom-mongers conjure with Roman and British analogies in order to trace the decay of American hegemony. In so doing they ignore Gibbon's warning about the danger of comparing epochs remote from one another." Rome was an agrarian society torn by internecine strife; the British Empire, based on a tiny island, was "an oak tree in a plant pot."[8]

The historical analogy with British decline is popular but misleading. Britain had an empire on which the sun never set, ruled over one-quarter of humankind, and enjoyed naval supremacy, but there were major differences in the relative power resources of imperial Britain and contemporary America. By the time of World War I, Britain ranked only fourth among the great powers in its share of military personnel, fourth in GDP, and third in military spending.[9] The costs of defense ranged from 2.5 to 3.4 percent of GDP, and the empire was ruled in large part through local troops. In 1914, Britain's net export of capital gave it an important financial kitty to draw upon (though some historians consider that it would have been better to have invested in home industry), and of the 8.6 million British forces in World War I, nearly one-third were provided by the overseas empire.[10] But with the rise of nationalism, it became increasingly difficult for London to declare war on behalf of the empire, and protecting the empire became more of a burden than an asset. In contrast, America has had a continental-scale economy immune from nationalist disintegration since 1865. For all the loose talk of American empire, the United States is less tethered and has more degrees of freedom than Britain had. And the geopolitics of the two states differs. Whereas Britain faced rising neighbors in Germany and Russia, America benefits from two oceans and weaker neighbors.

Despite these differences, Americans are prone to cycles of belief in their decline. Some see the American problem as imperial overstretch, some see it as relative decline caused by the rise of others, and some see it as a process of absolute decline or decay. Such projections are not new. The Founding Fathers worried about comparisons to the decline of the Roman republic. A strand of cultural pessimism is simply very American, extending back to Puritan roots. Charles Dickens observed a century and a half ago, "If its individual citizens, to a man, are to be believed, [America] always is depressed, and always is stagnated, and always is in an alarming crisis, and never was otherwise."[11]

More recently, polls showed a belief in decline after the Soviet Union launched *Sputnik* in 1957, after Nixon's economic adjustments and the oil shocks in the 1970s, and after the closing of rust belt industries and the budget deficits of the Reagan administration in the 1980s. At the end of that decade, the American people believed the country was in decline; yet within a decade they believed that the United States was the sole superpower, and now many believe in decline again.[12] Cycles of declinism tell us more about psychology than about underlying shifts in power resources.[13] Rather than relying on questionable historical analogies, or projections from short-term cycles, the next two sections will examine the issue of American power by looking first at decline relative to the power of other countries and then at absolute decline based on domestic change.

THE DISTRIBUTION OF POWER RESOURCES

The twenty-first century began with a very unequal distribution of power resources. With 5 percent of the world's population, the United States accounted for about a quarter of the world's product, nearly half of global military expenditures, and the world's most extensive cultural and educational soft power resources. According to two scholars, "No system of sovereign states has ever contained one state with comparable material preponderance."[14] As we saw earlier, however, power resources do not always translate into power outcomes, and even in the period after World War II, a preponderant United States was frequently thwarted in achieving its preferred outcomes. However, in relative power resources, the twenty-first century began with a distribution of power resources in which no country was in a position to balance the United States in terms of the classical realist understanding of the term. There was American primacy in the distribution of power resources, though not in all dimensions. As Table 6.1 shows, America ranked fourth in its share of world population, and the European Union had a slightly larger economy.

The future of this American primacy in the share of world resources is hotly debated. Although it is a mistake to project long-run trends from short-term events, the conventional wisdom at media events such as the Davos World Economic Forum in 2010 interpreted the global financial crisis as proof that the balance of power had already begun to shift.[15] As one strategist puts it, "Wall Street's crack-up presages a global tectonic shift: the beginning of the decline of American power. Great empires and great civilizations have a way of cresting that is pretty well set in historical stone."[16] Contrarily, others argue that American preeminence is so great that "systemic constraints on its security policy become generally inoperative."[17] Taking a longer-term view, the National Intelligence Council's projection for 2025 was that "the U.S. will remain the preeminent power, but that American dominance will be much diminished."[18] Much attention has been lavished on the so-called BRIC states (Brazil, Russia, India, and China), which some expect to outproduce the rich world by 2027. But as Table 6.1 shows, as measured by traditional power resources, Europe and Japan remain well ahead of the BRICs at the beginning of the century. We shall look first at America's rich allies, Europe and Japan, and then at the BRICs in assessing relative power resources.

Europe

The closest thing to an equal that the United States faces at the beginning of the twenty-first century is the European Union. Although the American economy is four times larger than Germany's, the total economy of the European Union is slightly larger than that of the United States and Europe's population of nearly 500 million is considerably larger than America's 300 million. American per capita income is higher than that of the EU, because a number of the new entrants into the European Union were poorer than the original Western European core countries, but in terms of human capital, technology, and exports, Europe is very much a peer competitor for the United States. Until the spring crisis of 2010, when fiscal problems in Greece and elsewhere created anxiety in financial markets, economists speculated that the Euro might soon replace the dollar as the world's primary reserve currency. Instead, European governments (and the IMF) had to organize a $925 million rescue program to try to restore market

TABLE 6.1 Distribution of Power Resources in the Early Twenty-First Century

BASIC	U.S.	JAPAN	EU	RUSSIA	CHINA	INDIA	BRAZIL
Territory in 1,000s of square km	9,827	378	4,325	17,098	9,597	3,287	8,515
Population in millions (2009)	307	127	492	140	1,339	1,166	199
% literate	99	99	99	99	91	61	89
MILITARY							
Deployed nuclear warheads (2009)[1]	2,702	0	460	4,834	186	60–70	0
Expenditures in $ billions (2008)[2]	607	46	285[3]	59 (est.)	85 (est.)	30	24[4]
Expenditures, as % of world shares (2008)[5]	42	3	20 (2007)	4 (est.)	6 (est.)	2	2
ECONOMIC							
GDP in $ billions, in ppp (2008)	14,260	4,329	14,940	2,266	7,973	3,297	1,993
GDP in $ billions (2008)	14,260	4,924	18,140	1,677	4,402	1,210	1,573
Per capita GDP in ppp (2008)	46,900	34,000	33,700	16,100	6,000	2,900	10,200
Internet users per 100 people (2007)	74 (2008)	69	50 (2006)	21	19 (2008)	7	32
SOFT							
Universities ranked in top 100 (2009)[6]	55	5	16	1	0	0	0
Films produced (2006)[7]	480	417	1,155 (est.)	67	260 (2005)	1,091	27
Foreign students in thousands (2008)[8]	623	132 (2010)	1,225 (est.)	89	195	18 (2007)	na

Source: *CIA World Handbook* unless otherwise cited.

1. "Chapter 8: World Nuclear Forces," *SIPRI Yearbook 2009* (Stockholm: Stockholm International Peace Research Institute, 2009), summary at www.sipri.org/yearbook/2009/08.

2. "Appendix 5A: Military Expenditure Data, 1999–2008," *SIPRI Yearbook 2009* (Stockholm: Stockholm International Peace Research Institute, 2009), summary at www.sipri.org/yearbook/2009/05/05A.

3. Calculated from % of GDP spending from *CIA World Factbook*.

4. National Congress of Brazil, Federal Budget, www.camara.gov.br/internet/comissao/index/mista/orca/orcamento/OR2009/Proposta/projeto/volume4/tomo2/07_md.pdf.

5. Ibid.

6. Institute of Higher Education of Shanghai Jiao Tong University, China, "Academic Ranking of World Universities—2009," www.arwu.org/ARWU2009.jsp.

7. United Nations Educational, Scientific and Cultural Organization, "Cinema: Production of Feature Films," http://stats.uis.unesco.org/unesco/TableViewer/tableView.aspx?ReportId=1391.

8. Institute of International Education, "Atlas of Student Mobility: Country Profiles," www.atlas.iienetwork.org/?p=48027. Statistics for Russia from Ministry of Education and Science of the Russian Federation, "Education in Russia for Foreigners," http://en.russia.edu.ru.

confidence, and German chancellor Angela Merkel warned that if the Euro fails, "then not only the currency fails. . . . Europe will fail, and with it the idea of European unity."[19]

In military terms, Europe spends less than one-half of what the United States does on defense but has more men under arms and includes two countries that possess nuclear arsenals. In soft power, European cultures have long had a wide appeal in the rest of the world, and the sense of a Europe uniting around Brussels has had a strong attraction for its neighbors. Europeans have also been important pioneers and played central roles in international institutions. The key question in assessing Europe's resources is whether Europe will develop enough political and social-cultural cohesion to act as one on a wide range of international issues, or whether it will remain a limited grouping of countries with strongly different nationalisms, political cultures, and foreign policies. In other words, what is Europe's power-conversion capability?

The answer varies with different issues. On questions of trade and influence within the World Trade Organization, Europe is the equal of the United States and able to balance American power. The creation of the European Monetary Union and the launching of the Euro at the beginning of 1999 made Europe's role in monetary affairs and the International Monetary Fund nearly equal to that of the United States (though the 2010 crisis over Greek debt dented confidence in the Euro). On antitrust issues, the size and attraction of the European market have meant that American firms seeking to merge have had to seek approval from the European Commission as well as the U.S. Justice Department. In the cyberworld, the EU is setting the global standards for privacy protection.

At the same time, Europe faces significant limits on its degree of unity. National identities remain stronger than a common European identity, despite six decades of integration, and national interests, although subdued in comparison to the past, still matter.[20] The enlargement of the European Union to include twenty-seven states (with more to come) means that European institutions are likely to remain sui generis and unlikely to produce a strong federal Europe or a single state. None of this is to belittle European institutions and what they have accomplished. Legal integration is increasing, and European Court verdicts have compelled member countries to change policies. However, legislative and executive branch integration has lagged, and even though Europe has created a president and a central figure for foreign relations, the integration of foreign and defense policy is still limited. In the words of Lord Patten, a former member of the European Commission, "Unlike the US we do not matter everywhere."[21]

Over the decades Europe has seen alternations between excessive optimism and bouts of "Euro-pessimism" such as characterize the current period. As one journalist reported in 2010, "Europe is starting to look like the loser in a new geopolitical order dominated by the U.S. and emerging powers led by China. . . . No Europeans were invited when U.S. President Barack Obama and Chinese Premier Wen Jiabao held the make-or-break meeting on Dec. 18 that brokered the modest Copenhagen accord. The Chinese invited the leaders of India, Brazil and South Africa. That meeting and Europe's absence was the 'seminal image' of 2009."[22] Moreover, after the 2008 financial crisis, the fiscal problems of several EU members, particularly Greece, exposed the limits of fiscal integration in the Eurozone.

As *The Economist* noted, "Talk of Europe's relative decline seems to be everywhere just now. . . . You may hear glum figures about Europe's future weight and with some reason. In 1900, Europe accounted for a quarter of the world's population. By 2060, it may account for just 6%—and almost a third of these will be more than 65 years old." Europe does face severe demographic problems, but the size of a population is not highly correlated with power, and "predictions of Europe's downfall have a long history of failing to materialize."[23] In the 1980s, analysts spoke of Euro-sclerosis and a crippling malaise, but in the ensuing decades Europe showed impressive growth and institutional development. "The EU's modus operandi—sharing power, hammering out agreements, resolving conflict by endless committee—can be boring and even frustrating to watch. But in an increasingly networked and interdependent world, it has become the global standard."[24] As the director of the European Council on Foreign Relations puts it, "The conventional wisdom is that Europe's hour has come and gone. Its lack of vision, divisions, obsession with legal frameworks, unwillingness to project military power, and sclerotic economy are contrasted with a United States more dominant even than Rome. . . . But the problem is not Europe—it is our outdated understanding of power."[25]

Political scientist Andrew Moravcsik makes a similar argument that European nations, singly and collectively, are the only states other than the United States able to "exert global influence across the full spectrum from 'hard' to 'soft' power. Insofar as the term retains any meaning, the world is *bipolar*, and is likely to remain so over the foreseeable future." The pessimistic prognosis is based on a nineteenth-century realist view in which "power is linked to the relative share of aggregate global resources and countries are engaged in constant zero-sum rivalry."[26] Moreover, as he points out, Europe is the world's second largest military power, with 21 percent of the world's military spending compared to 5 percent for China, 3 percent for Russia, 2 percent for India, and 1.5 percent for Brazil. Tens of thousands of troops have been deployed outside of home countries in Sierra Leone, Congo, Ivory Coast, Chad, Lebanon, and Afghanistan. In terms of economic power, Europe has the world's largest market and represents 17 percent of world trade compared to 12 percent for the United States, and Europe dispenses 50 percent of the world's foreign assistance compared to 20 percent for the United States.

In terms of relative power, if the EU overcame its internal differences and endeavored to become a global challenger to the United States in a traditional realist balance of power, these assets might counter American power. But if Europe and America remain loosely allied or even neutral, these resources could reinforce each other. As *The Economist* speculated a decade ago, in terms of military security, it is possible that "by about 2030, both Europe and America will be having the same trouble with some other part of the world," such as Russia, China, and Muslim southwest Asia.[27]

Nor is economic divorce likely. New technology, flexibility in labor markets, strong venture capital, and an entrepreneurial culture make the American market attractive to European investors. The United States spends 2.7 percent—twice as much as Europe—on universities and R&D. Direct investment in both directions is higher than with Asia and helps knit the economies together. More than one-third of trade occurs *within* transnational corporations. Moreover, even though trade inevitably produces some degree of friction in the domestic politics of democracies, it is a game from which both sides can profit if there is a will to cooperate, and U.S. trade with Europe is more balanced than U.S. trade with Asia.

At the cultural level, Americans and Europeans have sniped at and admired each other for more than two centuries. For all the complaints about Hollywood films or McDonald's, no one forces Europeans to eat there, though millions do each year. And despite the frictions between parts of Europe and the George W. Bush administration, Barack Obama became almost a cult figure in his popularity in much of Europe. In some ways, the inevitable frictions between the two continents show a closeness rather than a distance. And in a larger sense, Americans and Europeans share the values of democracy and human rights more with each other than with other regions of the world. Even in a traditional realist assessment of balance of power resources, neither the United States nor Europe is likely to threaten the vital or important interests of the other side.[28] Power struggles over conflicting interests are likely to remain at a more mundane level. And on issues that require power with rather than over others, the Europeans have impressive capacity.

Japan

Japan's economy has suffered two decades of slow growth because of poor policy decisions that followed the bursting of a speculative bubble in the early 1990s. In 2010, China's economy passed Japan's in total size as measured in dollars, though it is only one-sixth of Japan's in per capita terms (measured in purchasing power parity).[29] In 1988, eight of the top ten companies in the world by market capitalization were Japanese; today none are Japanese.[30] Despite its recent performance, Japan retains impressive power resources. It possesses the world's third largest national economy, highly sophisticated industry, and the most modern military in Asia. Although China has nuclear weapons and more men under arms, Japan's military is better equipped. It also has the technological capacity to develop nuclear weapons quite quickly if it chooses to do so.

Only two decades ago, many Americans feared being overtaken by Japan after Japanese per capita income surpassed that of the United States. A 1989 *Newsweek* article put it succinctly: "In boardrooms and government bureaus around the world, the uneasy question is whether Japan is about to become a superpower, supplanting America as the colossus of the Pacific and perhaps even the world's No. 1 nation."[31] Books predicted a Japanese-led Pacific bloc that would exclude the United States and even an eventual war between Japan and the United States.[32] Futurologist Herman Kahn forecast that Japan would become a nuclear superpower and that the transition in Japan's role would be like "the change brought about in European and world affairs in the 1870s by the rise of Prussia."[33] These views extrapolated an impressive Japanese record, but today they serve as a useful reminder about the danger of linear projections based on rapidly rising power resources.[34]

On the eve of World War II, Japan had accounted for 5 percent of world industrial production. Devastated by the war, it did not regain that level until 1964. From 1950 to 1974, Japan averaged a remarkable 10 percent annual growth, and by the 1980s Japan had become the world's second largest national economy, with 15 percent of world product.[35] It became the world's largest creditor and largest donor of foreign aid. Its technology was roughly equal with that of the United States and even slightly ahead in some areas of manufacturing. Japan armed only lightly (restricting military expenditures to about 1 percent of gross national product) and focused on economic growth as a highly successful strategy. Nonetheless, as mentioned, it created the most modern and best-equipped conventional military force in East Asia.

Japan has an impressive historical record of "reinventing itself" twice. A century and a half ago, Japan became the first non-Western country to successfully adapt to modern globalization. After centuries of isolation, Japan's Meiji Restoration chose selectively from the rest of the world, and within a half-century the country became strong enough to defeat a European great power in the Russo-Japanese War. After 1945, it rose from the ashes of World War II. In 2000, a prime minister's commission on Japan's goals in the twenty-first century called for a new reinvention.[36] Given the weakness of the political process, the need for further deregulation, the aging of the population, and the resistance to immigration, such change will not be easy.[37] Japan faces severe demographic problems, with its population projected to shrink to 100 million by 2050, and its culture is resistant to accepting immigrants.[38] But Japan retains a high standard of living, a highly skilled labor force, a stable society, and areas of technological leadership and manufacturing skills. Moreover, its culture (both traditional and popular), its overseas development assistance, and its support of international institutions provide some resources for soft power.

Could a revived Japan, a decade or two hence, become a global challenger to the United States, economically or militarily, as was predicted a decade ago? It seems unlikely. Roughly the size of California, Japan will never have the geographical or population scale of the United States. Its success in modernization and democracy and its popular culture provide Japan with some soft power, but ethnocentric attitudes and policies undercut it. Some politicians have started a movement to revise Article 9 of the Constitution, which restricts Japan's forces to self-defense, and a few have spoken of nuclear armament. If the United States were to drop its alliance with Japan, this could produce a sense of insecurity that might lead Japan to decide it had to develop its own nuclear capacity, but even so Japan would be far from a peer competitor.

Alternatively, if Japan were to ally with China, the combined resources of the two countries would make a potent coalition. In 2006, China became Japan's largest trade partner, and the new government formed by the Democratic Party of Japan in 2009 sought improved relations with China. However, a close alliance seems unlikely. Not only have the wounds of the 1930s failed to heal completely, but also China and Japan have conflicting visions of Japan's proper place in Asia and in the world. China would want to constrain Japan, but Japan might chafe at the restraints. In the highly unlikely prospect that the United States were to withdraw from the East Asian region, Japan might join a Chinese bandwagon. But given Japanese concerns about the rise of Chinese power, continued alliance with the United States is the more likely outcome. In terms of traditional balance of power resources, Japan is more likely to seek American support to preserve its independence from China, and this enhances the American position. An allied East Asia is not a plausible candidate to be the challenger that displaces the United States.[39]

In short, the two other entities in the world with per capita income and sophisticated economies similar to the American economy are both allied to the United States. In traditional realist terms of balances of power resources, that makes a large difference for the net position of American power. In addition, in a more positive-sum view of power with rather than over other countries, Europe and Japan provide the largest pools of resources for dealing with common transnational problems. Even though their interests are not identical to those of the United States, the large amount of overlap of social and governmental networks among these societies provides opportunities for cooperation on joint gains.

BRICs

The so-called BRICs are a different situation. Goldman Sachs coined the term in 2001 to call attention to profitable opportunities in what the investment firm considered "emerging markets." The BRICs' share of world product rose rapidly from 16 to 22 percent between 2000 and 2008, and collectively they did better than average in the global recession that began in 2008. Together, they accounted for 42 percent of world population and 33 percent of world growth in the first decade of the century.[40] Apart from the United States (which ranks third), of the four most populous countries of the world, China, India, Indonesia, and Brazil all had solid economic growth rates above 5 percent in the first decade of the century.[41] In contrast, the U.S. growth rate of 1.9 percent in the first decade was below its long-term average. China showed by far the best performance, and Russia performed poorly after the recession began.

Ironically, an economic term took on a political life of its own despite the fact that Russia fit poorly in the category. As the *Beijing Review* commented, "When Goldman Sachs created the acronym BRIC in 2001, neither the economists nor the rest of the world imagined that Brazil, Russia, India and China would finally sit together to build up a substantial platform one day."[42] In June 2009, the foreign ministers of the four countries met in Yekaterinburg, Russia, to transform "a catchy acronym into an international force to be reckoned with."[43] The BRICS held $2.8 trillion, or 42 percent, of global foreign reserves (though most of that was Chinese). Russian president Medvedev stated that "there can be no successful global currency system if the financial instruments that are used are denominated in only one currency," and after China eclipsed the United States as Brazil's largest trading partner, Beijing and Sao Paolo announced plans to settle trade in their national currencies rather than dollars. Although Russia accounts for only 5 percent of China's trade, the two countries announced a similar agreement.[44]

After the recent financial crisis, Goldman Sachs upped the ante and projected that "the combined GDP of the BRICs might exceed that of the G7 countries by 2027, about 10 years earlier than we initially believed."[45] Whatever the merits of this linear economic projection, the term makes little political sense for long-range assessments of power resources. Although a meeting of BRICs may be convenient for short-term diplomatic tactics, it lumps together countries that have deep divisions, and including Russia, a former superpower, with the three developing economies makes little sense. Of the four, Russia has the smallest and most literate population and a much higher per capita income, but, more importantly, many observers believe that Russia is declining while the other three are rising in power resources. Just two decades ago, "Russia was a scientific superpower, carrying out more research than China, India and Brazil combined. Since then it has been left behind not only by the world-beating growth of Chinese science but also by India and Brazil."[46] As we shall see, the heart of the BRIC acronym is the rise in the resources of China.

Russia

In the 1950s, many Americans feared that the Soviet Union would surpass the United States as the world's leading power. The Soviet Union had the world's largest territory, third largest population, and second largest economy, and it produced more oil and gas than Saudi Arabia. It possessed nearly one-half the world's nuclear weapons, had more men under arms than the United States, and had the highest number of people employed in research and development. It exploded a hydrogen bomb only one year after the United States did in 1952, and it was the first to launch a satellite into space in 1957. In terms of soft power, following World War II communist ideology was attractive in Europe because of its resistance to fascism and in the Third World because of its identification with the popular movement toward decolonization. Soviet propaganda actively fostered a myth of the inevitability of the triumph of communism.

Nikita Khrushchev famously boasted in 1959 that the Soviet Union would overtake the United States by 1970 or by 1980 at the latest. As late as 1976, Leonid Brezhnev told the French president that communism would dominate the world by 1995. Such predictions were bolstered by reported annual economic growth rates ranging between 5 and 6 percent and an increase in the Soviet share of world product from 11 to 12.3 percent between 1950 and 1970. After that, however, the Soviet growth rate and share of world product began a long decline. In 1986, Gorbachev described the Soviet economy as "very disordered. We lag in all indices."[47] A year later, Foreign Minister Eduard Shevardnadze told his officials, "You and I represent a great country that in the last 15 years has been more and more losing its position as one of the leading industrially developed nations."[48] What is surprising in retrospect is how wildly inaccurate were the American assessments of Soviet power. In the late 1970s, a "Committee on the Present Danger" argued that Soviet power was surpassing that of the United States, and the 1980 election reflected such fears.

The collapse of the Soviet Union in 1991 left a Russia significantly shrunken in territory (76 percent of the USSR), population (50 percent of the USSR), economy (45 percent of the USSR), and military personnel (33 percent of the USSR). Moreover, the soft power of communist ideology had virtually disappeared. Nonetheless, Russia had nearly 5,000 deployed nuclear weapons, and more than 1 million persons under arms, though its total military expenditure was only 4 percent of the world total (10 percent of the U.S. share), and its global power projection capabilities had greatly diminished. In economic resources, Russia's $2.3 trillion gross domestic product was 14 percent that of the United States, and its per capita income (in purchasing power parity) of $16,000 was roughly 33 percent that of the United States. Its economy was heavily dependent on export of oil and gas, with high-tech exports representing only 7 percent of its manufactured exports (compared to 28 percent for the United States). In terms of soft power, despite the attractiveness of traditional Russian culture, Russia has little global presence. In the words of one Russian analyst, Russia has to use "hard power, including military force, because it lives in a much more dangerous world and has no one to hide behind from it, and because it has little soft power—that is, social, cultural, political and economic attractiveness."[49]

Russia is no longer hampered by communist ideology and a cumbersome central planning system, and the likelihood of ethnic fragmentation, though still a threat, is less than in the past. Whereas ethnic Russians were only 50 percent of the former Soviet Union, they are now 81 percent of the Russian Federation. The political institutions for an effective market economy are largely missing, and corruption is rampant. Russia's robber baron capitalism lacks the kind of effective regulation that creates trust in market relationships. The public health system is in disarray, mortality rates have increased, and birthrates are declining. The average Russian male dies at fifty-nine, an extraordinarily low number for an advanced economy.[50] As President Medvedev puts it, "Every year there are fewer and fewer Russians."[51] Midrange estimates by UN demographers suggest that Russia's population may decline from 145 million today to 121 million by midcentury.[52] In the view of one expert, Russia will have to import 12 million immigrants by 2020 just to stand still demographically, and this seems unlikely.[53]

Many Russian futures are possible. At one extreme are those who project decline and see Russia as a "one-crop economy" with corrupt institutions and insurmountable demographic and health problems. Others argue that with reform and modernization, Russia will be able to surmount these problems and that the leadership is headed in this direction. Late in 2009, President Medvedev issued a sweeping call "for Russia to modernize its economy, wean itself from a humiliating dependence on natural resources and do away with Soviet-style attitudes" that he said were "hindering its effort to remain a world power."[54] But some critics argue that Russian leaders' concept of modernization is too state led and problematic because public institutions function so badly. "An innovative economy needs open markets, venture capital, free thinking entrepreneurs, fast bankruptcy courts and solid protection of intellectual property." Instead there are "wide-spread monopolies, ubiquitous corruption, stifling state-interferences, weak and contradictory laws."[55]

Dysfunctional government and pervasive corruption make modernization difficult. Peter Aven, president of Alfa Bank, argues that "economically, it looks like the Soviet Union more and more. There is a huge dependency on oil, a need for capital, a need for serious reforms, while the social burden is very strong. Stagnation is the main threat."[56] A Russian economist says flatly that "there is no consensus in favor of modernization."[57] Whatever the outcome, because of its residual nuclear strength, its great human capital, its skills in cybertechnology, its proximity to Europe, and the potential of alliance with China, Russia will have the resources to cause problems for the United States, even if it no longer has the capacity to balance American power that it had in the Cold War.

What are the prospects for a Russia-China axis? Traditional balance of power politics might predict such a response to American primacy in power resources. And there is historical precedent for such a union: In the 1950s, China and the Soviet Union were allied against the United States. After Nixon's opening to China in 1972, the triangle worked the other way, with the United States and China cooperating to limit what both saw as a threatening Soviet power. That alliance ended with the collapse of the Soviet Union. In 1992, Russia and China declared their relations a "constructive partnership"; in 1996, they called it a "strategic partnership"; and in July 2001, they signed a treaty of "friendship and cooperation." One theme of this partnership is common opposition to the present

(U.S.-dominated) "unipolar world."[58] Some Russians believe that "Russia is drifting fast towards prioritizing cooperation with China—even if as a 'younger brother.'"[59]

Despite the rhetoric, there are serious obstacles to an alliance between China and Russia that goes much beyond tactical diplomatic coordination. As a French analyst summarizes, "Despite some significant successes, their bilateral engagement continues to be partial and ambivalent. . . . Russia and China have contrasting world-views, different approaches to foreign policy and sometimes conflicting priorities."[60] The demographic situation in the Far East, where the population on the Russian side of the border is 6 million and on the China side is up to 120 million, creates a degree of anxiety in Moscow. Russia's economic and military decline have increased its concern about the rise of Chinese power. As President Medvedev says, "If Russia does not secure its presence in the Far East, it could eventually 'lose everything' to the Chinese."[61] In 2009, Russia announced a new military doctrine that explicitly reserved the right to first use of nuclear weapons, and it continued to hold a large number of short-range tactical nuclear weapons. During the Cold War, the United States used a similar nuclear posture to counter Russian conventional military superiority in Europe. Many military observers believe the new Russian doctrine is a similar response to Chinese conventional superiority in East Asia. A traditional realist might even expect an improvement in Russian-Indian, Russian-Japanese, and even Russian-American relations as Chinese power grows.

Russia still poses a potential threat to the United States, largely because it is the one country with enough missiles and nuclear warheads to destroy the United States, and Russia's relative decline has made the country more reluctant to renounce its nuclear status. Russia also possesses enormous scale, an educated population, skilled scientists and engineers, and vast natural resources. But it seems unlikely that Russia would again possess the resources to present the same sort of balance to American power that the Soviet Union presented during the four decades after World War II.

India

India is often mentioned as a future great power, and its population of 1.2 billion is four times that of the United States and is likely to surpass that of China by 2025. Some Indians predict a tripolar world by midcentury: the United States, China, and India.[62] One economist argues that "if we extrapolate present trends, India will have the world's third largest national income (after the U.S. and China) within 25 years from now."[63]

For decades, India suffered from what some called the "Hindu rate of economic growth" of a little more than 1 percent per capita. After independence in 1947, India followed an inward-looking policy focused on heavy industry. But the rate of economic growth turned out to owe less to Hindu culture than to imported British Fabian (and other) socialist economic planning. After market-oriented reforms in the early 1990s, the pattern changed, and growth rates rose to 7 percent overall growth, with projections of double-digit rates in the future. British columnist Martin Wolf calls India a "premature superpower," meaning a country with low living standards but a huge economy. He thinks that the Indian economy will be bigger than Britain's in a decade and bigger than Japan's in two.[64] India has an emerging middle class of several hundred million, and English is an official language spoken by some 50–100 million people. Building on that base, Indian information industries are able to play a major role in global markets, and India has an active space program.

India has significant military power resources, with an estimated 60–70 nuclear weapons, intermediate-range missiles, a space program, 1.3 million military personnel, and annual military expenditure of nearly $30 billion, or 2 percent of the world total. In terms of soft power, India has an established democracy and a vibrant popular culture with transnational influence. India has an influential diaspora, and its motion picture industry, Bollywood, is the largest in the world in terms of the number of films produced yearly, outcompeting Hollywood in parts of Asia and the Middle East.[65]

At the same time, India remains very much an underdeveloped country, with hundreds of millions of illiterate citizens living in poverty. "Around a third of India's 1.1 billion people live in conditions of acute poverty, and around a third of the world's poor live in India."[66] India's GDP of $3.3 trillion (ppp) is little more than 33 percent of China's $8 trillion (ppp) and 20 percent that of the United States. India's per capita income of $2,900 (in purchasing power parity) is 50 percent of China's and less than 7 percent of the United States'. Even more striking, whereas 91 percent of the Chinese population is literate and 43 percent urban, the numbers for India are only 61 percent and 29 percent, respectively. Each year, India produces about twice as many "engineering and computing geeks as America . . . but only 4.2 percent are fit to work in a software product firm, and just 17.8 percent are employable by an IT [information technology] services company, even with six months training."[67] A symptom of this is India's poor performance in international comparisons of universities: "The 2009 Asian University Rankings, prepared by the higher education consultancy QS, shows the top Indian institution to be the IIT Bombay at number 30; 10 universities in China and Hong Kong are higher."[68] India's high-tech exports are only 5 percent of its total exports compared to 30 percent for China.

India is unlikely to develop the power resources to become a global challenger to the United States in the first half of this century, but it has considerable assets that could be added to the scales of a Sino-Indian coalition. Because of the rapid growth and increased trade of these two countries, some observers began to use the term "Chindia" to refer to the combination of them, but enormous differences remain.[69] The likelihood that such a coalition would become a serious anti-American alliance is small. Just as there is lingering suspicion in the Sino-Russian relationship, so there is a similar rivalry between India and China. Even though the two countries signed agreements in 1993 and 1996 that promised peaceful settlement of the border dispute that had led them to war in 1962, it is also worth noting that India's defense minister labeled China as India's "potential enemy number one" just prior to India's nuclear tests in March 1998, and the border dispute became controversial again in 2009. Even though Indian officials have become more discrete in public about relations with China, their concerns remain intense in private.[70] Rather than becoming an ally, India is more likely to become part of the group of Asian nations that will tend to balance China.

Brazil

Brazilians sometimes joked that "we are a country with a great future—and always will be!"[71] Former president Ignacio Lula da Silva said, "Brazil always behaved like a second-class country. We always told ourselves we were the country of the future, but we never transformed these qualities into something concrete."[72] After Brazil gained independence from Portugal in 1825, real income remained stagnant throughout the century. A growth spurt in the mid-twentieth century was financed with foreign debt within a semiclosed economy, which collapsed among the oil shocks of the 1970s. Two volatile decades of rampant inflation followed, reaching more than 700 percent a year by the early 1990s. In 1994, Brazil introduced a new floating exchange rate, instructed the Central Bank to target inflation, and stabilized government finances.

Brazil's future is a joke no longer. When the BRIC acronym was first invented, some observers objected that "a country with a growth rate as skimpy as its swimsuits, prey to any financial crisis that was around, a place of chronic political instability, whose infinite capacity to squander its obvious potential was as legendary as its talent for football and carnivals, did not seem to belong with those emerging titans." As *The Economist* further commented, now "in some ways, Brazil outclasses the other BRICs. Unlike China, it is a democracy. Unlike India, it has no insurgents, no ethnic and religious conflicts nor hostile neighbors. Unlike Russia, it exports more than oil and arms and treats foreign investors with respect." Brazil is attracting foreign investment, and "has established some strong political institutions. A free and vigorous press uncovers corruption—though there is plenty of it, and it mostly goes unpunished."[73]

Since curbing inflation and instituting market reforms in the 1990s, Brazil has shown an impressive rate of economic growth in the range of 5 percent in the 2000s, which some analysts believe might increase in the future.[74] With a territory nearly three times the size of India's, 90 percent of its 200 million people literate, a $2 trillion GDP equivalent to Russia's, and per capita income of $10,000 (three times India's and nearly twice China's), Brazil has impressive power resources. In 2007, the discovery of massive offshore oil reserves promised to make Brazil a significant power in the energy arena as well. Brazil's military is much smaller, and unlike the other BRICs, the country has no nuclear weapons. But it is the largest state on its continent and has no real peer competitors among its neighbors. In soft power terms, Brazil's popular culture of carnival and football has transnational appeal, and it has adopted a foreign policy designed to project a positive image in Latin America and beyond.

Brazil also faces serious problems. Its infrastructure is inadequate, its legal system is overburdened, it has a very high murder rate, and corruption abounds. It ranks 75th out of 180 countries on Transparency International's corruption perceptions index (compared to 79th for China, 84th for India, and 146th for Russia). In economic competitiveness, the World Economic Forum ranks Brazil as 56th among 133 countries (compared to 27th for China, 49th for India, and 63rd for Russia). Brazil spends less than the OECD average on research and development; and South Korea, with a population 25 percent of Brazil's, registers about thirty times more patents. Productivity growth is sluggish, and although Brazil is the home of some successful transnational corporations, as one Brazilian manager puts it, "we are not going to have a Harvard or a Google here."[75] Some Brazilians believe that they will not be able to raise their productivity rate unless they increase their savings and invest more in education.[76]

Poverty and inequality have been a serious problem for Brazil. The nation has a Gini coefficient index of 0.55 (1.0 is perfect inequality, with one person receiving all income) compared to 0.45 for the United States, 0.42 for China, 0.37 for India, and 0.42 for Russia. Brazil has recently taken a number of steps to reduce poverty and inequality. It reduced extreme poverty by 50 percent between 2003 and 2008, and inequality dropped by 5.5 percent.[77] The number of people living in poverty fell from 28 percent of the total population in 2003 to 16 percent in 2008.[78]

In terms of foreign policy objectives, "Brazil is just starting to realize the weight it has," and it has resisted a number of entreaties from the United States to alter its policy toward countries such as Iran and Venezuela.[79] But Brazil has not made notable progress on the three foreign policy objectives it set for itself in 2003: a permanent seat on the UN Security Council, a world trade deal in the Doha Round of WTO talks, and creation of a powerful South American block.[80] And when China's artificially pegged exchange rates began to create problems for Brazil in 2010, "unfortunately, Brazil has no stomach for arguments with China. Its diplomats prize solidarity among the emerging BRIC nations . . . even when that solidarity could threaten the growth on which Brazil's BRIC status is premised."[81] Only belatedly did Brazil say that it would prefer a Chinese revaluation. It is also the case that, although the new Brazil will complicate American diplomacy compared to the past, Brazil is not likely to try becoming a peer competitor to the United States in this century. That role will be left to China.

China

Among the BRICs, China is by far the giant, with a population and an economy equal to those of the other three countries combined. Moreover, it has the largest army, the largest military budget, the highest rate of economic growth, and the most Internet users of the four. China lags behind Russia and Brazil in income per capita and in Internet and mobile phone users per capita, but this may change if China maintains its recent high growth rates. At any figure above 7 percent per year, the Chinese economy will double in a decade. China recovered quickly from the 2008 economic crisis, and as mentioned previously, Goldman Sachs expects the total size of the Chinese economy to surpass that of the United States in 2027. One Nobel Laureate economist looks even further into the future and estimates that by 2040, China will produce 40 percent of global GDP.[82]

China is another of Wolf's premature superpowers. China's current reputation for power benefits from projections about the future. In one poll, 44 percent of respondents mistakenly thought that China already had the world's largest economy, compared to 27 percent who accurately picked the United States (which is three times larger).[83] For more than a decade, many have viewed China as the most likely contender to balance American power or surpass it.[84] One recent book is even entitled *When China Rules the World: The End of the Western World and the Birth of a New Global Order*.[85] Already in the 1990s, polls showed that 50 percent of the American public thought China would pose the biggest challenge to U.S. world power status in the twenty-first century (compared with 8 percent for Japan and 6 percent for Russia and Europe).[86]

Although most projections of Chinese power are based on the rapid growth rate of the nation's GDP, China has other significant power resources. In terms of basic resources, its territory is equal to that of the United States and its population is four times greater. It has the world's largest army, about 200 nuclear weapons, and modern capabilities in space and cyberspace (including the world's largest number of Internet users). In soft power resources, as we saw in Chapter 4, China still lacks cultural industries able to compete with Hollywood or Bollywood, its universities are not yet the equal of America's, and it lacks the many NGOs that generate much of America's soft power. However, China is making major efforts to increase it soft power. China has always had an attractive traditional culture, and it has created several hundred Confucius

Institutes around the world to teach its language and culture. China has also adjusted its diplomacy to use more multilateral arrangements to alleviate fears and reduce the likelihood of other countries allying to balance a rising power.

China does have impressive power resources, but we should be skeptical about projections based primarily on current growth rates and political rhetoric. In both China and the United States, perceptions of the other country are heavily colored by domestic political struggles, and there are people in both countries who want to see the other as an enemy. Even without such distortions, the military on both sides would be seen by its countrymen and -women as derelict in its duties if it did not plan for all contingencies. As for the historical analogies mentioned earlier, remember that by 1900 Germany had surpassed Britain in industrial power and the kaiser was pursuing an adventurous, globally oriented foreign policy that was bound to bring about a clash with other great powers. In contrast, China still lags far behind the United States economically and has focused its policies primarily on its region and on its economic development. Even though China's "market Leninist" economic model (the so-called Beijing Consensus) provides soft power in authoritarian countries, it has the opposite effect in many democracies.[87] Nonetheless, the rise of China recalls Thucydides's warning that belief in the inevitability of conflict can become one of its main causes.[88] Each side, believing it will end up at war with the other, makes reasonable military preparations, which then are read by the other side as confirmation of its worst fears.

In fact, the rise of China is a misnomer. Reemergence would be more accurate, because by size and history the Middle Kingdom has long been a major power in East Asia. Technically and economically, China was the world's leader (though without global reach) from 500 to 1500. Only in the last half-millennium was it overtaken by Europe and America, which were first to benefit from the Industrial Revolution. After Deng Xiaoping's market reforms in the early 1980s, China's high annual growth rates of 8–9 percent led to a remarkable tripling of its GNP in the last two decades of the twentieth century, and this pragmatic economic performance, along with its Confucian culture, enhanced China's soft power in the region.

China has a long way to go to equal the power resources of the United States and still faces many obstacles to development. At the beginning of the twenty-first century, the American economy was about twice the size of China's in purchasing power parity and more than three times as large at official exchange rates. All such comparisons and projections are somewhat arbitrary, however. For example, purchasing power parity is an estimate that economists make to judge the equivalence in welfare in different societies. A few years ago, when World Bank economists revised their methodology, China's GDP at purchasing power parity dropped 40 percent at the stroke of a pen or, more likely, the click of a mouse.[89] Meanwhile, comparisons in terms of current exchange rates (by which the United States is much further ahead) depend on fluctuations in currency values, and China has used an artificially low exchange rate as a means to subsidize its exports. Nonetheless, exchange rate comparisons are often more accurate in estimating power resources. The price of a meal or a haircut or a house is best compared by using purchasing power parity, but the cost of imported oil or an advanced fighter aircraft is better judged at the exchange rates that must be used to pay for it.

Even if overall Chinese GDP passes that of the United States around 2030, the two economies would be equivalent in size but not equal in composition. China would still have a vast underdeveloped countryside, and it will begin to face demographic problems from the delayed effects of the one child per couple policy it enforced in the twentieth century.[90] Newcomers to China's labor force will start declining in 2011, and China's labor force will peak in 2016. Moreover, as countries develop, there is a tendency for growth rates to slow. If we assume a 6 percent Chinese growth and only 2 percent American growth after 2030, China would not equal the United States in per capita income until sometime in the second half of the century (depending on the measures of comparison).[91]

Per capita income provides a measure of the sophistication of an economy. In other words, China's impressive growth rate combined with the size of its population will likely lead it to pass the American economy in total size at some point. This has already provided China with impressive power resources, but that is not the same as equality. And because the United States is unlikely to be standing still during that period, China is a long way from posing the kind of challenge to American preponderance that the kaiser's Germany posed when it passed Britain at the beginning of the last century. Even if fuzzy hegemonic transition theory were more clearly specified than it is, the facts do not at this point justify alarmist predictions of a coming war.[92]

Moreover, linear projections of economic growth trends can be misleading. Countries tend to pick the low-hanging fruit as they benefit from imported technologies in the early stages of economic takeoff, and growth rates generally slow as economies reach higher levels of development. At per capita incomes above $10,000, rates of growth slow down. In addition, the Chinese economy faces serious obstacles of transition from inefficient state-owned enterprises, growing inequality, massive internal migration, an inadequate social safety net, corruption, and inadequate institutions that could foster political instability. The north and east of the country have outpaced the south and west. Only ten of thirty-one provinces have per capita income above the national average, and underdeveloped provinces include those with higher proportions of minorities, such as Tibet and Xinjiang. Almost alone among developing countries, China is aging extraordinarily fast. By 2030, China will have "more elderly dependents than children," and some Chinese demographers worry about "getting old before getting rich."[93]

During the 2000s, China moved from being the ninth largest exporter to the largest in the world, but China's export-led development model will probably need to be adjusted as global trade and financial balances become more contentious in the aftermath of the 2008 financial crisis. World Bank president Robert Zoellick argues that China's export-led growth model is unsustainable over time, because to maintain 8 percent growth would require a doubling of China's share of exports by 2020. Reducing saving and increasing consumption are the obvious but not easy answers, because an aging population may keep household savings high, and high corporate savings reflect special interests and limited competition in some sectors.[94]

In 2010, China was home to the two largest and four of the ten largest banks in the world, though rankings by size can be misleading until China cleans up the many financial institutions that remain in government hands and enforces commercial discipline and transparency.[95] Some economists think China could experience a painful financial contraction but a collapse is unlikely: "Chinese growth will almost certainly slow dramatically, but the country will nonetheless continue to grow faster than the rest of the world."[96] And although China holds huge foreign currency reserves (as we saw in Chapter 3), China will have difficulty increasing its financial leverage by lending overseas in its own currency. "Until China has a deep and open bond market where interest rates are set by the market and not the government, there will be only limited takers for such renminbi assets."[97]

China's authoritarian political system has thus far shown an impressive power-conversion capability in relation to specific targets—for example, the ability to stage a successful Olympic Games, build high-speed rail projects, or even stimulate the economy to recover from the global financial crisis. Whether China can maintain this capability over the longer term is a mystery both to outsiders and to Chinese leaders. Unlike India, which was born with a democratic constitution, China has not yet found a way to solve the problem of demands for political participation (if not democracy) that tend to accompany rising per capita income. The ideology of communism is long gone, and the legitimacy of the ruling party depends upon economic growth and ethnic Han nationalism. One expert argues that the Chinese political system lacks legitimacy, suffers from a high level of corruption, has no clear vision for self-improvement, and is vulnerable to political unrest should the economy falter. "Despite its economic successes and growing defense capabilities, China's international influence will remain limited as long as it fails to evolve an attractive political system."[98] Another expert believes that economic change will bring political change, and by 2020, when per capita GDP will reach $7,500 (in purchasing power parity [ppp]), China will join countries such as Singapore that are rated by Freedom House as "partly free."[99] Singapore's senior leader, Lee Kwan Yew, believes that political change may come in ten or fifteen years when a younger overseas-educated generation rises to power. "They understand the problems of the system, and while bargaining hard for Chinese interests, will have a broader view of change."[100] Whether China can develop a formula that can manage an expanding urban middle class, regional inequality, and resentment among ethnic minorities remains to be seen. The basic point is that no one, including the Chinese, knows how China's political future will evolve and how that will affect its economic growth.[101]

Cyberpolitics presents another complication. As we saw in the previous chapter, with over 400 million users, China has the largest Internet population, as well as a highly developed system of governmental controls and filters. Not only are many Internet users intensely nationalistic, but also minority liberal views are filtered out and dissent is punished. Nonetheless, some leakage of information is inevitable. Coping with greatly increasing flows of information at a time when restrictions can hinder economic growth presents a sharp dilemma for Chinese leaders. Indeed, some observers fear instability caused by a collapsing, rather than a rising, China. In the words of China expert Susan Shirk, "It is China's internal fragility, not its growing strength, that presents the greatest danger. The weak legitimacy of the Communist Party and its leaders' sense of vulnerability could cause China to behave rashly in a crisis."[102] Or as President Bill Clinton put it in 1999, while most people worry about the challenge of a strong China, "let us not forget the risk of a weak China, beset by internal conflict, social dislocation and criminal activity; becoming a vast zone of instability in Asia."[103] A China that cannot control flows of migration, environmental effects on the global climate, and internal conflict poses serious problems. Politics sometimes has a way of confounding economic projections.

As long as China's economy does grow, its military power will likely increase, thus making China appear more dangerous to its neighbors. Official Chinese reports of military expenditure do not include many items listed in the American defense budget, but regardless of composition, from 1989 to 2008 China's official military budget increased by double digits every year. The Gulf War in 1991, the tensions over Taiwan in 1995–1996, and the Kosovo campaign of 1999 showed Chinese leaders how far China lagged behind in modern military capabilities, and as a result they nearly doubled military expenditures over the course of the 1990s. China has imported military technology from Russia, and its own industries are producing some weapons systems that are approaching the capability of those in the American inventory. A 2010 Pentagon report estimated China's total military spending to be $150 billion (compared to $719 billion for the United States), or about 2 percent of GDP (compared to 4 percent for the United States).[104] A RAND study projects that by 2025, China's military expenditure will be more than $185 billion (in 2001 dollars), or about 25 percent of current American military expenditure.[105]

Although China has not developed impressive capabilities for global force projection, it is able to complicate American naval operations off its coast with long-range missiles and a growing submarine fleet, and this has raised questions about China's new assertions of a "core interest" in control of the South China Sea. In the words of China expert Kenneth Lieberthal, "There is an overall feeling in China that there is a narrowing of the gap in power with the United States that is belied by reality. Nevertheless, there is a sort of national hyperbole in China."[106] At the same time, China is only at the beginning of the complex process of developing a blue water navy with carrier battle groups.[107] Nonetheless, growing Chinese military capacity would mean that any American military role to reassure allies in Asia would require more resources. In addition, as we saw in Chapters 2 and 5, China has been making impressive efforts to develop asymmetrical conflict capabilities in cyberspace.

Deng told the UN General Assembly in 1974 that "China is not a superpower, nor will it ever seek to be one."[108] The current generation of Chinese leaders, realizing that rapid economic growth is the key to domestic political stability, has focused on economic development and on what it calls a "harmonious" international environment that will not disrupt China's growth. But generations change, power often creates hubris, and appetites sometimes grow with eating. Martin Jacques argues that "rising powers in time invariably use their newfound economic strength for wider political, cultural and military ends. That is what being a hegemonic power involves, and China will surely become one."[109] Traditionally, China saw itself as the center, or "middle kingdom," of a tributary system of states in East Asia and will seek to re-create this order.[110] Others such as John Ikenberry argue that the current international order has the openness, economic integration, and capacity to absorb China rather than be replaced by a Chinese-led order.[111] Thus far, Chinese leaders have taken only minor steps toward a major global role, whether as a hegemon or as a "responsible stakeholder." They still act as free-riders, but "for the first time are becoming dependent on a world which they cannot control rather than an empire which they can control."[112]

As we saw earlier, some skeptics have argued that China aims "in the near term to replace the United States as the dominant power in East Asia and in the long term to challenge America's position as the dominant power in the world."[113] Even if this were an accurate assessment of China's intentions (and even the Chinese cannot know the views of future generations), it is doubtful that China will have the military capability to make this possible. Moreover, Chinese leaders will have to contend with the reactions of other countries as well as the constraints created by their own objectives of economic growth and the need for external markets and resources. Too aggressive a Chinese military posture could produce a countervailing coalition among its regional neighbors that would weaken both its hard and soft power. In 2010, for example, as China became more assertive in its claims to the Paracel Islands that lie 250 miles off the east coast of Vietnam, the Vietnamese denounced the move and began "pushing hard behind the scenes to bring more foreign players into negotiations so that China will have to bargain in a multilateral setting," which goes against China's preference to negotiate one on one with each country.[114] Moreover, a Pew poll of sixteen countries around the world found a positive attitude toward China's economic rise but not toward its military rise. "If China is perceived as mainly an economic actor, that person is likely to both approve China's rise and being pro-U.S. By contrast, if an individual mainly sees China as an increasing military power, then his or her pro-American sentiments will often mean disapproval of China's rise."[115]

That China is not likely to become a peer competitor to the United States on a global basis does not mean that it could not challenge the United States in Asia, but as mentioned earlier, the rise of Chinese power in Asia is contested by both India and Japan (as well as other states), and that provides a major power advantage to the United States.[116] The U.S.-Japan alliance, which the Clinton-Hashimoto declaration of 1996 reaffirmed as the basis for stability in post–Cold War East Asia, is an important impediment to Chinese ambitions, as is the improvement in U.S.-Indian relations that advanced under the Bush administration. This means that in the great power politics of the region, China cannot easily expel the Americans. From that position of strength, the United States, Japan, India, Australia, and others can work to engage China and provide incentives for it to play a responsible role, while hedging against the possibility of aggressive behavior as China's power grows.

AMERICAN POWER: DOMESTIC DECAY?

Some argue that the costs of exercising power eventually overburden all empires and that a power transition will occur because of America's imperial overstretch.[117] Thus far, the facts do not fit this theory very well because external burdens have not increased over time. Instead, defense and foreign affairs expenditures have declined as a share of GNP over the past several decades. Nonetheless, the United States could decline in terms of relative power not because of imperial overstretch, but because of domestic underreach. As historians remind us, Rome rotted from within. People lost confidence in their culture and institutions, elites battled for control, corruption increased, and the economy failed to grow adequately.[118]

Could the United States lose its ability to influence world events because of domestic battles over culture, collapse of institutions, and economic stagnation? If American society and institutions appear to be collapsing, the United States will be less attractive to others. If the economy fails, the United States will lose hard as well as soft power. And even if the United States continues to hold impressive military, economic, and soft power resources, it could lack the capacity to transform those resources into effective influence. After all, some card players lose despite being dealt high hands.

Society and Culture

Although the United States has many social problems—and always has—they do not seem to be getting worse in any linear manner. Some are even improving, such as crime, divorce rates, and teenage pregnancy. There are culture wars over issues such as same-sex marriage and abortion, but polls nevertheless show an overall increase in tolerance. Civil society is robust, and church attendance is high at 42 percent.[119] Nonetheless, polls show an "optimism gap" between perceptions and reality. In part, this reflects the media's tendency to emphasize stories consistent with a bad news theme.

Reaction to national-level trends is a mediated phenomenon. To the extent that people have direct experience with public affairs, the majority tell pollsters that their own lives, communities, schools, and congressmen are fine, though they worry about the national level. If everyone "knows" from the media that things are a mess at the national level and they have no direct experience at the national level, they tell pollsters the conventional wisdom about the national condition. The resulting optimism gap is not convincing evidence of decline. Past culture battles over immigration, slavery, evolution, temperance, McCarthyism, and civil rights were arguably more serious than any of today's issues of contention. Polls show that people often attribute a golden glow to the past. It is always easy to show decay by comparing the good in the past with the bad in the present (or progress by doing the converse).

There are two ways in which such cultural judgments could adversely affect American national power. First, if Americans were so distracted or divided by internal battles over social and cultural issues that the United States lost the capacity to act collectively in foreign policy, hard power would diminish. That appeared to be a problem in the 1970s in the aftermath of deep divisions over Vietnam. In contrast, even though support for the Iraq War fell from 72 percent in 2003 to 36 percent by 2008, American public opinion continued to support an active foreign policy.[120]

Second, a decline in the quality of American social conditions could reduce soft power. Although America has made progress on some social issues, the United States lags behind other rich countries on infant mortality, life expectancy, children in poverty, and homicides. Such comparisons can be costly for American soft power, but the United States is not alone in many of the cultural changes that cause controversy. When such problems are shared, comparisons are less invidious and less damaging to soft power. For example, respect for authority and some standards of behavior have declined since 1960 throughout the Western world. But there is little indication that American levels of personal responsibility are lower than those of other advanced Western societies, and levels of charitable giving and community service are generally higher.[121]

Immigration

A more serious concern would be if the United States turned inward and seriously curtailed immigration. With its current levels of immigration, America is one of the few developed countries that may avoid demographic decline and keep its share of world population, but this might change if reactions to terrorist events or public xenophobia closed the borders. Fears over the effect of immigration on national values and on a coherent sense of American identity have existed since the early years of the nation. The nineteenth-century Know Nothing Party was built upon opposition to immigrants, particularly the Irish. Asians were singled out for exclusion from 1882 onward, and with the Immigration Restriction Act of 1924 the influx of immigrants slowed for the next four decades. During the twentieth century, the nation recorded its highest percentage of foreign-born residents in 1910—14.7 percent of the population. Today, 11.7 percent are foreign born.[122]

Despite being a nation of immigrants, more Americans are skeptical about immigration than are sympathetic to it. Various polls show that a plurality or majority wants fewer immigrants coming into the country.[123] The recession exacerbated such views, and in 2009, 50 percent of Americans favored decreasing immigration, up from 39 percent in 2008.[124] Both the numbers and origins of the new immigrants have caused concerns about immigration's effects on American culture. Data from the 2000 census showed a soaring Hispanic population driven largely by waves of new immigrants, legal and illegal, with Hispanics about to replace blacks as the nation's largest minority.[125] Demographers have portrayed a country in 2050 in which non-Hispanic whites will be only a slim majority. Hispanics will be 25 percent; blacks, 14 percent; and Asians, 8 percent.[126]

Communications and market forces produce a powerful incentive for immigrants to master the English language and accept a degree of assimilation. Most of the evidence suggests that the latest immigrants are assimilating at least as quickly as their predecessors. Modern media help new immigrants to know more about their new country beforehand than immigrants did a century ago. Although rapid illegal immigration can cause social problems, proponents argue that over the long term legal immigration strengthens the power of the United States. Most developed countries will experience a shortage of people as the century progresses. Some eighty-three countries and territories currently have fertility rates that are below the level necessary for a constant population level. To maintain its current population size, Japan would have to accept 350,000 newcomers a year for the next fifty years, which is difficult for a culture that has historically been hostile to immigration.[127] Despite American ambivalence, it remains a country of immigration. The Census Bureau projects that the American population will grow 49 percent over the next four decades.

Today, the United States is the world's third most populous country; fifty years from now it is still likely to be third (after only India and China). Not only is this relevant to economic power, but also with nearly all developed countries aging and facing a burden of providing for the older generation, immigration could help reduce the sharpness of the policy problem. In addition, the economic benefits of skilled immigrants can be important to particular sectors, even though studies suggest that the short-term directly measurable economic benefits at the national level are relatively small and unskilled workers may suffer from competition. There is a strong correlation between the number of H-1B visas and the number of patents filed in the United States. A 1 percent increase in the number of immigrant college graduates leads to a 6 percent increase in patents per capita.[128] In 1998, Chinese- and Indian-born engineers were running one-quarter of Silicon Valley's high-technology businesses, which accounted for $17.8 billion in sales, and in 2005, foreign-born immigrants had participated in one of every four American technology start-ups during the previous decade.[129]

Equally important are immigration's benefits for America's soft power. That people want to come to the United States enhances America's appeal, and the upward mobility of immigrants is attractive to people in other countries. America is a magnet, and many people can envisage themselves as Americans. Many successful Americans "look like" people in other countries. Moreover, connections between immigrants and their families and friends back home help to convey accurate and positive information about the United States. In addition, the presence of multiple cultures creates avenues of connection with other countries and helps create an important broadening of American attitudes in an era of globalization. Rather than diluting hard and soft power, immigration enhances both. When Lee Kwan Yew, an acute longtime observer of both the United States and China, concludes that China will not surpass the United States as the leading power of the twenty-first century, he cites as a major reason the ability of the United States to attract the best and brightest from the rest of the world and meld them into a diverse culture of creativity. China has a larger population to recruit from domestically, but in his view, its Sino-centric culture will make it less creative than the United States.[130]

The Economy

Although the cultural and social problems discussed thus far do not seem likely to weaken American power, a failure in the performance of the American economy would be a real showstopper. Economic failure does not mean recessions that are normal in all capitalist economies, but a long-term slump in the level of productivity and the capacity for sustained growth. Even though macroeconomic forecasts (like weather forecasts) are notoriously unreliable, it appears that the United States will experience slower growth in the decade after the 2008 financial crisis. The International Monetary Fund expects economic growth in the aftermath of the current recession to average about 2 percent in 2014. Harvard economist Martin Feldstein projects a similar rate for the next decade. This is lower than the average over the past several decades but "roughly the same as the average rate over the past ten years."[131]

In the 1980s, many observers believed that the U.S. economy had run out of steam. Technological dominance had been lost in several manufacturing sectors, including automobiles and consumer electronics. The annual rate of increase of labor productivity, which averaged 2.7 percent in the two decades after World War II, had slipped to 1.4 percent in the 1980s. Although the American standard of living was still the highest among the seven largest market economies, it had grown only one-quarter as fast as the others since 1972. According to a leading business magazine in 1987, "The nation is in a growth crisis. . . . Both personal and national agendas that were once unquestioned suddenly seem too expensive."[132] Japan and Germany were believed to be overtaking America, and this undercut American hard and soft power. The United States seemed to have lost its competitive edge. Even after the financial crisis and ensuing recession, the World Economic Forum ranked the United States fourth (after Switzerland, Sweden, and Singapore) in global economic competitiveness. In comparison, China ranked twenty-seventh.[133] And the American economy leads in many new sectors, such as information technology, biotechnology, and nanotechnology. The United States spends more on research and development than the next seven countries combined.[134] Some economists argue that America's "venturesome consumption is a vital counterpart to the country's entrepreneurial business culture."[135]

Will productivity growth support American power well into this century? Optimists cite the U.S. lead in the production and use of information technologies. After 1995, a noticeable change in the rate of decline in the cost of computing power enhanced American productivity. Productivity is crucial because the more that workers can produce per hour, the more the economy can grow without shortages and inflation. And sustained noninflationary growth provides the resources that can be invested in hard power and that can enhance soft power. Productivity can increase because of new investment in tools or new forms of organization.

Information technology is not the only source of American productivity. The United States has seen significant agricultural innovation, and openness to globalization also plays a role, but the computer and electronics industry generated 44 percent of productivity growth from 1960 to 2006, and the IT sector accounts for a larger share of GDP than in the other major industrial countries. As a leading expert concludes, "Surprisingly, productivity growth in the U.S. economy has continued to rise at a rapid pace since the dot-com crash in 2000, indicating a high rate of innovation," and this growth is now spreading to user industries. The acceleration of American productivity growth was not equaled in the major economies of the EU.[136] Some economists project that American productivity growth will slow to 2.25 percent, whereas others forecast a rate closer to 1.5 percent in the next decade.[137]

In terms of investment in research and development, the United States was the world leader with $369 billion in 2007, followed by Asia ($338 billon) and the European Union ($263 billion), though the North American share of the global total dropped from 40 percent in 1996 to 35 percent in 2007, while Asia's rose to 31 percent. The United States spent 2.7 percent of its GDP on research and development, nearly double that of China, but slightly less than the 3 percent for Japan and Korea.[138] In 2007, American inventors registered about 80,000 patents in the United States, or more than the rest of the world combined.[139] A number of reports have expressed concern about matters such as corporate tax rates, human capital, and the growth of overseas patents. Others argue that Americans are more innovative at using and commercializing technologies because of the country's entrepreneurial culture. Venture capital firms in the United States invest 70 percent of their money in start-ups in this country rather than overseas. A survey of global entrepreneurship ranked the United States ahead of other countries because it had a favorable culture, the most mature venture capital industry, a tradition of close relations between universities and industry, and an open immigration policy.[140]

In addition to the question of whether the new rates of productivity are sustainable, other concerns about the future of American economy include the low rate of personal savings, the current account deficit (which means that Americans are becoming more indebted to foreigners), and the rise in government debt. Personal savings are difficult to calculate and subject to serious measurement errors, but the trend was clearly down from 9.7 percent of personal incomes in the 1970s to near zero in 2001, recovering to about 4 percent after the financial crisis of 2008–2009.[141] In part this decline was attributed to an increased culture of consumerism and easier access to credit. How much this decline matters is difficult to determine. The national savings rate includes government and corporate saving and is based on outdated measures.[142] Japan kept up a high personal savings rate, but its economy stagnated. When corrected for the fact that capital goods are cheaper in the United States, American real investment compares favorably with other OECD countries.[143] The danger is that in a severe recession foreigners might withdraw their investments rapidly and add to instability in the economy, though contrary to some predictions, the dollar remained a safe haven and the Treasury bonds sold easily in the aftermath of the 2008 crisis. Nonetheless, American income would be higher and dangers of instability lessened if the United States financed more of its investment through higher savings.

After the financial crisis, a major source of concern became the level of government debt. In the words of British historian Niall Ferguson, "This is how empires decline. It begins with a debt explosion." Not only did the bank bailout and Keynesian stimulus package add to debt, but also the costs of entitlement programs for social security and health care and servicing of the debt will claim large shares of future revenue. "Unless entitlements are cut or taxes are raised, there will never be another balanced budget." Ferguson goes on to say that "the idea that the US is a 'safe haven' is nonsense. Its government debt is a safe haven the way Pearl Harbor was in 1941."[144] But America is not Greece.

The Congressional Budget Office calculates that total government debt will reach 100 percent of GDP by 2023. Many economists worry when debt levels in rich countries exceed 90 percent, "but America has two huge advantages over other countries that have allowed it to face its debt with relative equanimity: possessing both the world's reserve currency and its most liquid asset market, in Treasury bonds."[145] During the financial crisis, the dollar rose and bond yields fell, making it easier for America to finance its deficit. A sudden crisis of confidence is less the problem than is a gradual increase in the cost of servicing the debt, affecting the long-term health of the economy. Studies suggest that interest rates rise 0.03 percent for every 1 percent increase in the debt-to-GDP ratio, and higher interest rates mean lower private-sector investment and slower growth over the long term. "All of these effects can be mitigated by good policies, or exacerbated by bad ones."[146] Increased debt need not lead to decline, though it certainly increases the risks.

A well-educated labor force is another key to economic success in an information age. At first glance, the United States does well. In 2006, 84 percent of adults had graduated from high school and 27 percent had graduated from college.[147] The United States spends twice as much on higher education as a percentage of GDP than does France, Germany, Britain, or Japan.[148] The American higher education system is rated the best in the world, and American universities have widened their lead in academic reputation over competitors in Britain, Continental Europe, and Japan over the past few decades. The *Times Higher Education Supplement* lists six of the top ten universities as American; and a Chinese study by Shanghai Jiao Tong University places seventeen of the top twenty in the United States (and none in China).[149] Americans win more Nobel prizes than do citizens of any other country and publish more scientific papers in peer-reviewed journals (including three times as many as

Chinese do).[150] These accomplishments enhance both economic power and soft power.

However, even though American education is strong at the top, it is less impressive at lower levels. American education at its best—much of the university and the top slice of the secondary system—meets or sets the global standard. But American education at its worst—too many primary and secondary schools, especially in less-affluent districts—lags badly. This may mean that the quality of the labor force will not keep up to the rising standards needed in an information-based economy. A National Assessment of Educational Progress in 2007 found only 39 percent of fourth graders were at or above the proficient level in math and 33 percent scored at that level in reading, though there had been a slight improvement during the previous decade.[151] There is no reliable evidence that students are performing worse than in the past, but America's educational advantage is eroding because more countries are doing better than in the past. Among the thirty richest countries, only New Zealand, Spain, Turkey, and Mexico now have lower high school completion rates.[152] The situation is also true in higher education. America's 40 percent rate of young adults earning at least an associate degree has not changed, but it used to lead the world and now earns twelfth place among thirty-six developed countries.[153] American students do not seem to be improving their knowledge and skills enough to keep pace with an advancing economy. Improvement in the American educational system will be necessary if the country is to meet the standards needed in an information-driven economy.

The changing shape of the nation's income distribution also poses a problem for the American economy. According to the Census Bureau, from 1947 to 1968 family income inequality decreased. After 1968, inequality increased. The American Gini coefficient of 0.45 is high by international standards and "has risen steadily over the past several decades . . . and the gap between the highest earners and the mid-level earners has increased over the past decade."[154] Shifts in labor demand away from less-educated workers are perhaps the most important explanation of eroding wages.[155] The problem is not only a question of justice, but also of whether inequality may lead to political reactions that could curb the productivity of the economy and slow the high rates of economic growth that are the foundation of hard and soft power.

Soft power generated by the American economy is an open question. Many people admire the success the American economy has had over the long term but have not seen it as a model, even before the financial crisis tarnished its reputation. Government plays a lighter role in the U.S. economy, spending one-third of GDP, whereas Europe is nearer one-half. Competitive market forces are stronger, social safety nets weaker. Unions are weaker and labor markets less regulated. American health care has been both costly and exceptional in its inequality. Cultural attitudes, bankruptcy laws, and financial structures more strongly favor entrepreneurship. Regulations are more transparent, and shareholders have more influence on company managers. Although foreigners extol some of these virtues, others object to the price of inequality, insecurity, and macroeconomic instability that accompanies this greater reliance on market forces.

Political Institutions

Despite these problems and uncertainties, and despite some slowing, with the right policies the American economy seems likely to continue producing hard power for the country. Greater uncertainty surrounds the question of American institutions. Many observers argue that the gridlock of the American political system will prevent it from translating its power resources into power outcomes. In the view of James Fallows, an experienced journalist who lived in China for years, "America still has the means to address nearly any of its structural weaknesses . . . energy use, medical costs, the right educational and occupational mix to rebuild a robust middle class. . . . That is the American tragedy of the early 21st century: a vital and self-renewing culture that attracts the world's talent and a governing system that increasingly looks like a joke."[156] Although political gridlock in a period of recession often looks bad, the difficulty is ascertaining whether the situation is much worse than it was in the past.

Power conversion—translating power resources into effective influence—is a long-standing problem for the United States. The Constitution is based on an eighteenth-century liberal view that power is best controlled by fragmentation and countervailing checks and balances. In foreign policy, the Constitution has always invited the president and Congress to struggle for control. Strong economic and ethnic pressure groups struggle for their self-interested definitions of the national interest, and a political culture of American exceptionalism complicates matters by making foreign policy uniquely moralistic. Congress always pays attention to squeaky wheels, and special interests press it to legislate the tactics of foreign policy and codes of conduct with sanctions for other countries. As Kissinger once pointed out, "What is presented by foreign critics as America's quest for domination is very frequently a response to domestic pressure groups." The cumulative effect "drives American foreign policy toward unilateral and bullying conduct. For unlike diplomatic communications, which are generally an invitation to dialogue, legislation translates into a take-it-or-leave-it prescription, the operational equivalent of an ultimatum."[157]

There is also a concern about the decline of public confidence in institutions. In 2010, one poll found that 61 percent of poll respondents thought the country was in decline and only 19 percent trusted the government to do what is right all or most of the time. Another poll found 22 percent trusting the government in Washington almost always or most of the time.[158] As William Galston puts it, "Trust is never more important than when citizens are asked to make sacrifices for a brighter future. Mistrust of the government making this request could be the harbinger—even the cause—of national decline.[159]

In 1964, three-quarters of the American public said they trusted the federal government to do the right thing most of the time. Today, only one-fifth of the public admits to trust at this high standard. The numbers have varied somewhat over time, rising after September 11, 2001, before gradually declining, and the numbers for state and local government have been slightly better in the past—32 to 38 percent—but they sunk to a new low in 2009.[160] Government is not alone. Over the past few decades, public confidence has dropped in half for many major institutions: 61 to 30 percent for universities, 55 to 21 percent for major companies, 73 to 29 percent for medicine, and 29 to 14 percent for journalism. Over the past decade, confidence rose in educational institutions and the military but fell for Wall Street and major companies.[161]

The United States was founded in part on a mistrust of government, and the American Constitution was deliberately set up to resist centralized power. A long Jeffersonian tradition says Americans should not worry too much about the level of confidence in government. Moreover, when asked not about day-to-day government but about the underlying constitutional framework, the public is very positive. If you ask Americans what is the best place to live, 80 percent say the United States. If asked whether they like their democratic system of government, 90 percent say yes. Few people feel the system is rotten and must be overthrown.[162]

Some aspects of the current mood are probably cyclical, whereas others represent discontent with current bickering and deadlock in the political process. Compared with the recent past, party politics has become more polarized, but nasty politics is nothing new. Part of the problem of assessment is that faith in government became abnormally high among the generation that survived the Depression and won World War II. In that case, over the long view of American history, the anomaly was overconfidence in government in the 1950s and early 1960s, not low levels thereafter. Moreover, much of the evidence for loss of trust in government comes from polling data, and responses are sensitive to the way questions are asked.

What cannot be dismissed is that there has been a downward trend to answers to the same questions over time, but the significance of this decline is still uncertain. After all, the sharpest decline occurred over four decades ago in the Johnson and Nixon administrations of the late 1960s and early 1970s.

This does not imply that there are no problems with expressions of declining confidence in government. Whatever the reasons for the decline, if the public becomes unwilling to provide such crucial resources as tax dollars or to voluntarily comply with laws, or if bright young people refuse to go into government service, governmental capacity would be impaired and people would become more dissatisfied with government. Moreover, a climate of distrust can trigger extreme actions by deviant members of the population, such as the bombing of a federal office building in Oklahoma City in 1995. Such results could impair both American hard and soft power.

As yet, however, these behavioral results do not seem to have materialized. The Internal Revenue Service sees no increase in cheating on taxes.[163] By many accounts, government officials have become less corrupt than in earlier decades, and the World Bank gives the United States a high score (above the ninetieth percentile) on "control of corruption."[164] Voluntary mail return of census forms increased to 67 percent in 2000, and rose slightly in 2010, reversing a thirty-year decline since 1970.[165] Voting rates declined from 62 percent to 50 percent in the forty years after 1960, but the decline stopped in 2000 and returned to 58 percent in 2008. Behavior does not seem to have changed as dramatically as have responses to poll questions. Despite predictions of institutional crisis expressed in the aftermath of the tightly contested 2000 presidential election, the incoming Bush administration was able to govern and achieve reelection.

Nor does the decline in confidence in government institutions seem to have greatly diminished American soft power, if only because most other developed countries seem to be experiencing a similar phenomenon. Canada, Britain, France, Sweden, Japan—just to name a few—have seen a similar trend. The causes of the expressed loss of confidence in institutions may be rooted in deeper trends in attitudes toward greater individualism and less deference to authority that are characteristic of all postmodern societies. As we saw with regard to social change, when such attitudes are typical of most advanced societies, it is difficult to make invidious comparisons that undercut American attractiveness compared to the others.[166]

How serious are these changes in social capital for the effectiveness of American institutions? Robert Putnam notes that community bonds have not weakened steadily over the last century. On the contrary, American history carefully examined is a story of ups and downs in civic engagement, not just downs—a story of collapse and renewal.[167] He suggests a number of policies that might contribute to a renewal early in the twenty-first century analogous to that created by the progressive movement at the beginning of the last century. Three-quarters of Americans feel connected to their communities and say the quality of life there is excellent or good. According to a Pew poll, 111 million Americans say they volunteered their time to help solve problems in their communities in the previous twelve months, and 60 million volunteered on a regular basis. Forty percent said working together with others in their community was the most important thing they could do.[168]

In recent years, American politics and political institutions have become more polarized than the distribution of opinions in the American public would suggest. The situation was exacerbated by the economic downturn after 2008. As a British observer suggests, "America's political system was designed to make legislation at the federal level difficult, not easy. . . . So the basic system works; but that is no excuse for ignoring areas where it could be reformed," such as the gerrymandered safe seats in the House of Representatives and the blocking procedures of Senate rules and filibusters.[169] Whether the American political system can reform itself and cope with the problems described here remains to be seen, but it is not as broken as implied by critics who draw analogies to the domestic decay of Rome or other empires. American decline is unlikely to lead to a rapid power transition to Chinese dominance in the first decades of this century.

NET ASSESSMENT

Any net assessment of American power in the coming decades encounters a number of difficulties. As we have seen, many earlier efforts have been wide of the mark. It is chastening to remember how wildly exaggerated were American estimates of Soviet power in the 1970s and of Japanese power in the 1980s. Today, some confidently predict the twenty-first century will see China replace the United States as the world's leading state, whereas others equally confidently argue that "the United States is only at the beginning of its power. The twenty-first century will be the American century."[170] But unforeseen events often confound such projections. There are a range of possible futures, not one.

On American power relative to China, much will depend on the uncertainties of future political change in China. Barring such political uncertainties, China's size and high rate of economic growth will almost certainly increase its relative strength vis-à-vis the United States. This will bring it closer to the United States in power resources but will not necessarily mean that China will surpass the United States as the most powerful country. Even if China suffers no major domestic political setback, many current projections based on GDP growth alone are too one-dimensional and ignore U.S. military and soft power advantages, as well as China's geopolitical disadvantages in the internal Asian balance of power compared to America's likely favorable relations with Europe, Japan, India, and others. My own estimate is that among the range of possible futures, the more likely are ones in which China gives the United States a run for its money but does not surpass it in overall power in the first half of this century. Looking back at history, British strategist

Lawrence Freedman notes two features that distinguish the United States from "the dominant great powers of the past: American power is based on alliances rather than colonies and is associated with an ideology that is flexible . . . to which America can return even after it has overextended itself."[171] And looking to the future, Anne-Marie Slaughter argues that America's culture of openness and innovation will keep it central in a world where networks supplement, if not fully replace, hierarchical power.[172] The United States is more likely to benefit from such networks and alliances.

On question of absolute, rather than relative, American decline, the United States faces serious problems in areas such as debt, secondary education, and political gridlock, but they are only part of the picture. It is important to look beyond current conventional wisdom and not to let preferences determine analysis. Among the negative futures are ones in which the United States overreacts to terrorist attacks by closing inward and thus cuts itself off from the strength it obtains from openness. But barring such mistakes, in principle and over a longer term, there are solutions to major American problems that preoccupy us today, such as long-term debt (for example, consumption taxes and expenditure cuts that pay for entitlements when the economy recovers) and political gridlock (for example, changes in redistricting procedures to reduce gerrymandering, changes in Senate rules, and so forth). Of course, such solutions may forever remain out of reach. But it is worth distinguishing situations where there are no solutions from those that could in principle be solved (even without a constitutional amendment).

Describing power transition in the twenty-first century as an issue of American decline is inaccurate and misleading. Such analysis can lead to dangerous policy implications if it encourages China to engage in adventurous policies or the United States to overreact out of fear. America is not in absolute decline, and it is likely to remain more powerful than any single state in the coming decades, although American economic and cultural preponderance will become less dominant than at the beginning of the century. At the same time, the United States will certainly be faced with a rise in the power resources of many others—both states and nonstate actors. The United States will also face an increasing number of issues in which solutions will require power *with* others as much as power *over* others. American capacity to maintain alliances and create networks will be an important dimension of the nation's hard and soft power. In such circumstances, it will be more important than ever to combine domestic reforms with smart strategies for the conversion of American resources into external power, as we shall see in the next chapter.

PART III

POLICY

CHAPTER 7

Smart Power

Power is not good or bad per se. It is like calories in a diet; more is not always better. Having too few power resources means a lower probability of obtaining preferred outcomes, but too much power (in terms of resources) can be a curse, rather than a benefit, if it leads to overconfidence and inappropriate strategies for power conversion. Good evidence exists to support Lord Acton's famous dictum that "power corrupts and absolute power corrupts absolutely," and studies show that it particularly corrupts those who think they deserve it.[1] One psychologist defines "the power paradox" as the fact that power is given to those individuals, groups, or states that advance the interests of the greater good in socially intelligent fashion, but "what people want from leaders—social intelligence—is what is damaged by the possession of power."[2] Just as we sometimes say that a man or a woman may be too handsome or too smart for his or her own good, so people and states may suffer from a "power curse."[3] In the biblical story of David and Goliath, the Philistine's superior power resources misled him into an inferior strategy, which in turn led to defeat and death.[4]

A smart power narrative for the twenty-first century is not about maximizing power or preserving hegemony. It is about finding ways to combine resources into successful strategies in the new context of power diffusion and the "rise of the rest." As the largest power, American leadership remains important in global affairs, but the old twentieth-century narrative about an American century and primacy or, alternatively, narratives of American decline are both misleading about the type of strategy that will be necessary.

A strategy relates means to ends, and that requires clarity about goals (preferred outcomes), resources, and tactics for their use. A smart strategy provides the answers to five questions. First, *what goals or outcomes are preferred?* Because we can't usually have everything we want in life, this answer requires more than the mere construction of an infinite wish list. It means setting priorities that will structure trade-offs. It also requires understanding the relationship between tangible possession goals and general structural goals, as well as which goals involve zero-sum power over others and which involve joint gains that require power with others. One historian said of Secretary of Defense Dick Cheney's "Defense Strategy for the 1990s," that it "sought to assure U.S. dominance without any clear purpose beyond just that."[5]

A smart strategy must also answer a second question: *What resources are available and in which contexts?* Not only an accurate and complete inventory of resources is needed, but also an understanding of when they will (or will not) be available and how their availability is likely to change in different situations. Then a smart power–conversion strategy asks a third question: *What are the positions and preferences of the targets of influence attempts?* As a survey of classical strategies emphasized, it is essential to have "an accurate view of the capabilities and proclivities of potential opponents."[6] What do they have, and, more importantly, what do they think? What are the intensity, malleability, and likelihood of changes in their preferences and strategies over what periods in which domains? Sometimes, as in extreme acts of violent destruction, the preferences of the target do not matter much to success—for example, it may not matter what you think if all I want to do is to assassinate you—but in most instances good intelligence about the target is essential for adjusting the tactics used to combine power resources.

That leads to the fourth question: *Which forms of power behavior are most likely to succeed?* In a given situation, are you more likely to succeed at reasonable time and cost with the command behavior of hard power or with the co-optive behavior of agenda-setting, persuasion, and attraction or a combination of the two. How will the tactics for using these behaviors lead to competition or reinforcement among them? For example, when will the use of hard and soft power reinforce or undercut each other? How will that change over time?

Fifth, *what is the probability of success?* Noble causes can have terrible consequences if they are accompanied by excessive optimism or willful blindness about the probabilities of success. For example, no matter what the quality of the objectives for the American invasion of Iraq, it was accompanied by what proved to be hubristic blindness about the eventual time and costs involved. It is worth remembering that the ancient tradition of just-war theory asks not only about proportionality and discrimination in means, but also about how the probability of success will affect consequences. That is the case for prudence that realists properly extol in a smart power strategy. And, finally, if the probabilities of success fail the test of prudent judgment, a return to the first question is in order, along with a reassessment of goals, priorities, and trade-offs. After adjusting goals, a smart power strategy then runs down the list again.

STATE SMART POWER STRATEGIES

According to a high State Department official, "The concept of 'smart power'—the intelligent integration and networking of diplomacy, defense, development, and other tools of so-called 'hard and soft' power—is at the very heart of President Obama and Secretary Clinton's policy vision."[7] Because the term has been adopted by the Obama administration, some analysts think it refers only to the

United States, and critics complain that it is merely a slogan like "tough love" that sugarcoats nasty stuff. But even though the term "smart power" lends itself to slogans (no one wants to be "dumb," though counterproductive strategies fit that description), smart power can also be used for analysis and is by no means limited to the United States.

Small states are often adept at smart power strategies. Singapore has invested enough in its military resources to make itself appear indigestible in the eyes of neighbors it wishes to deter, but it has combined this approach with active sponsorship of diplomatic activities in the Association of Southeast Asian Nations, as well as efforts to have its universities serve as the hubs of networks of nongovernmental activities in the region. Switzerland long used the combination of mandatory military service and mountainous geography as resources for deterrence, while making itself attractive to others through banking, commercial, and cultural networks. Qatar, a small peninsula off the coast of Saudi Arabia, allowed its territory to be used as the headquarters for the American military in the invasion of Iraq, while at the same time sponsoring Al Jazeera, the most popular television station in the region, which was highly critical of American actions. Norway joined NATO for defense but developed forward-leaning policies on overseas development assistance and peace mediation to increase its soft power above what would otherwise be the case.

Historically, rising states have used smart power strategies to good avail. In the nineteenth century, Otto von Bismarck's Prussia employed an aggressive military strategy to defeat Denmark, Austria, and France in three wars that led to the unification of Germany, but once Bismarck had accomplished that goal by 1870, he adapted German diplomacy to create alliances with neighbors and make Berlin the hub of European diplomacy and conflict resolution. One of the kaiser's great mistakes two decades later was to fire Bismarck, fail to renew his "reinsurance treaty" diplomacy with Russia, and challenge Britain for naval supremacy on the high seas. After the

Meiji Restoration, Japan built the military strength that enabled it to defeat Russia in 1905, but it also followed a conciliatory diplomatic policy toward Britain and the United States and spent considerable resources to make itself attractive overseas.[8] After the failure of its Greater East Asia Co-Prosperity imperial scheme of the 1930s (which had a soft power component of anti-European propaganda) and defeat in World War II, Japan turned to a strategy that minimized military power and relied on an American alliance. Its single-minded focus on economic growth was successful on that dimension, but it developed only modest military and soft power.

China under Mao built its military strength (including nuclear weapons) and used the soft power of Maoist revolutionary doctrine and Third World solidarity to cultivate allies abroad, but after the exhaustion of the Maoist strategy in the 1970s, Chinese leaders turned to market mechanisms to foster economic development. Deng warned his compatriots to eschew external adventures that might jeopardize this internal development. In 2007, President Hu proclaimed the importance of investing in China's soft power. From the point of view of a country that was making enormous strides in economic and military power, this was a smart strategy. By accompanying the rise of its hard power with efforts to make itself more attractive, China aimed to reduce the fear and tendencies to balance Chinese power that might otherwise grow among its neighbors.

In 2009, China was justly proud of its success in managing to emerge from the world recession with a high rate of economic growth. Many Chinese concluded that this represented a shift in the world balance of power and that the United States was in decline. One dated the year 2000 as the peak of American power. "People are now looking down on the West, from leadership circles, to academia, to everyday folks," said Professor Kang Xiaoguong of Renmin University.[9] But such narratives can lead to conflict. Overconfidence in power assessment (combined with insecurity in domestic affairs) led to more assertive Chinese foreign policy behavior in the latter part of 2009. Some observers wondered if China was beginning to deviate from the smart strategy of a rising power and violating the wisdom of Deng, who advised that China should proceed cautiously and "skillfully keep a low profile."[10]

Dominant states also have incentives to combine hard and soft power resources. Empires are easier to rule when they rest on the soft power of attraction as well as the hard power of coercion. Rome allowed conquered elites to aspire to Roman citizenship, and France co-opted African leaders such as Leopold Senghor into French political and cultural life. Victorian Britain used expositions and culture to attract elites from the empire, and as we saw earlier, it was able to rule a vast empire in large part with locals and very few British troops. Of course, this became progressively more difficult as rising nationalism changed the context and eroded the soft power of the British Empire. The development of the British Commonwealth of Nations was an effort to maintain a residual of that soft power in the new postcolonial context.

A state's "grand strategy" is its leaders' theory and story about how to provide for its security, welfare, and identity ("life, liberty, and the pursuit of happiness" in Jefferson's terms), and that strategy has to be adjusted for changes in context. Too rigid an approach to strategy can be counterproductive. Strategy is not some mystical possession at the top of government. It can be applied at all levels.[11] A country must have a general game plan, but it also must remain flexible in the face of events. In the words of one historian, a sound grand strategy is "an equation of ends and means so sturdy that it triumphs despite serial setbacks at the level of strategy, operations and campaigns."[12] Some American analysts of the post–Cold War world look for narratives that can be reduced to bumper stickers, such as "containment" served in the past. They forget that the same slogan covered policies that sometimes conflicted with each other.[13] For some, containment justified the Vietnam War; for George Kennan, author of the strategy, it did not. More important than simple formulas or clever slogans is the contextual intelligence that leads to accurate assessment of trends in power and thinking ahead about smart policy responses.[14]

As we have seen, academics, pundits, and presidents have often been mistaken in their assessment of America's position in the world. For example, two decades ago the conventional wisdom was that the United States was in decline, suffering from imperial overstretch. A decade later, with the end of the Cold War, the new conventional wisdom was that the world was a unipolar American hegemony. Some observers concluded that the United States was so powerful that it could decide what it thought was right and others would have no choice but to follow. Charles Krauthammer celebrated this view as "the new unilateralism," and this narrative of dominance heavily influenced the Bush administration even before the shock of the attacks on September 11, 2001, produced a new "Bush Doctrine" of preventive war and coercive democratization.[15] But the new unilateralism was based on a profound misunderstanding of the nature of power in world politics and the context under which the possession of preponderant resources will produce preferred outcomes.

What are the main features of the current world environment, and how are they changing?[16] In the Preface, I likened the context of politics today to a three-dimensional chess game in which interstate military power is highly concentrated in the United States; interstate economic power is distributed in a multipolar manner among the United States, the EU, Japan, and the BRICs; and power over transnational issues such as climate change, crime, terror, and pandemics is highly diffused. Assessing the distribution of resources among actors varies with each domain. The world is neither unipolar, multipolar, nor chaotic—it is all three at the same time. Thus, a smart grand strategy must be able to handle very different distributions of power in different domains and understand the trade-offs among them. It makes no more sense to see the world through a purely realist lens that focuses only on the top chessboard or a liberal institutional lens that looks primarily at the other boards. Contextual intelligence today requires a new synthesis of "liberal realism" that looks at all three boards at the same time. After all, in a three-level game, a player who focuses on only one board is bound to lose in the long run.

That will require an understanding of how to exercise power with as well as power over other states. On issues arising on the top board of interstate military relations, an understanding of ways to form alliances and balance power will remain crucial. But the best order of military battle will do little good in solving many of the problems on the bottom chessboard of nonstate actors and transnational threats, such as pandemics or climate change, even though these issues can present threats to the security of millions of people on the order of magnitude of military threats that traditionally drive national strategies. Such issues will require cooperation, institutions, and pursuit of public goods from which all can benefit and none can be excluded.

Theorists of hegemony have looked at issues of transition and the prospects of conflict, as we saw in the last chapter, but they have also examined the beneficial effects of hegemony on the provision of public goods. This led to a theory of hegemonic stability. Public goods from which all can benefit are underproduced because the incentives to invest in their production are reduced by the inability to prevent others from enjoying the benefits without paying for their production. If everyone has an incentive to "free-ride," no one has an incentive to invest. The exception may be situations where one state is so much larger than the others that it will notice the benefits of its investment in public goods even if smaller states free-ride. In this "case for Goliath,"[17] hegemonic states are necessary for global governance and must take the lead in production of global public goods because smaller states lack the incentives or capacity to do so.

When the largest states do not step up to the task, the results can be disastrous for the international system. For example, when the United States replaced Britain as the world's leading financial and trading state after World War I, it did not live up to these obligations, and that failure contributed to the onset and severity of the Great Depression. Some analysts worry about a repeat of that experience.[18] As China approaches the United States in its share of the distribution of economic resources, will it assume the role of responsible stakeholder (to use the phrase developed by the Bush administration), or will it continue to free-ride as the United States did in the interwar period?

Fortunately, hegemonic preponderance is not the only way to produce global public goods. Robert Keohane argues that it is possible to design international institutions to solve problems of coordination and free riding in the period "after hegemony."[19] Moreover, as other theorists have pointed out, hegemonic stability theory is an oversimplification because pure public goods are rare and large governments can often exclude some countries from some of the benefits they provide.[20] Some broad goods, such as security or trade agreements, can be turned into "club goods" that benefit many but from which some can be excluded.

Global government is unlikely in the twenty-first century, but degrees of global governance already exist. The world has hundreds of treaties, institutions, and regimes for governing areas of interstate behavior ranging from telecommunications, civil aviation, ocean dumping, trade, and even the proliferation of nuclear weapons. But such institutions are rarely self-sufficient. They still benefit from the leadership of great powers. And it remains to be seen whether the largest countries in the twenty-first century will live up to this role. As the power of China and India increases, how will their behavior in this dimension change? Some, such as liberal scholar John Ikenberry, argue that the current set of global institutions are sufficiently open and adaptable that China will find it in its own interests to be co-opted into them.[21] Others believe that China will wish to impose its own mark and create its own international institutional system as its power increases. Ironically, for those who foresee a tripolar world at midcentury composed of the United States, China, and India, all three of these large powers are among the most protective of their sovereignty and the most reluctant to accept a post-Westphalian world.

Even if the EU retains a leading role in world politics and pushes for more institutional innovation, it is unlikely that, barring a disaster such as World War II, the world will see "a constitutional moment" such as it experienced with the creation of the UN system of institutions after 1945. Today, as a universal institution the United Nations plays a crucial role in legitimization, crisis diplomacy, peacekeeping, and humanitarian missions, but its very size has proven to be a disadvantage for many other functions. For example, as the 2009 UN Framework Conference on Climate Change (UNFCCC) at Copenhagen demonstrated, meetings of nearly two hundred states are often unwieldy and subject to bloc politics and tactical moves by players that are largely extraneous because they otherwise lack resources to solve functional problems.

One of the dilemmas of multilateral diplomacy is how to get everyone into the act and still get action. The answer is likely to lie in what Europeans have dubbed "variable geometry." There will be many multilateralisms that will vary with the distribution of power resources in different issues. For instance, on monetary affairs the Bretton Woods conference created the International Monetary Fund in 1944, and it has since expanded to include 186 nations, but the preeminence of the dollar was the crucial feature of monetary cooperation until the 1970s. After the weakening of the dollar and President Nixon's ending of its convertibility into gold, France convened a small group of five countries in 1975 to meet in the library of the Chateau of Rambouillet to discuss monetary affairs.[22] It soon grew to the Group of Seven and later broadened in scope and membership to the Group of Eight (which included Russia and a vast bureaucratic and press attendance). Subsequently, the Group of Eight began the practice of inviting five guests from the BRICs and other countries. In the financial crisis of 2008, this framework evolved into a new Group of 20, with a more inclusive membership.

At the same time, the Group of 7 continued to meet at the ministerial level on a narrower monetary agenda; new institutions such as the Financial Stability Board were created, and bilateral discussions between the United States and China continued to play an important role. As one experienced diplomat puts it, "If you're trying to negotiate an exchange rate deal with 20 countries or a bailout of Mexico, as in the early Clinton days, with 20 countries, that's not easy. If you get above 10, it just makes it too darn hard to get things done."[23] After all, with 3 players, there are 3 pairs of relationships; with 10 players, there are 45; with 100 players, there are nearly 5,000. Or to take issues of climate change, the UNFCCC will continue to play a role, but more intensive negotiations are likely to occur in smaller forums where fewer than a dozen countries account for 80 percent of greenhouse gas emissions.[24]

Much of the work of global governance will rely on formal and informal networks. Network organizations (such as the G-20) are used for agenda-setting and consensus-building, policy coordination, knowledge exchange, and norm-setting.[25] As we discussed in Chapter 1, centrality in networks can be a source of power, but "the power that flows from this type of connectivity is not the power to impose outcomes. Networks are not directed and controlled as much as they are managed and orchestrated. Multiple players are integrated into a whole that is greater than the sum of its parts"[26]— in other words, the network provides power to achieve preferred outcomes with other players rather than over them. We saw that power in networks can come from both strong ties and weak ties. Strong ties, such as alliances, "multiply a nation's power through everything from basing rights, intelligence sharing, weapons system collaborations and purchases, and shared military deployments to support in multilateral institutions, mutual trade benefits and mutual security guarantees." And weak ties, such as global multilateral institutions, "for all of their manifest deficiencies . . . still matter, and a nation cannot be a great power without at least having a significant voice as the UN, the IMF and the World Bank."[27] In this dimension, predictions of an Asian century remain premature; the United States will remain more central in a dense global web of governance than other countries.

AN AMERICAN SMART POWER STRATEGY

Returning to the five questions about a successful strategy that we discussed earlier suggests five steps in the construction of an American smart power strategy.

The First Step

As argued previously, the first step in designing a smart power strategy is clarity about objectives. In terms of grand strategy, Americans have long debated the proper purposes of their power. Most recently, there has been a debate about whether a dominant goal should be to seek to retain primacy or preponderance in power resources or to promote values either by perfecting democracy at home or by practicing liberal interventionism abroad. This is sometimes cast as a struggle between realism and idealism, but a successful American narrative must include both.[28] Values are an intrinsic part of American foreign policy. American exceptionalism dates from the earliest days of a republic founded in reaction to the old world, seeing itself as a city on the hill with universal values to share with others. As Kissinger notes, realists seek equilibrium and stability, whereas idealists strive for conversion. But he goes on to say that the debate between them is overstated. Realists can acknowledge the importance of ideal and values, and idealists do not necessarily reject all geopolitical restraints.[29] Nevertheless, there has been a long-standing tension between them.

Traditional realists often distinguish between a foreign policy based on values and a foreign policy based on interests. They describe as "vital" those interests that would directly affect security and thus merit the use of force: for example, to prevent attacks on the United States, to prevent the emergence of hostile hegemons in Asia or Europe, to prevent hostile powers on the borders or in control of the seas, and to ensure the survival of American allies.[30] Promoting human rights or democracy or specific economic sectors is relegated to a lower priority. But this traditional approach is analytically too narrow, and it fits poorly with the nature of American political culture.

Vital national interests deserve priority because survival is at stake, but the connection between a particular event and a threat to national survival may involve a long chain of causes. People can disagree about how probable any link in the chain is and how much "insurance" they want against remote threats before pursuing other values such as human rights. In a democracy, the national interest is simply what citizens, after proper deliberation, say it is. It is broader than vital strategic interests, though they are a crucial part. It can include values such as human rights and democracy, particularly if the American public feels that those values are so important to our identity or sense of "who we are" that people are willing to pay a price to promote them. Values are simply an intangible national interest. If the American people think that our interests include certain values and their promotion abroad, then they become part of the national interest. Leaders and experts may point out the costs of indulging certain values, but if an informed public disagrees, experts cannot deny the legitimacy of their opinion.

In practice, the American tradition in foreign policy objectives is broader than the simple dichotomy between realism and idealism.[31] Americans debate how attentive to be to the interests of others both in the ends that we seek and in the means that we use. Nationalists debate cosmopolitans and unilateralists debate multilateralists. And most presidents and opinion-makers wind up borrowing from many traditions—witness Harry Truman, Dwight Eisenhower, and John Kennedy.

As a result, trade-offs in objectives are inevitable. The question is how they should be reconciled. Realists warn against unlimited crusades and stress the importance of prudence in judging the probability of success in achieving objectives. Many call for a "modest foreign policy" that stays within American means, and this is sound advice as far as it goes. But modesty is an ambiguous goal, and its proponents define it in different ways. For some, "the first virtue of a restraint strategy is that it husbands American power."[32] But that still leaves the question of how to use the power that is husbanded. We can take the argument a step further by recalling the importance of the largest state in the provision of global public goods. As we saw earlier, if the largest beneficiary of a public good (such as the United States) does not take the lead in providing disproportionate resources toward its provision, the smaller beneficiaries are unlikely to be able to produce it because of the difficulties of organizing collective action when large numbers are involved.[33]

A grand strategy starts with ensuring survival but then should focus on providing public goods. To a large extent, international order is a global public good—something everyone can consume without diminishing its availability to others.[34] A small country can benefit from peace in its region, freedom of the seas, open trade, control of infectious diseases, or stability in financial markets at the same time that the United States does without diminishing the benefits to either the United States or others. Of course, as we saw earlier, pure public goods are rare. When some countries can be excluded, the result is club goods or partial public goods. And sometimes things that look good in American eyes may look bad in the eyes of others. Too narrow an appeal to public goods can become a self-serving ideology, but that is a reminder to listen to others, not a reason to discard an important strategic principle. The United States would gain doubly from such a strategy: from the public goods themselves and from the soft power they can create. If the United States defines its national interest in terms of goods that include the interest of others, it can create a narrative that is more likely to obtain the broad support required to accomplish its objectives, particularly as the United States faces the rise of new state and nonstate actors and is seeking to coordinate action in networks.

The United States can learn from the lesson of Great Britain in the nineteenth century, when it focused on maintaining the balance of power among the major states in Europe, promoting an open international economic system, and maintaining open international commons such as the freedom of the seas. All three are relevant to the American situation in the twenty-first century. Maintaining regional balances of power and dampening local incentives to use force to change borders provide a public good for many (but not all) countries. The American military presence helps to "shape the environment" in important regions, particularly in Europe and Asia. Promoting an open international economic system is good for American economic growth and is good for other countries as well. Openness of global markets is a necessary (though not sufficient) condition for alleviating poverty in poor countries even as it benefits the United States. In addition, in the long term economic growth is also more likely to foster stable democratic middle-class societies in other countries, though the time scale may be quite lengthy. Like nineteenth-century Britain, America has an interest in keeping international commons, such the oceans, open to all. Today, however, the international commons include new issues such as global climate change, preservation of endangered species, and the uses of outer space, as well as the imperfect "virtual commons" of cyberspace.

There are additional dimensions of global public goods in this century. One is the development and maintenance of international regimes of laws and institutions to organize international actions for dealing with trade and environment as well as nuclear proliferation, peacekeeping, human rights, and other concerns. A global public good narrative for this century also includes international development. Much of the poor majority of the world is mired in vicious circles of disease, poverty, and political instability. Aid can sometimes be helpful, but it is far from sufficient for development; opening markets, strengthening accountable institutions, and discouraging corruption are even more important. Development will take a long time, and we must explore better ways to make sure that help actually reaches the poor, but both prudence and a concern for soft power suggest that we should make development a high priority.

Finally, as a preponderant power, the United States can provide an important public good by acting as a mediator and convener of coalitions. By using its good offices to mediate conflicts in places such as Sudan and the Middle East, the United States can help in shaping international order in ways that are beneficial to itself as well as to other nations. Some ethnic and religious conflicts are intractable, and there are some situations where other countries can more effectively play the mediator's role, but often the United States can bring parties together, and when successful, it can enhance its reputation and increase its soft power at the same time that it reduces a source of instability.

The Second Step

After setting manageable objectives that combine values and interests, the second step in the development of a smart power strategy is an accurate inventory of the resources available and an assessment of how that inventory will change with changing contexts.

In terms of military resources, with the United States spending nearly half the global budget on these resources and possessing the most advanced technology, no country can balance American power in the traditional sense. Maintaining that edge and preventing a peer competitor challenging military primacy have been major objectives of American strategy since the end of the Soviet Union in 1991. But that approach has limits. America's military resources allow it to master command of the commons of air above 15,000 feet, space, and the open oceans. This capacity is not likely to be matched by China or others for well into the century. That allows unmatched global force projection, but the United States can still be challenged in contested zones, such as urban areas, remote regions, and littoral seas.[35] And in the imperfect commons of cyberspace, the United States may have the world's leading capability for cyberoffense, but it is also highly vulnerable because of its reliance on cybernetworks, and the playing field is much more level when it comes to the problems of cyberdefense.

Controlling socially mobilized populations can be very costly. Simple technologies such as improvised explosive devices used by insurgents are far cheaper than smart weapons developed by the United States. At a ratio of one troop per twenty populations in occupied countries, a full counterinsurgency doctrine requires enormous resources. For example, the costs of each American soldier or marine deployed in Afghanistan are estimated to be nearly $1 million per head per year.[36] Even if the budgetary costs can be met, the question of how long the public in the United States and its allies will support such efforts gives a psychological advantage to the insurgents. In short, the United States is likely to retain its lead in military resources, but their utility and cost-effectiveness will be limited in a number of important future contexts.

America is well endowed in economic resources, but the EU is able to balance American economic power on some issues, and by some projections the Chinese economy may surpass that of the United States in total size in another two decades. American power resources are already balanced by others in the economic area, and this is likely to be even more true in the future. The development of the G-20 network organization and the redistribution of voting power in the IMF are illustrations of this point. Even though the United States will retain certain demographic, technological, and entrepreneurial advantages, it will have to bargain more often with other countries as equals. Moreover, in a period of budget deficits, means will be constrained and must be selected in a manner that fits with a realistic assessment of economic resources. To the extent that the United States undertakes domestic reforms to strengthen its economy and works with international economic institutions that magnify its power as a center of networks, it will do better in such bargaining.

In soft power as well, the United States has more resources than most countries, though this depends upon varying degrees of attraction to American culture and values in other countries. Of the means of projecting American values, the city on the hill approach is less costly than active intervention abroad. American universities and media are likely to remain preeminent for quite some time into the future, but as other countries develop their capabilities in these areas, the American lead will narrow. And policies that are seen as heavy-handed or illegitimate can undercut the soft power produced by culture and values.

The Third Step

The third step in a smart American grand strategy is an assessment of the resources and preferences of the targets of attempts at influence. For example, it makes little sense to make blanket statements about military power becoming obsolete when the three categories of postindustrial countries (such as Europe), industrializing countries (such as the BRICs), and preindustrial countries (as in much of Africa) are each so different. The attitudes toward the legitimate use of military power vary with these contexts. For example, on the question of war, only 25 percent of Europeans (compared to 71 percent of Americans) believe that under some conditions war is necessary to obtain justice, and Europeans tend to think that economic power is more important than military power.[37] In the web of complex interdependence among postindustrial democracies, economic and soft power resources are likely to play larger roles and the use of military force may become unacceptable. Even though military power remains important in its protective dimension, America's role in institutions and networks becomes even more important in the context of relations among the rich democracies. In contrast, for countries in Asia concerned about balancing the increase in China's hard power resources, an American military presence is often welcome, and for countries such as Liberia and Sierra Leone, an active peacekeeping military presence can be important.

In addition to differences among states, there are also important differences among nonstate actors. In dealing with terrorist groups, for instance, too weak a response can encourage the extremists, but the wrong type of military response can be counterproductive. As Rumsfeld once observed, winning a war against terrorists depends on whether the numbers being killed and deterred (by our hard power) are greater than the numbers the terrorists are able to recruit with their soft power. Defeating extreme Islamist terrorism, for example, requires international intelligence and police cooperation, as well as a drying up of the sources of radical recruits. Hard military power will remain crucial, but if its use is perceived as unjust, such as at Abu Ghraib or Guantánamo, then hard power undercuts the soft power needed to win the minds of mainstream Muslims and creates more new terrorists than are destroyed. For example, a leading terrorism expert concludes that anti-Americanism was exacerbated by the war in Iraq and the U.S. failure to tailor strategies for key countries. International jihadist groups increased their membership and carried out twice as many attacks in the three years after 2001 as before it.[38] Similarly, the former head of Britain's MI5 intelligence service told the commission investigating the origins of the Iraq War that the war had increased, rather than decreased, terrorists' success at recruitment.[39]

The Fourth Step

The fourth step for a smart strategy is choosing among power behaviors, choosing command power or co-optive power in different situations, and adjusting tactics so that they reinforce, rather than undercut, each other. During the Cold War, military deterrence helped to prevent Soviet aggression in Europe, while the soft power of culture and ideas ate away at belief in communism behind the Iron Curtain. Kennan's original grand strategy of containment relied heavily on the idea of change occurring behind the Iron Curtain over time, and Eisenhower believed strongly in public diplomacy and exchanges. But in other areas such as Southeast Asia, the strategy of containment was less successfully applied. Americans failed to understand the motivations and tenacity of the Vietnamese nationalists, and military actions in Vietnam greatly eroded American soft power.[40]

Eisenhower's prudence at the peak of American twentieth-century power contrasts with the way the United States entered the twenty-first century believing that leadership rested on taking a strong initiative with hard power and leaving others with little choice but to follow. "Vice President Cheney believed that when other governments recognized they could not thwart U.S. action, they would rally to the American cause. He believed that the U.S. could create its own realities."[41] But the net effect of the invasion of Iraq was instead to unite American enemies and divide its friends, with polls showing a drop in American attractiveness around the world. Even though it is useful for deterrence and protection of allies to retain American military primacy, it would be a mistake to think that American military preponderance will be great enough to follow the type of strategy adopted in 2001 and enshrined in the National Security Strategy of 2002.

At the tactical level, counterinsurgency doctrine places great emphasis on the trade-off between the necessary military force to clear insurgents from an area and the damage to civilians whose hearts and minds are being sought. And in some instances, trade-offs are unavoidable. For instance, drone strikes against Taliban and Al Qaeda fighters are one of the few instruments available in northern Pakistan (given Pakistani opposition to American boots on the ground), but they damage American soft power in the eyes of Pakistan's public. Such tactical issues will have to be decided on a case-by-case basis.

This is not just a question of whether to use military resources or not, for military resources can be used to produce hard and/or soft power behavior. Fighting and threatening are hard power behaviors; protecting and assisting are soft power behaviors. Sometimes the fit between the different behaviors is difficult to manage. For example, in 2008 the Pentagon established a unified regional command for Africa, and according to Pentagon officials, "AFRICOM at its core is about public diplomacy," but no African government offered to host its headquarters. As one observer puts it, "As a traditional military command, it would make perfect sense. . . . As an instrument of public diplomacy, however, AFRICOM has yet to prove that it is capable of performing this role and convincing skeptics."[42] Earlier, the Pentagon's SOUTHCOM for Latin America, which had previously emphasized direct military action, "now focuse[d] on programs to train and support local forces, and assist economic development, health services and counternarcotics efforts."[43] But although some approved the new goals as admirable, they also worried about overmilitarization of foreign policy and draining of authority from the State Department. The percentage of development assistance controlled by the Defense Department grew to nearly one-quarter in the first decade of the century, while the percentage controlled by AID shrank from 65 to 40 percent.[44] This is not to deny the value of unified military commands combining hard and soft power behavior, but to draw attention to the problems of perceptions and unintended consequences.

Among economic behaviors, structuring markets is important but often runs into resistance by private interests and companies that benefit or lose from alternative structures, and this makes the instrument difficult to wield. Sometimes the incentives of companies and the U.S. government are aligned, and sometimes they are at cross-purposes. On sanctions, we found that the behavior is often oversold but is nonetheless better than alternatives in terms of cost-effectiveness and signaling. Development assistance is more problematic as an instrument because of uncertainties about the causes of development, but assistance for specific purposes and institutional structures could sometimes be effective, and development is an important part of the smart power narrative. State-building efforts are often oversold, but like sanctions, they can prove useful in particular contexts. The problem is that they are often difficult to scale. Small and targeted efforts have often been more successful than large bureaucratic endeavors, but the government is not organized that way. Nongovernmental actors are often (but not always) more flexible.

Soft power behaviors ranging from public diplomacy to aid programs often help to create an enabling environment, but their effects are sometimes difficult to measure in terms of outcomes in the short term. With the advent of a new administration in 2009, President Obama was able to raise American standing (as measured by polls) with a series of speeches and symbols, but the changes measured by the international behavior of others was limited in the short term. At the same time, it is important to consider time horizons and types of goals in such judgments. As former British foreign secretary David Milliband puts it, often "we underestimate the impact of soft power in the long term and overestimate the impact of hard power in the short term."[45]

In general, the United States has not worked out an integrated plan for combining hard and soft power. A survey of reports by twenty nongovernmental commissions in 2008 and 2009 found a "bipartisan consensus on implementing a new 'smart power' strategy to elevate and strengthen our civilian capacities, particularly in development and diplomacy, as essential tools for advancing U.S. interests alongside a strong defense."[46] But many official instruments of soft power—public diplomacy, broadcasting, exchange programs, development assistance, disaster relief, military-to-military contacts—are scattered around the government, and there is no overarching strategy or budget that even tries to integrate them with hard power into an overarching smart power strategy. The United States spends about five hundred times more on the military than it does on broadcasting and exchanges. Is this the right proportion in an information age? How would we know? How would we make trade-offs? And there is little planning for how the government relates to the nonofficial generators of soft power—everything from Hollywood to Harvard to the Bill and Melinda Gates Foundation—that emanate from civil society. As we saw earlier, Defense Secretary Gates argued for more investment in soft power, and in arguing for a new agency in early 2008, former defense secretary Rumsfeld said the United States was "sitting on the sidelines in the global battle of ideas. . . . We're barely competing and for that reason we are losing."[47] As two astute analysts conclude, "Strategy is one thing.

Executing is another. Though a unique coalition of military and civilian leaders now support using American soft power more effectively, we need to move urgently from strategy to action and permanently build the civilian capacity to wield soft power well. The alternative to soft power is not only less effective hard power, but less power, period."[48]

The Fifth Step

Finally, the fifth step for a smart power strategy is a careful assessment of the probability of success in achieving its objectives, both at the grand strategy level and in the tactics of any particular influence attempt. This requires a clear assessment of international limits. As Paul Kennedy points out, "Smart, long-standing empires such as that of the Romans, recognized their limits and rarely went beyond them. After losing three entire legions in the dense German forests, Augustus and his successors decided to establish a boundary along the western side of the Rhine."[49] The number one power does not have to man every boundary and be strong everywhere. The attempt to do so would violate Eisenhower's prudence in resisting direct intervention on the side of the French in Vietnam.

Also relevant today is Eisenhower's belief that it is essential to preserve the strength of the American economy that undergirds military strength. Applied to today's world, this suggests avoidance of involvement in land wars on the Asian continent. Whatever the difficulty of getting from where the United States is today to such a preferable position in the future ("build up to build down?"), such an approach would be useful. As President Obama said in announcing his surge in Afghanistan, "Our prosperity provides the foundation for our power. . . . That's why our troop commitment in Afghanistan cannot be open-ended," and his National Security Strategy of 2010 states that "our strategy starts by recognizing that our strength and influence abroad begins with the steps we take at home."[50] As strategist Anthony Cordesman observes, "Taken at face value, this is a return to the more classic American foreign policy of engagement and partnership—with a few changes it could have been written by the Eisenhower administration."[51] A return to traditional prudence must be part of a twenty-first-century smart power narrative. Global leadership does not require global interventionism.

Counterinsurgency is attractive as a doctrine in the way that it pays careful attention to the tactical balancing of hard and soft power, but in a strategic sense it is not likely to be appropriate for all places. Avoiding major land wars in Asia does not mean withdrawing a forward military presence from places such as Japan and Korea or ending military assistance of various types to countries such as Pakistan or Yemen, but it sets clear limits like the Rhine boundary for military presence in contested places. Some analysts call this a strategy of "offshore balancing," but that term must be interpreted to mean more than just naval and air force activity.[52] For example, an American troop presence that is welcome and supported in Europe and Japan should not be ruled out by a slogan. With prudence, American military primacy can represent an economic asset, not a liability.

Finally, a clear assessment of the probability of success also requires an understanding of what is possible in terms of American domestic institutions and public attitudes. British historian Niall Ferguson, an enthusiast for empire, lamented at the time of the Iraq War that the United States lacked the capacity for empire because of three domestic deficits: manpower (not enough boots on the ground), attention (not enough public support for long-term occupation), and finance (not enough savings and not enough taxation relative to public expenditure).[53] He was correct. A stomach for empire or colonial occupation is one of the important ways in which the American political culture differs from that of nineteenth-century Britain. Whether with applause or lament, such is the nature of the American political culture. At the same time, universalistic values and a temptation to intervene on the side of "the good" are also in the nature of the political culture. Prudence rests in understanding both international and domestic limits and adjusting objectives accordingly. Efforts to remake other nations in the American image will be a recurring temptation, but pragmatic tailoring of the foreign policy garment to the power resource cloth is the essence of a smart power strategy and narrative for this century.

CONCLUSION

A smart power strategy requires that the old distinction between realists and liberals needs to give way to a new synthesis that we might call liberal realism. What should go into a liberal realist smart power strategy?

First, it would start with an understanding of the strength and limits of American power. Preponderance is not empire or hegemony. The United States can influence but not control other parts of the world. Power always depends upon context, and in the context of transnational relations (such as climate change, illegal drugs, pandemics, and terrorism), power is diffuse and chaotically distributed. Military power is a small part of the solution in responding to these new threats. These solutions require cooperation among governments and international institutions. Even on the top board (where America represents nearly one-half of world defense expenditures), its military is supreme in the global commons of air, sea, and space, but much more limited in its ability to control nationalistic populations in occupied areas. As Richard Haass observes, "While the US remains the world's most powerful single country, it cannot maintain, much less expand, international peace and prosperity on its own."[54] Success will require partners, and that will mean maintaining old alliances as well as developing new networks that involve emerging powers such as China, India, and Brazil.

Second, a liberal realist strategy would stress the importance of developing an integrated grand strategy that combines hard power with soft attractive power into smart power of the sort that won the Cold War. In a struggle against terrorism, the United States needs to use hard power against the hard-core terrorists, but we cannot hope to win unless we win the hearts and minds of main-stream Muslims.

Third, the objective of a liberal realist strategy would have the key pillars of providing security for the United States and its allies, maintaining a strong domestic and international economy, avoiding environmental disasters (such as pandemics and negative climate change), and encouraging liberal democracy and human rights at home and abroad where feasible at reasonable levels of cost. This does not mean imposing American values by force. Democracy pro-motion is better accomplished by soft attraction than hard coercion, and it takes time and patience. Here we should learn from the past and lead by example, remembering the effective narrative of being Reagan's shining city on a hill. The United States would be wise to try encouraging the gradual evolution of democracy but in a manner that accepts the reality of diversity. It needs fewer Wilsonian calls to make the world safe for democracy, unless combined with Kennedy's rhetoric of "making the world safe for diversity."

Such a strategy should place priority on five major challenges. Prob-ably the greatest danger to the American way of life would be the intersection of terrorism with nuclear materials. Preventing this re-quires policies for countering terrorism, achieving nonproliferation, ensuring better protection of foreign nuclear materials, creating sta-bility in the Middle East, and giving attention to failed states.

Political Islam and how it develops are the second challenge. The current struggle against extreme Islamist terrorism is not a "clash of civilizations" but a civil war within Islam. A radical minority is using violence to enforce a simplified and ideological version of its religion upon a mainstream that has more diverse views. Even though there are more Muslims in Asia than anywhere else, they are influenced by the heart of this struggle in the Middle East, an area that has lagged behind the rest of the world in globalization, openness, in-stitutions, and democratization. More open trade, economic growth, education, development of civil society institutions, and gradual increases in political participation may help strengthen the mainstream over time, but so also will the way Muslims are treated in Europe and America. Equally important will be Western policies toward the Middle East and whether they attract mainstream Muslims or reinforce the radicals' narrative of a war against Islam.

The third major challenge would be the rise of a hostile hegemon as Asia gradually regains the share of the world economy that corresponds to its more than half of the world population. This requires a policy that welcomes China as a responsible stakeholder but hedges against possible hostility by maintaining close relations with Japan, India, and other countries in Asia that welcome an American presence.

The fourth major challenge would be an economic depression that could be triggered by financial mismanagement or a crisis that disrupts global access to the Persian Gulf, where two-thirds of world oil reserves are located. A strategic response to this challenge will require policies that gradually reduce dependence on oil while realizing that the American economy cannot be isolated from global energy markets and that the United States must not succumb to costly and counterproductive protectionism.

The fifth major challenge would be ecological breakdowns such as pandemics and negative climate change. Solutions to this challenge will require prudent energy policies and leadership on climate change as well as greater cooperation through international institutions.

Finally, a smart power strategy should look to the long-term evolution of world order and realize the responsibility of the largest country in the international system to produce global public or common goods. In the nineteenth century, Britain defined its national interest broadly to include promoting freedom of the seas, an open international economy, and a stable European balance of power. Such common goods helped Britain but benefited other countries as well. They also contributed to Britain's legitimacy and soft power. As the largest country of the twenty-first century, the United States should similarly promote an open international economy and commons (seas, space, Internet), mediate international disputes before they escalate, and develop international rules and institutions.

Because globalization will spread technical capabilities, and information technology will allow broader participation in global communications, American economic and cultural preponderance will become less dominant than at the start of this century. But that is not a narrative of decline. The United States is unlikely to decay like ancient Rome or even to be surpassed by another state, including China. The first half of the twenty-first century is not likely to be a "post-American world," but the United States will need a strategy to cope with the "rise of the rest"—among both states and nonstate actors.[55] The United States will need a smart power strategy and narrative that stress alliances, institutions, and networks that are responsive to the new context of a global information age. In short, for success in the twenty-first century, the United States will need to rediscover how to be a smart power.

ACKNOWLEDGMENTS

Since this book is the culmination of several decades of thinking about power, I owe more intellectual debts than I can possibly remember. No man is an island, and I have many bells to toll. I have learned from my teachers, from those with whom I have co-taught courses, from many undergraduate and graduate students, and from colleagues both in government and the academy. Friends at Oxford University and the Aspen Strategy Group heard and commented on some of these ideas. In particular, however, I have to thank my friend Robert O. Keohane, who scrubbed first drafts of every chapter with his usual wire brush criticisms. In addition, over the years, Bob and I have co-authored so many books and articles that I no longer know whether my ideas are really mine or his. And while I have tried to do justice with endnotes, I am sure that I have borrowed ideas from many other friends and colleagues. I am grateful for the institutional support of the Center for Public Leadership and the Belfer Center for Science and International Affairs at the Harvard Kennedy School. I am blessed to have worked among thoughtful and generous people. To all, thanks.

And special thanks to those who commented or helped on particular parts of the book: Graham Allison, Robert Axelrod, Tyson Belanger, Steven Biddle, Steve Chan, Nazli Choucri, Jeffrey Cooper, Richard Cooper, Michael Doyle, Peter Feaver, Allan Friedman, Jack Goldsmith, Fen Hampson, Andrew Hurrell, Roger Hurwitz, Sean Lynn Jones, Dale Jorgenson, Vijay Joshi, Peter Katzenstein, Andrew Kohut, Matt Kohut, Jennifer Lerner, Itamara Lochard, John Mallery, Sarah Sewall, Debra Sinnott, Allison Stanger, Greg Treverton, Alexander Vuving, Steven Walt, David Welch, Jed Willard, Ali Wynne. In addition, Scott Moyers and Clive Priddle provided very helpful editorial advice. Maia Usui and

Jack Sun were excellent research assistants, while Jeanne Marasca was a terrific personal assistant.

Above all, I am grateful to Molly, my full partner in life, and the support of our sons John, Ben, and Dan, and their progeny: Tupper, Hannah, Sage, Avery, Maggie, Ellie, Cole, Brooke, and Molly, to whom this book is dedicated.

NOTES

PREFACE

1. White House Press Office, "Inaugural Address by President Barack Hussein Obama," January 20, 2009, www.whitehouse.gov/the-press -office/president-barack-obamas-inaugural-address; National Public Radio, "Transcript of Clinton's Confirmation Hearing," January 13, 2009, www.npr.org/templates/story/story.php?storyId=99290981.

2. Thom Shanker, "Defense Secretary Urges More Spending for U.S. Diplomacy," *New York Times*, November 27, 2007.

3. Leslie Gelb, *Power Rules: How Common Sense Can Rescue American Foreign Policy* (New York: HarperCollins, 2009), 32.

4. Dominique Moisi, "Russia's Neurotic Invasion," *Project Syndicate*, August 21, 2008; Edward Luttwak, "Georgia Conflict: Moscow Has Blown Away Soft Power," *Telegraph*, August 16, 2008.

5. Alexei Mukhin, director of the Center for Political Information, quoted in Ellen Barry, "Russia's Neighbors Resist Wooing and Bullying," *New York Times*, July 3, 2009.

6. Fu Mengzhi, quoted in Geoff Dyer, "The Dragon Stirs," *Financial Times*, September 25, 2009.

7. Pew Research Center, "13 of 25—China Will Be World's Top Superpower," htpp://pewresearch.org/databank/?NumberID=832.

8. National Intelligence Council, "Global Trends 2025: A Transformed World" (Washington, DC: GPO, 2008); Dmitri Medvedev, quoted in Andrew Kramer, "Moscow Says U.S. Leadership Era Is Ending," *New York Times*, October 3, 2008; Michael Ignatieff, quoted in "The Ignatieff Revival," *The Economist*, April 25, 2009, 42.

9. Horace Walpole, quoted in Barbara Tuchman, *The March of Folly* (New York: Random House, 1984), 221.

10. John Arquilla and David Ronfeldt, *The Emergence of Noopolitik: Toward an American Information Strategy* (Santa Monica, CA: RAND, 1999), ix–xii.

11. Richard Armitage and Joseph S. Nye, "CSIS Commission on Smart Power: A Smarter, More Secure America" (Washington, DC: Center for Strategic and International Studies, 2007).

12. August Cole, "Defense Industry Pursues Gold in Smart Power Deals," *Wall Street Journal*, March 23, 2010.

13. Peter Morriss, *Power: A Philosophical Analysis*, 2nd ed. (Manchester, UK: Manchester University Press, 2002), 33–35.

14. Contextual intelligence is discussed at length in Chapter 5 of my book *The Powers to Lead* (Oxford, UK: Oxford University Press, 2008).

CHAPTER 1 WHAT IS POWER IN GLOBAL AFFAIRS?

1. For a classic exploration of this problem, see James G. March, "The Power of Power," in David Easton, ed., *Varieties of Political Theory* (Englewood Cliffs, NJ: Prentice-Hall, 1966), 39–70. Other classic articles on power by Robert Dahl, John C. Harsanyi, Hebert Simon, and others are collected in Roderick Bell, David V. Edwards, and R. Harrison Wagner, eds., *Political Power: A Reader in Theory and Research* (New York: Free Press, 1969).

2. Bertrand Russell, *Power: A New Social Analysis* (London: Allen and Unwin, 1938), quoted in Dacher Keltner, Cameron Anderson, and Deborah Gruenfeld, "Power, Approach, and Inhibition," *Psychological Review* 110 (2003): 265.

3. Ray S. Cline, *World Power Assessment* (Boulder, CO: Westview Press, 1977). For a canonical approach, see Hans J. Morgenthau, *Politics Among Nations: The Struggle for Power and Peace* (New York: Knopf, 1948).

4. Ashley Tellis, Janice Bially, Christopher Layne, Melissa McPherson, and Jerry Solinger, *Measuring National Power in the Postindustrial Age: Analyst's Handbook* (Santa Monica, CA: RAND, 2000).

5. A. J. P Taylor, *The Struggle for Mastery in Europe, 1848–1918* (Oxford, UK: Oxford University Press, 1954), xxix.

6. "In bargaining, weakness may be strength." Thomas C. Schelling, *The Strategy of Conflict* (Oxford, UK: Oxford University Press, 1960), 62.

7. Christian Oliver and Geoff Dyer, "Kim Holds Ace as Visit Shows Limits of Chinese Influence," *Financial Times*, May 8, 2010.

8. Stefano Guzzini argues that the dependence of power on theory means that "there is no single concept of power applicable to every type of explanation." Stefano Guzzini, "Structural Power: The Limits of Neo-realist Power Analysis," *International Organization* 47, no. 3 (Summer 1993): 446.

9. David A. Baldwin, "Power and International Relations," in Walter Carlsnaes, Thomas Risse, and Beth A. Simmons, eds., *Handbook of International Relations* (London: Sage, 2002), 179.

10. Kenneth E. Boulding uses both in *Three Faces of Power* (London: Sage, 1989), 15.

11. Power implies causation and is like the word "cause." When we speak of causation, we choose to pick out the relation between two items in a long and complex chain of events because we are interested in them more than the myriad other things that we might focus upon. We do not say in the abstract that "an event causes" without specifying what it causes.

12. Peter J. Katzenstein, ed., *Civilizations in World Politics: Plural and Pluralist Perspectives* (New York: Routledge, 2009).

13. As one economist put it, "One of the main purposes for which social scientists use the concept of A's power over B is for the description of the policy possibilities open to A." John Harsanyi, "The Dimension and Measurement of Social Power," reprinted in K. W. Rothschild, *Power in Economics* (Harmondsworth, UK: Penguin Books, 1971), 80.

14. Max Weber, *The Theory of Social and Economic Organization* (New York: Oxford University Press, 1947), 152.

15. Jack Nagel, *The Descriptive Analysis of Power* (New Haven, CT: Yale University Press, 1975), 14.

16. This general power is stressed by Susan Strange, *States and Markets* (New York: Blackwell, 1988).

17. On intentions and power, see Peter Morriss, *Power: A Philosophical Analysis*, 2nd ed. (Manchester, UK: Manchester University Press, 2002), 25–28. See also Baldwin, "Power and International Relations," 181. "There is no need for a fundamental reformulation of the concept of power in order to account for its unintended effects." For example, President Woodrow Wilson's ideas influenced rising anticolonial activism in Asia and the Middle East. This was unintended power in the broad sense of the capacity to make change, but not in the sense of achieving preferred

outcomes because Wilson was not interested in freeing Asian nations. See Erez Manela, *The Wilsonian Moment: Self-Determination and the International Origins of Anticolonial Nationalism* (New York: Oxford University Press, 2007).

18. Harold Lasswell and Abraham Kaplan, *Power and Society: A Framework for Political Inquiry* (New Haven, CT: Yale University Press, 1950).

19. It is worth noting that after fighting Russia at the beginning of World War II, Finland was cautious not to challenge the Soviet Union during the Cold War and was able to preserve its independence. Outcomes are not always all or nothing.

20. Philosophers such as Antony Kenny and Peter Morriss argue that reducing power to resources constitutes the "vehicle fallacy," but Keith Dowding contends that "the vehicle fallacy is not a fallacy if resources are measured relationally, for example, the power of money is relative to its distribution. It follows that strategic considerations must enter into the very essence of the concept of power." Keith Dowding, "Power, Capability, and Ableness: The Fallacy of the Vehicle Fallacy," *Contemporary Political Theory* 7 (2008): 238–258.

21. Baldwin, "Power and International Relations," 185–186, contests my statement but does not offer compelling evidence that would make me change it. In my experience in government, policymakers do tend to focus on resources.

22. Leslie Gelb, *Power Rules: How Common Sense Can Rescue American Foreign Policy* (New York: HarperCollins, 2009), 28.

23. Alan Axelrod, *Eisenhower and Leadership: Ike's Enduring Lessons in Total Victory Management* (San Francisco: Jossey-Bass, 2006), 120, 283.

24. Robert A. Dahl, *Who Governs: Democracy and Power in an American City* (New Haven, CT: Yale University Press, 1961).

25. Preferences and strategies are closely related. Preferences rank outcomes in a given environment, and a strategy is an actor's effort to come as close as possible to preferred outcomes in that setting. From an analytical point of view, preferences in one setting may become strategies in another. See Jeffry A. Frieden, "Actors and Preferences in International Relations," in David A. Lake and Robert Powell, eds., *Strategic Choice and International Relations* (Princeton, NJ: Princeton University Press, 1999), 41. Thus, in the gunman example, in the original setting A's preferences include both life and money, and his strategy is to keep both.

The gunman's threat changes the environment so that A must now rank his preferences and adopt a strategy of handing over his wallet. A's preferences do not change (life ranks over money), but when the gunman changes the environment, A has to change his strategy.

26. Peter Bachrach and Morton Baratz, "Decisions and Nondecisions: An Analytical Framework," *American Political Science Review* 57, no. 3 (September 1963): 632–642. William H. Riker has developed a somewhat similar concept that he calls "heresthetics," which "involves structuring the situation so that others accept it willingly." William H. Riker, "The Heresthetics of Constitution-Making: The Presidency in 1787, with Comments on Determinism and Rational Choice," *American Political Science Review* 78, no. 1 (March 1984): 8.

27. Steven Lukes, *Power: A Radical View*, 2nd ed. (London: Palgrave Macmillian, 2005).

28. As Lukes points out, my concept of soft power is similar but not identical to his third face of power. My concept includes voluntaristic dimensions of agenda-setting as well as preference-setting by attraction and persuasion. It is more concerned with the actions of agents and less concerned with the problematic concept of "false consciousness."

29. Lukes calls soft power "a cousin" of his concept of the third face of power. He is concerned, however, about distinguishing degrees of freedom or voluntarism. "Both the agent-centered, strategic view of Nye and the subject-centered structural view of Foucault lack this distinction. . . . We need to focus on both agents and subjects and ask the question: exactly how do agents succeed in winning the hearts and minds of those subject to their influence—by wielding power over them or by contributing to their empowerment?" Steven Lukes, "Power and the Battle for Hearts and Minds: On the Bluntness of Soft Power," in Felix Berenskoetter and M. J. Williams, eds., *Power in World Politics* (London: Routledge, 2007), 97.

30. "Humans are wired to form social bonds, and such scraps of kindness can deepen even a relationship built on manipulation and abuse. Some victims have profoundly ambivalent feelings toward abusive captors, psychologists say." Benedict Carey, "For Longtime Captive, a Complex Road Home," *New York Times*, September 1, 2009.

31. A French Muslim woman who objected to laws against veils complained, "Don't believe for a moment that I am submissive to my husband. I'm the one who takes care of the documents and the money."

Steven Erlanger, "Burqa Furor Scrambles the Political Debate in France," *New York Times*, September 1, 2009.

32. John Gaventa, "Levels, Spaces, and Forms of Power," in Berenskoetter and Williams, *Power in World Politics*, 206.

33. Clarissa Hayward, *De-facing Power* (Cambridge, UK: Cambridge University Press, 2000), 37.

34. Martin J. Smith, *Power and the State* (Basingstoke, UK: Palgrave Macmillan, 2009), 36.

35. Bob Woodward, *The Agenda: Inside the Clinton White House* (New York: Simon and Schuster, 1994), 139.

36. See Keith Dowding, "Agency and Structure: Interpreting Power Relationships," *Journal of Power Studies* 1, no. 1 (2008): 21–36.

37. The second and third faces of power incorporate structural causes such as institutions and culture but also leave room to focus on agents who make choices, albeit constrained by structural forces. Many power relations, like many markets, are imperfect in their structure and allow some voluntarism and choice for agents within the structures. Some writers have suggested a "fourth face" of power that would encompass primarily structural forces. For some purposes this can be fruitful, but it is less useful for understanding the policy options that leaders confront. Peter Digeser has used this term to refer to Michel Foucault's view that subjects and social practices are the effects of a power that one cannot escape, and knowledge presupposes power, but Digeser admits that "Foucault's use of power departs significantly from ordinary usage." Peter Digeser, "The Fourth Face of Power," *Journal of Politics* 54, no. 4 (November 1992): 990. See also Michael Barnett and Raymond Duvall, "Power in International Politics," *International Organization* 59, no. 1 (Winter 2005): 39–75, for an abstract fourfold typology that goes beyond the three faces of power categories. For my purposes, the insights that Foucault and other structuralists provide are purchased at too high a price in terms of conceptual complexity and clarity.

38. Baldwin, "Power and International Relations," 179.

39. In terms of the earlier example of the teenager choosing an attractive shirt, this can take the indirect form of shaping preferences (as in the advertisement example) or the direct form of using existing preferences to attract by wearing a stylish shirt.

40. Arnold Wolfers, *Discord and Collaboration: Essays on International Politics* (Baltimore, MD: Johns Hopkins University Press, 1962), 73–77.

41. Ronald Burt, *Structural Holes: The Social Structure of Competition* (Cambridge, MA: Harvard University Press, 1992), chap. 1.

42. Mark Granovetter, "The Myth of Social Network Analysis as a Special Method in the Social Sciences," *Connections* 13, no. 2 (1990): 13–16.

43. Boulding, *Three Faces of Power*, 109–110.

44. Dacher Keltner, "The Power Paradox," *Greater Good*, Winter 2007–2008, 15.

45. Hannah Arendt, *The Human Condition* (Chicago: University of Chicago Press, 1998), 200.

46. G. John Ikenberry, *Liberal Order and Imperial Ambition* (Cambridge, UK: Polity, 2006).

47. Anne Marie Slaughter, "America's Edge: Power in the Networked Century," *Foreign Affairs* 88, no. 1 (January–February 2009): 94–113.

48. I am indebted to Tyson Belanger for this point.

49. Leslie Gelb, *Power Rules*, 69.

50. At various times, in trying to explain soft power, I have shortened my formulation to statements such as "Soft power is attractive power," "Soft power is the ability to shape or reshape preferences without resort to force or payment," and "Soft power is the ability to get others to want what you want." These short forms are consistent with the longer, more formal definition of the concept.

51. The behaviors in the spectrum in Table 1.1 sometimes overlap, but they can be conceived in terms of the degree of voluntarism in B's behavior. In the middle of the spectrum, payment has a degree of voluntarism and agenda-setting can be affected by institutions and discourses that B may not fully accept. That aspect of agenda-setting is determined by hard power, but to the extent that hard power in one period can create in a later period institutions that limit the agenda but are widely regarded as legitimate, then agenda-setting is part of co-optive and soft power. The effect of World War II in changing power relations that set the framework for the postwar United Nations and Bretton Woods institutions is a case in point.

52. Baldwin and others have criticized my earlier discussion of tangibility. I should have made clearer that intangibility is not a *necessary* condition for soft power. I defined soft power in behavioral terms as the ability to affect others to obtain preferred outcomes by co-option and attraction rather than by coercion or payment, and I was careful to use language that suggested an imperfect relationship ("tend to be associated," "are usually associated") between soft power behavior and the intangibility of the resources that can produce it. But the criticism is justified, and that explains this restatement.

53. Admiral Gary Roughead, Chief of Naval Operations, General James T. Conway, Commandant of the Marine Corps, and Admiral Thad W. Allen, Commandant of the Coast Guard, *A Cooperative Strategy for 21st Century Seapower* (Washington, DC: U.S. Navy, October 2007), 3.

54. Niall Ferguson, "Think Again: Power," *Foreign Policy* 134 (January–February 2003): 18–22.

55. See Joseph S. Nye, *Soft Power: The Means to Success in World Politics* (New York: PublicAffairs, 2004), 32, 147. I am grateful to Fen Hampson for the term. Suzanne Nossel also deserves credit for using the term in "Smart Power," *Foreign Affairs* 83, no. 2 (March–April 2004): 131–142, but I was not aware of this until later.

56. Christopher Layne, "The Unbearable Lightness of Soft Power," in Inderjeet Parmer and Michael Cox, eds., *Soft Power and U.S. Foreign Policy* (London: Routledge, 2010), 67ff.

57. Angus Taverner, "The Military Use of Soft Power–Information Campaigns: The Challenge of Applications, Their Audiences, and Effects," in Parmar and Cox, *Soft Power and U.S. Foreign Policy*, 149.

58. "Why It Will Take So Long to Win," *The Economist*, February 23, 2006, www.economist.com/opinion/displaystory.cfm?story_id=E1_VV QRTTV.

CHAPTER 2 MILITARY POWER

1. Scholars agree on the decline in interstate wars, but disagree on whether intrastate conflicts have also declined since the early 1990s. Skeptics are critical of the definitions and coding practices used in major data projects. See Oyvind Osterud, "Towards a More Peaceful World? A Critical View," *Conflict, Security & Development* 8, no. 2 (June 2008): 223–240.

2. Thucydides, *History of the Peloponnesian War*, trans. Martin Hammonds (New York: Oxford University Press, 2009), liii.

3. Richard Wrangham and Dale Peterson, *Demonic Males: Apes and the Origins of Human Violence* (New York: Houghton Mifflin, 1996).

4. See the essays in Robert I. Rotberg and Theodore Raab, eds., *The Origin and Prevention of Major Wars* (Cambridge, UK: Cambridge University Press, 1989).

5. David Hume, "Of the First Principles of Government," in David Hume, *Essays Moral, Political and Literary*, ed. Eugene Miller (Indianapolis, IN: Liberty Classics, 1985), 32–33.

6. The fascinating case of Byzantium is described in Edward N. Luttwak, *The Grand Strategy of the Byzantine Empire* (Cambridge, MA: Harvard University Press, 2009).

7. See Brian C. Schmidt, "Realist Conceptions of Power," in Felix Berenskoetter and M. J. Williams, eds., *Power in World Politics* (London: Routledge, 2007), 43–63. See also Kenneth Waltz, "The Origins of War in Neo-Realist Theory," in Rotberg and Rabb, *The Origin and Prevention of Major Wars*.

8. See, for example, Michael Doyle, "Kant, Liberal Legacies, and Foreign Affairs," *Philosophy and Public Affairs* 12, no. 3 (Summer 1983): 205–235; John M. Owen, "How Liberalism Produces Democratic Peace," *International Security* 19, no. 2 (Fall 1994): 87–125; Sebastian Rosato, "The Flawed Logic of Democratic Peace Theory," *American Political Science Review* 97, no. 4 (November 2003): 585–602; and Bruce Russett, *Grasping the Democratic Peace: Principles for a Post–Cold War World* (Princeton, NJ: Princeton University Press, 1993). See also Robert Cooper, *The Post-Modern State and the World Order* (London: Demos, 2000).

9. See Edward D. Mansfield and Jack Snyder, *Electing to Fight: Why Emerging Democracies Go to War* (Cambridge, MA: MIT Press, 2005). See also Nils Petter Gleditsch, "The Liberal Moment Fifteen Years On," *International Studies Quarterly* 52, no. 4 (2008).

10. National Intelligence Council, "Global Trends 2025: A Transformed World" (Washington, DC: GPO, November 2008).

11. Nina Tannenwald, "Stigmatizing the Bomb: Origins of the Nuclear Taboo," *International Security* 29, no. 4 (2005): 5–49.

12. Graham Allison, "Nuclear Disorder: Surveying Atomic Threats," *Foreign Affairs* 89, no. 1 (January–February 2010): 74–85.

13. See Karl W. Deutsch, *Nationalism and Social Communication* (Cambridge, MA: MIT Press, 1953). See also Benedict Anderson, *Imagined Communities* (London: Verso, 1991).

14. Joseph Joffee, "Power Failure: Why Force Doesn't Buy Order," *American Interest*, July–August 2007, 50.

15. Robert Pape, *Dying to Win: The Strategic Logic of Suicide Terrorism* (New York: Random House, 2005). See also Robert Pape, "Dying to Kill Us," *New York Times*, September 22, 2003.

16. Peter Feaver and Christopher Gelpi, *Choosing Your Battles* (Princeton, NJ: Princeton University Press, 2004).

17. William S. Lind, Colonel Keith Nightengale, Captain John F. Schmidt, Colonel Joseph W. Sutton, and Lieutenant Colonel Gary I.

Wilson, "The Changing Face of War: Into the Fourth Generation," *Marine Corps Gazette*, October 1989, 22–26.

18. Colonel Thomas X. Hammes, *The Sling and the Stone: On War in the 21st Century* (St. Paul, MN: Zenith Press, 2004), 31.

19. Martin van Creveld, "Through a Glass Darkly: Some Reflections on the Future of War," *Naval War College Review* 53, no. 4 (Autumn 2000): 29.

20. John Mueller, *Retreat from Doomsday: The Obsolescence of Major War* (New York: Basic Books, 1989).

21. See Raymond Aron, *The Century of Total War* (Garden City, NY: Doubleday, 1954). See also Morton Halperin, *Limited War* (Cambridge, MA: Center for International Affairs, Harvard University, 1962).

22. Mikael Eriksson, Peter Wallensteen, and Margareta Sollenberg, "Armed Conflict, 1989–2002," *Journal of Peace Research* 5 (2003): 593–607.

23. Richard Schultz, Roy Godson, and Querine Hanlon, *Armed Groups and Irregular Warfare* (Washington, DC: National Strategy Information Center, 2009).

24. Rupert Smith, *The Utility of Force: The Art of War in the Modern Age* (New York: Random House, 2006), 5–6, 19–20.

25. F. G. Hoffman, "Hybrid Threats: Neither Omnipotent or Unbeatable," *Orbis* 54, 3 (Summer 2010): 443.

26. See Cori E. Dauber, *YouTube War: Fighting in a World of Cameras in Every Cell Phone and Photoshop on Every Computer* (Carlisle, PA: U.S. Army War College, 2009).

27. Patrick M. Cronin, ed., *America's Security Role in a Changing World: Global Strategic Assessment 2009* (Washington, DC: National Defense University Press, 2009), 157–158.

28. Colonel Qiao Liang, quoted in David Kilcullen, *The Accidental Guerilla: Fighting Small Wars in the Midst of a Big One* (Oxford, UK: Oxford University Press, 2009), 3.

29. The term comes from counterterrorism expert Michael Scheuer, quoted in Kilcullen, *The Accidental Guerilla*, 28.

30. "A Nation at War: Casualties," *New York Times*, March 31, 2003. Cited source is the U.S. Department of Defense.

31. Oddly, nuclear weapons do not make Boot's list, though van Crevald, "Through a Glass Darkly," places great emphasis on the effect of nuclear weapons on war.

32. Max Boot, *War Made New: Technology, Warfare, and the Course of History, 1500 to Today* (New York: Gotham Books, 2006), 455.

33. "Insurgents Hack U.S. Drones," *Wall Street Journal*, December 17, 2009.

34. P. W. Singer, *Wired for War: The Robotics Revolution and Conflict in the Twenty-First Century* (New York: Penguin Press, 2009).

35. See John Nagl, "Let's Win the Wars We're In," *Joint Force Quarterly* 52, no. 1 (2009): 20–26.

36. Sarah Sewall, "Introduction to the University of Chicago Press Edition," in *The U.S. Army/Marine Corps Counterinsurgency Field Manual* (Chicago: University of Chicago Press, 2007), xxvi–xxvii.

37. Thom Shanker, "Joint Chiefs Chairman Readjusts Principles on Use of Force," *New York Times*, March 4, 2010.

38. Yunus-Bek Yevkurov, quoted in Ellen Barry, "In Cauldron of Caucasus Region, Two Leaders Vie for the Loyalty of a Generation," *New York Times*, April 18, 2010.

39. Richard A. Oppel, Jr., "Tighter Rules Fail to Stem Deaths of Innocent Afghans at Checkpoints," *New York Times*, March 27, 2010.

40. See Allison Stanger, *One Nation Under Contract: Outsourcing of American Power and the Future of Foreign Policy* (New Haven, CT: Yale University Press, 2009).

41. Haider Mullick, "Beefing Up COIN-Lite in Afghanistan and Pakistan," *World Politics Review*, December 11, 2009.

42. David Gompert and John Gordon IV, *War by Other Means: Building Complete and Balanced Capabilities for Counterinsurgency* (Washington, DC: RAND/National Defense Research Institute, 2008), xxiv–xxv.

43. Christopher Paul, Colin P. Clarke, and Beth Grill, *Victory Has a Thousand Fathers: Sources of Success in Counterinsurgency* (Washington, DC: RAND/National Defense Research Institute, 2010), xvi. See also John Mackinlay and Alison Al-Baddawy, *Rethinking Counterinsurgency* (Washington, DC: RAND/National Defense Research Institute, 2008).

44. Gian P. Gentile, "A (Slightly) Better War: A Narrative and Its Defects," *World Affairs* 171, no. 1 (Summer 2008): 61.

45. Kilcullen, *The Accidental Guerilla*, 268.

46. Michele Flournoy, quoted in Thom Shanker, "Pentagon to Outline Shift in War Planning Strategy," *New York Times*, June 23, 2009.

47. U.S. Department of Defense, *Quadrennial Defense Review Report* (Washington, DC: U.S. Department of Defense, February 2010).

48. Army Capstone Concept Team, presentation at Harvard Kennedy School, Cambridge, Massachusetts, November 10, 2009. H. R. McMaster, quoted in Sydney J. Freedberg, Jr., "The Army Looks Beyond Afghanistan," *National Journal*, December 12, 2009, 39.

49. Robert M. Gates, "A Balanced Strategy: Reprogramming the Pentagon for a New Age," *Foreign Affairs* 88, no. 1 (January–February 2009): 28–40.

50. Ashley Tellis, Janice Bially, Christopher Layne, Melissa McPherson, and Jerry Sollinger, *Measuring National Power in the Postindustrial Age: Analyst's Handbook* (Santa Monica, CA: RAND, 2000), 26, 39.

51. Stephen Biddle, *Military Power: Explaining Victory and Defeat in Modern Battle* (Princeton, NJ: Princeton University Press, 2004), 6.

52. This is not always the case. Japan attacked the United States in 1941 despite an inferiority in resources because Japan felt it had no alternative given the American oil embargo.

53. Richard Halloran, "Strategic Communication," *Parameters* (Fall 2007): 4. I am indebted to Colonel Debra Sinnott for reminding me of this exchange.

54. Biddle, *Military Power*, 192.

55. Allen Buchanan and Robert O. Keohane, "The Legitimacy of Global Governance Institutions," *Ethics and International Affairs* 20, no. 4 (2006): 409.

56. Thom Shanker, "Top U.S. Commander Sees Progress in Afghanistan," *New York Times*, February 5, 2010.

57. Kim Gamel, "Afghanistan Needs More Than Military Force, Petraeus Says," *Atlanta Journal-Constitution*, September 15, 2008.

58. Joseph Berger, "U.S. Commander Describes Marja Battle as First Salvo in Campaign," *New York Times*, February 22, 2010.

59. Alissa J. Rubin, "Taliban Overhaul Image to Win Allies," *New York Times*, January 21, 2010.

60. Kilcullen, *The Accidental Guerilla*, 14.

61. The outcome was actually more complex than the public relations costs imply. Edward Luttwak argues that Israel was able to further deter Hezbollah attacks. See Edward Luttwak, "In Praise of Aerial Bombing," *Foreign Policy* 178 (March–April 2010), 69.

62. Sarah Sewall, "Leading Warriors in the Long War," in Robert Taylor, William E. Rosenbach, and Eric B. Rosenbach, eds., *Military Leadership in Pursuit of Excellence* (Boulder, CO: Westview Press, 2009), 121–123.

63. Kilcullen, *The Accidental Guerilla*, 24.

64. Barry Blechman and Stephen Kaplan, *Force Without War* (Washington, DC: Brookings Institution, 1978), chap. 4.

65. Rowan Callick, "China's Netizens Menace Vietnam," *The Australian*, September 11, 2008.

66. "Disquiet on the Eastern Front," *The Economist*, November 28, 2009, 60.

67. Rachel Bronson, *Thicker Than Oil: America's Uneasy Partnership with Saudi Arabia* (New York: Oxford University Press, 2006).

68. General Charles C. Krulak, "The Strategic Corporal: Leadership in the Three Block War," *Marines Magazine*, January 1999, 28–34.

69. Admiral Gary Roughead, Chief of Naval Operations, General James T. Conway, Commandant of the Marine Corps, and Admiral Thad W. Allen, Commandant of the Coast Guard, *A Cooperative Strategy for 21st Century Seapower* (Washington, DC: U.S. Navy, October 2007).

70. We could add to this mix other modalities, such as nation-building and the overthrowing of tyrannies.

71. Office of the Press Secretary, "Remarks by the President at the Acceptance of the Nobel Peace Prize," December 10, 2009, www.white house.gov/the-press-office/remarks-president-acceptance-nobel-peace -prize.

72. David Baldwin, *Paradoxes of Power* (New York: Basil Blackwell, 1989), 151.

73. Robert J. Art, "The Fungibility of Force," in Robert J. Art and Kenneth N. Waltz, eds., *The Use of Force: Military Power and International Politics* (Lanham, MD: Rowman and Littlefield, 2004), 9.

CHAPTER 3 ECONOMIC POWER

1. Richard N. Rosecrance, *The Rise of the Trading State* (New York: Basic Books, 1986), 16, 160.

2. Ronald Robinson, John Gallagher, and Alice Denny, *Africa and the Victorians: The Official Mind of Imperialism* (London: Macmillan, 1981).

3. Robert Gilpin, *U.S. Power and the Multinational Corporation* (New York: Basic Books, 1975), 24.

4. David A. Baldwin, *Economic Statecraft* (Princeton, NJ: Princeton University Press, 1985), 30–31.

5. Klaus Knorr, *The Power of Nations: The International Political Economy of International Relations* (New York: Basic Books, 1975), 80.

6. Robert Powell, "Absolute and Relative Gains in International Relations Theory," *American Political Science Review* 85, no. 4 (December 1991): 1303–1320; Joseph Grieco, "Anarchy and the Limits of Cooperation: A Realist Critique of the Newest Liberal Institutionalism," *International Organization* 4, no. 3 (Summer 1988): 485–507.

7. Charles P. Kindleberger, *Power and Money: The Politics of International Economics and the Economics of International Politics* (New York: Basic Books, 1970), 56.

8. Richard N. Cooper, "Can China Be Effectively Punished Through Global Economic Isolation?" in Richard N. Rosecrance and Arthur A. Stein, eds., *No More States? Globalization, National Self-Determination, and Terrorism* (New York: Rowman and Littlefield, 2006), 77–78.

9. John Kay, "The Fallacy of Equating Economic Power with Influence," *Financial Times*, March 25, 2009.

10. Baldwin lists eighteen examples of negative economic sanctions and twelve examples of positive sanctions affecting trade and capital. Baldwin, *Economic Statecraft*, 41–42.

11. Albert Hirschman, *National Power and the Structure of Foreign Trade* (Berkeley: University of California Press, 1945), describes Germany's strategy to control eastern and southeastern Europe in the 1930s as a classical study of this phenomenon.

12. This draws heavily on work done jointly with my friend Robert Keohane. See Robert O. Keohane and Joseph S. Nye, *Power and Interdependence: World Politics in Transition* (Boston: Little, Brown, 1977).

13. Yao Yang, "Smart Power Is What China Needs," *China Daily*, August 2, 2010, www.chinadaily.com.cn/usa/2010–08/02/cpmtemt_1108 2125.htm.

14. Bill Geertz, "Chinese See U.S. Debt as Weapon in Taiwan Dispute," *Washington Times*, February 10, 2010.

15. Jamil Anderlini, "China Still Keen to Buy US Bonds," *Financial Times*, March 10, 2010.

16. Daniel Drezner, "Bad Debts: Assessing China's Financial Influence in Great Power Politics," *International Security* 34 (Fall 2009): 7–45.

17. See Jonathan Kirshner, *Currency and Coercion: The Political Economy of International Monetary Power* (Princeton, NJ: Princeton University Press, 1995).

18. Ibid., 68ff.

19. Charles de Gaulle, quoted in Harold James, *The Creation and Destruction of Value: The Globalization Cycle* (Cambridge, MA: Harvard University Press, 2009), 206.

20. McKinsey & Company, "An Exorbitant Privilege? Implications of Reserve Currencies for Competitiveness," discussion paper, December 2009, http://root.transitionmonetaire.org/mtm/reserve_currencies_full _discussion_paper.pdf.

21. James, *The Creation and Destruction of Value*, 211.

22. Carla Norloff, *America's Global Advantage: US Hegemony and International Cooperation* (Cambridge, UK: Cambridge University Press, 2010), 172.

23. Kenneth Rogoff, "Europe Finds That the Old Rules Still Apply," *Financial Times*, May 6, 2010.

24. Richard N. Cooper, "The Future of the Dollar" (unpublished paper, May 2009). For alternative views, see Eric Helleiner and Jonathan Kirshner, eds., *The Future of the Dollar* (Ithaca, NY: Cornell University Press, 2009).

25. John Paul Rathbone, "Brics Balance Shared Interests with Rivalries," *Financial Times*, April 14, 2010.

26. For evidence, see Keohane and Nye, *Power and Interdependence*, chap. 7.

27. See Paul Collier, *The Bottom Billion: Why the Poorest Countries Are Failing and What Can Be Done About It* (Oxford, UK: Oxford University Press, 2007).

28. "Testing Their Metal," *The Economist*, October 24, 2009, 75.

29. David Barboza, "Chinese Court Hands Down Stiff Sentences to Four Mining Company Employees," *New York Times*, March 30, 2010.

30. For general background, see Daniel Yergin, *The Prize: The Epic Quest for Oil, Money, and Power* (New York: Simon and Schuster, 1991).

31. See Raymond Vernon, *Sovereignty at Bay: The Multinational Spread of U.S. Enterprises* (New York: Basic Books, 1971).

32. PetroStrategies, Inc., "World's Largest Oil and Gas Companies," www.petrostrategies.org/Links/Worlds_Largest_Oil_and_Gas_Companies_Sites.htm.

33. See Robert Stobaugh, "The Oil Companies in the Crisis," *Daedalus* 104 (Fall 1975): 179ff.

34. Rachel Bronson, *Thicker Than Oil: America's Uneasy Partnership with Saudi Arabia* (Oxford, UK: Oxford University Press, 2006), 120.

35. "Tilting to Moscow," *Financial Times*, April 27, 2010.

36. Bernard A. Gelb, "Russian Natural Gas: Regional Dependence" (Washington, DC: Congressional Research Service Report, January 2007), http://italy.usembassy.gov/pdf/other/RS22562.pdf.

37. Amy Myers Jaffee, "Shale Gas Will Rock the World," *Wall Street Journal*, May 10, 2010. See also "Gas Industry Special Report," *Financial Times*, May 26, 2010.

38. Thomas Schelling, "Promises," *Negotiations Journal*, April 1989, 117. I thank Tyson Belanger for bringing this anecdote to my attention.

39. Baldwin, *Economic Statecraft*, 41–42.

40. "Beijing Tightens Technology Noose," *Financial Times*, February 23, 2010.

41. Jamil Anderlini, "Frustrated Foreign Groups Rethink Their Positions," *Financial Times*, January 14, 2010.

42. Rose Gottemoeller, "The Evolution of Sanctions in Practice and Theory," *Survival* 49, no. 4 (Winter 2007–2008): 100.

43. Gary Clyde Hufbauer, Jeffrey J. Schott, and Kimberly Ann Elliott, *Economic Sanctions Reconsidered*, 2nd ed. (Washington, DC: Institute for International Economics, 1990).

44. See Robert A. Pape, "Why Economic Sanctions *Still* Do Not Work," *International Security* 23, no. 1 (Summer 1998): 67–77; and Kimberly Ann Elliott, "The Sanctions Glass: Half Full or Completely Empty?" *International Security* 23, no. 1 (Summer 1998): 50–65.

45. Baldwin, *Economic Statecraft*, 119, 174ff.

46. Meaghan O'Sullivan, *Shrewd Sanctions: Statecraft and State Sponsors of Terrorism* (Washington, DC: Brookings Institution Press, 2003), 288.

47. Francesco Giumelli, "Coercing, Constraining, and Signaling: Exploring the Purposes of UN and EU Sanctions" (paper presented at American Political Science Association, Toronto, Ontario, September 2009).

48. James Lindsay, "Trade Sanctions as Policy Instruments: A Reexamination," *International Studies Quarterly* 30, no. 2 (June 1986): 154.

49. Mark Landler and Nazila Fathi, "President of Iran Defends His Legitimacy" *New York Times*, September 4, 2009.

50. O'Sullivan, *Shrewd Sanctions*, 291–292. On Libya, see Ian Hurd, *After Anarchy: Legitimacy and Power in the United Nations Security Council* (Princeton, NJ: Princeton University Press, 2007), chap. 6.

51. See "Beats Shoveling Bird Droppings on Nauru," *New York Times*, December 19, 2009.

52. Sharon LaFraniere and John Grobler, "China Spreads Aid in Africa, with a Catch," *New York Times*, September 21, 2009. See also Simon Romero and Alexei Barrionuevo, "Deals Help China Expand Its Sway in Latin America," *New York Times*, April 16, 2009.

53. Adam Nossiter, "Defying Pariah Status, Guinea Boasts of a Deal with a Chinese Company," *New York Times*, October 14, 2009. The article goes on to say that "in Conakry, human rights campaigners had a different view, drawing a sharply unfavorable comparison between the Chinese approach and heavy American criticism of the junta."

54. "Crumbs from the BRICs-man's Table," *The Economist*, March 20, 2010, 68.

55. "Pentagon Taking over U.S. Foreign Policy," *Atlantic Free Press*, September 26, 2009, www.atlanticfreepress.com/news/1/11732-pentagon-taking-over-us-foreign-policy.html.

56. Jeffrey Sachs, *The End of Poverty: Economic Possibilities of Our Time* (New York: Penguin Books, 2005); William Easterly, *The White Man's Burden: Why the West's Efforts to Aid the Rest Have Done So Much Ill and So Little Good* (New York: Penguin Books, 2006). See also Collier, *The Bottom Billion*; and Jagdish Bhagwati, "Banned Aid: Why International Assistance Does Not Alleviate Poverty," *Foreign Affairs* 89, no. 1 (January–February 2010): 120–125.

57. Jeffrey Gittleman, "Shower of Aid Brings Flood of Progress," *New York Times*, March 9, 2010.

58. David Bearce and Daniel Tirone, "Foreign Aid Effectiveness and the Strategic Goals of Donor Governments," *Journal of Politics* 72, no. 3 (July 2010): 833–851.

59. Mark Landler, "Clinton Heads to Pakistan to Confront Rising Anti-Americanism," *New York Times*, October 28, 2009.

60. Sabrina Tavernise, "An Afghan Development Model: Small Is Better," *New York Times*, November 13, 2009. This view is confirmed by David Mansfield, Carr Center for Human Rights seminar, Harvard Kennedy School, Cambridge, Massachusetts, October 2009. For a more complete discussion, see Clare Lockhart, "Afghanistan: Framing the Context and Options for the Way Forward" (paper prepared for the Aspen Strategy Group, Aspen, Colorado, August 2010).

61. "The Rise of the Hybrid Company," *The Economist*, December 5, 2009, 78.

CHAPTER 4 SOFT POWER

1. Although I developed the concept in the context of a debate over American power at the end of the twentieth century, soft power is not restricted to states or to international relations or to modern times. Leaders in democratic societies have always relied on their power of attraction to get elected, and presidents of universities and other nonprofit organizations often find that their soft power is far greater than their hard power. For example, "the importance of soft power is now widely accepted in the analysis of international affairs. And it is becoming increasingly important in the world of philanthropy. Over time, soft power may very well eclipse the hard power of grants and other financial transactions. . . . The Gates and Ford foundations, and most other large philanthropies, have far more soft power at their disposal than the hard power

represented by their grant-making budgets." Sean Stannard-Stockton, "Philanthropists' Soft Power May Trump the Hard Pull of Purse Strings," *Chronicle of Philanthropy*, April 22, 2010, 33. I thank Brad Voigt for calling this article to my attention.

2. It is in the dimension of means that we might construct a normative preference for greater use of soft power, even if international relations cannot be based solely on reasoned persuasion. Ethical judgments have three dimensions: intentions, means, and consequences. Although soft power can be used with bad intentions and wreak horrible consequences, it does differ in terms of means. Power defined in behavioral terms is a relationship, and soft power depends more upon the target's role in that relationship than does hard power. Attraction depends upon what is happening in the mind of the subject. Even though there may be instances of coercive verbal manipulation, there are more degrees of freedom for the subject when the means involve soft power. I may have few degrees of freedom if the person with the gun demands my money or my life. I have even fewer degrees of freedom if he kills me and simply takes my wallet from my pocket. But to persuade me that he is a guru to whom I should donate my money leaves open a number of degrees of freedom as well as the possibility of other outside influences arising and influencing the power relationship. After all, minds can change over time, whereas the dead cannot be revived. See Joseph Nye, *The Powers to Lead* (Oxford, UK: Oxford University Press, 2008), chap. 5.

3. Joshua Cooper Ramo, *The Age of the Unthinkable* (New York: Little, Brown, 2009), 76–77.

4. Daniel Byman and Kenneth Pollack, "Let Us Now Praise Famous Men: Bringing the Statesman Back In," *International Security* 25, no. 4 (Spring 2001): 107.

5. Robert H. Wiebe, *The Search for Order, 1877–1920* (New York: Hill and Wang, 1967), 264.

6. For example, some critics portray the difference between hard and soft power as a contrast between realism and idealism. To them, "soft power is nothing more than a catchy term for the bundle of liberal international policies that have driven U.S. foreign policy since World War II and which are rooted in the Wilsonian tradition." But they are mistaken. Christopher Layne, "The Unbearable Lightness of Soft Power," in Inderjeet Parmar and Michael Cox, eds., *Soft Power and U.S. Foreign Policy* (London: Routledge, 2010), 73.

7. Kenneth Waltz, *Theory of International Politics* (Reading, MA: Addison-Wesley, 1979).

8. The term comes from Steven Lukes, *Power: A Radical View*, 2nd ed. (London: Palgrave Macmillan, 2005).

9. Alan Cowell, "Power of Celebrity at Work in Davos," *International Herald Tribune*, January 29, 2005.

10. Helene Cooper, "Darfur Collides with Olympics, and China Yields," *New York Times*, April 13, 2010.

11. John S. Dryzek, *Deliberative Global Politics: Discourse and Democracy in a Divided World* (Cambridge, UK: Polity Press, 2006), 82.

12. There are almost as many definitions of culture as power. A prominent one by Clifford Geertz defines culture as "an historically transmitted pattern of meanings embodied in symbols, a system of inherited conceptions expressed in symbolic forms by means of which men communicate, perpetuate, and develop their knowledge about and attitudes toward life." Clifford Geertz, *The Interpretation of Cultures* (New York: Basic Books, 1973), 89.

13. Norimitsu Onishi, "For China's Youth, Culture Made in South Korea," *New York Times*, January 2, 2006.

14. Qian Ning, quoted in Carol Atkinson, "Does Soft Power Matter? A Comparative Analysis of Student Exchange Programs 1980–2006," *Foreign Policy Analysis* 6, no. 1 (January 2010): 3.

15. Rasmus Bertelsen calls this "reverse soft power." Rasmus Bertelsen and Steffen Moller, "The Direct and Reverse Soft Power of American Missionary Universities in China and Their Legacies" (paper presented at the International Studies Association, New Orleans, Louisiana, February 21, 2010).

16. Martin Wolf, "Soft Power: The EU's Greatest Gift," *Financial Times*, February 2, 2005, 17.

17. Yanzhong Huang and Bates Gill, "Sources and Limits of Chinese 'Soft Power,'" *Survival* 48, no. 2 (June 2006): 17–36. See also Sheng Ding, *The Dragon's Hidden Wings: How China Rises with Its Soft Power* (Lanham, MD: Lexington Books, 2008).

18. "How to Improve China's Soft Power?" *People's Daily Online*, March 11, 2010, http://english.people.com.cn/90001/90785/6916487 .html.

19. Ingrid d'Hooghe, *The Limits of China's Soft Power in Europe: Beijing's Public Diplomacy Puzzle*, Clingendael Diplomacy Papers No. 25

(The Hague: Netherlands Institute of International Relations Clingendael, 2010).

20. Geraldo Zahran and Leonardo Ramos, "From Hegemony to Soft Power: Implications of a Conception Change," in Parmer and Cox, *Soft Power and U.S. Foreign Policy*, 12–31.

21. Janice Bially Mattern, "Why Soft Power Isn't So Soft: Representational Force and Attraction in World Politics," in Felix Berenskoetter and M. J. Williams, eds., *Power in World Politics* (London: Routledge, 2007), 98–119.

22. Steven Lukes, "Power and the Battle for Hearts and Minds: On the Bluntness of Soft Power," in Felix Berenskoetter and M. J. Williams, eds., *Power in World Politics* (London: Routledge, 2007), 83–97.

23. Tyler Cowen, "For Some Developing Countries, America's Popular Culture Is Resistable," *New York Times*, February 22, 2007.

24. Parama Sinha Palit, "China's Soft Power in South Asia," RSIS Working Paper 200 (Singapore: Rajaratnam School of International Studies, 2010), 1.

25. See Joseph Nye and Wang Jisi, "The Rise of China's Soft Power and Its Implications for the United States," in Richard Rosecrance and Gu Guoliang, eds., *Power and Restraint: A Shared Vision for the U.S.-China Relationship* (New York: PublicAffairs, 2009), 28.

26. David Shambaugh, *China Goes Global* (forthcoming), chap. 6, presents a very thorough account of China's efforts to increase its soft power.

27. Huang and Gill, "Sources and Limits of Chinese 'Soft Power.'" See also Joel Wuthnow, "The Concept of Soft Power in China's Strategic Discourse," *Issues and Studies* 44, no. 2 (June 2008): 2–24; and the essays in Mingjiang Li, ed., *Soft Power: China's Emerging Strategy in International Politics* (Lanham, MD: Lexington Books, 2009).

28. David Shambaugh, "China Flexes Its Soft Power," *International Herald Tribune*, June 7, 2010.

29. Joshua Kurlantzick, *Charm Offensive: How China's Soft Power Is Transforming the World* (New Haven, CT: Yale University Press, 2007).

30. Yee-Kuang Heng, "Mirror, Mirror on the Wall, Who Is the Softest of Them All? Evaluating Japanese and Chinese Strategies in the Soft Power Competition Era," *International Relations of the Asia-Pacific* 10 (2010): 298.

31. Toshi Yoshihara and James R. Holmes, "Chinese Soft Power in the Indian Ocean" (paper delivered at the American Political Science Association, Toronto, Ontario, September 3, 2009).

32. David Barboza, "China Yearns to Form Its Own Media Empires," *New York Times*, October 5, 2009.

33. Geoff Dyer, "China's Push for Soft Power Runs Up Against Hard Absolutes," *Financial Times*, January 4, 2010.

34. Chicago Council on Global Affairs, *Soft Power in Asia: Results of a 2008 Multinational Survey of Public Opinion* (Chicago: Chicago Council on Global Affairs, 2009), 34.

35. BBC News, "World Warming to US Under Obama," http://news .bbc.co.uk/1/hi/world/8626041.stm.

36. Jacques Hymans, "India's Soft Power and Vulnerability," *India Review* 8 (July–September 2009): 2344–2365.

37. Donna Byrne, Gerald Clore, and George Smeaton, "The Attraction Hypothesis: Do Similar Attitudes Affect Anything?" *Journal of Personality and Social Psychology* 51, no. 6 (1986): 1167–1170; Fang Fang Chen and Douglas Kenrick, "Repulsion or Attraction?: Group Membership and Assumed Attitude Similarity," *Journal of Personality and Social Psychology* 83, no. 1 (2002): 111–125; Alice Eagly, Richard Ashmore, Mona Makhijani, and Laura Longo, "What Is Beautiful Is Good, but . . . : A Meta-analytic Review of Research on the Physical Attractiveness Stereotype," *Psychological Bulletin* 110, no. 1 (1991): 109–128.

38. Alexander L. Vuving, "How Soft Power Works" (paper presented at the American Political Science Association, Toronto, Ontario, September 3, 2009), 7–8.

39. Robert O. Keohane, "Subversive Realism and the Problem of Persuasion" (paper delivered at Stanford University, Palo Alto, California, December 3–5, 2009).

40. See Richard E. Petty and Duane T. Wegener, "Thought Systems, Argument Quality, and Persuasion," *Advances in Social Cognition* 4 (1991): 147–162; Blain T. Johnson and Alice H. Eagly, "Effects of Involvement on Persuasion: A Meta-analysis," *Psychological Bulletin* 106, no. 2 (1989): 290–314.

41. "Obama Wins More Food Aid but Presses African Nations on Corruption," *New York Times*, July 10, 2009.

42. Alan B. Krueger, "Attitudes and Action: Public Opinion and the Occurrence of International Terrorism," CEPS Working Paper No. 179 (January 2009).

43. Layne, "The Unbearable Lightness of Soft Power," 57.

44. See Atkinson, "Does Soft Power Matter?" 3. See also Antonio Spilimbergo, "Democracy and Foreign Education," *American Economic Review* 99, no. 1 (March 2009): 528–543.

45. Julie Cencula Olberding and Douglas J. Olberding, "Ripple Effects in Youth Peacebuilding and Exchange Programs: Measuring Impacts Beyond Direct Participants," *International Studies Perspectives* 11 (2010): 75–91.

46. See Joseph Nye, *Soft Power: The Means to Success in World Politics* (New York: PublicAffairs, 2004), chap. 2.

47. Raymond Bonner and Jane Perlez, "British Report Criticizes U.S. Treatment of Terror Suspects," *New York Times*, July 28, 2007.

48. See Matthew Kroenig, Melissa McAdam, and Steven Weber, "Taking Soft Power Seriously" (unpublished paper, February 23, 2009), for a very interesting, though limited approach to causal inference.

49. Richard Pells, *Not Like Us* (New York: Basic Books, 1997), xxii.

50. Geir Lundestad, *Empire by Integration: The United States and European Integration, 1945–1997* (New York: Oxford University Press, 1998), 155.

51. Bertelsen and Moller, "The Direct and Reverse Soft Power of American Missionary Universities."

52. "Europe and an inscrutable China," *The Economist*, January 23, 2010, 52.

53. Testimony of Andrew Kohut, president of Pew Research Center, before the House Subcommittee on International Organizations, Human Rights, and Oversight, March 4, 2010.

54. Simon Anholt, "The $2 Trillion Man," *Foreign Policy* (December 2009). See also "Briefing Barack Obama's First Year," *The Economist*, January 16, 2010, 29.

55. Nicholas Kulish, "Obama Gets High Marks Abroad, Survey Finds," *New York Times*, June 17, 2010.

56. Testimony of Andrew Kohut.

57. Thomas Erdbrink, "Iranians Seek Out Abuses by US," *Washington Post*, August 24, 2009.

58. Clifford J. Levy, "Russia Prevailed on the Ground but Not in the Media," *New York Times*, August 22, 2008.

59. Inderjeet Parmar, "Challenging Elite Anti-Americanism in the Cold War," in Parmar and Cox, *Soft Power and U.S. Foreign Policy*, 115.

60. Emily Rosenberg, *Spreading the American Dream* (New York: Hill and Wang, 1981), 79, 100.

61. Herbert A. Simon, "Information 101: It's Not What You Know, It's How You Know It," *Journal for Quality and Participation*, July–August 1998, 30–33.

62. John Arquila and D. Ronfeldt, *The Emergence of Noopolitik: Toward an American Information Strategy* (Santa Monica, CA: RAND, 1999), ix–x.

63. "President Kikwete's Hard Road Ahead," *The Economist*, September 1, 2007, 45.

64. For a thorough survey of American public diplomacy, see Kennon Nakamura and Matthew Weed, *U.S. Public Diplomacy: Background and Current Issues* (Washington, DC: Congressional Research Service, 2009).

65. Mark Leonard, *Public Diplomacy* (London: Foreign Policy Center, 2002).

66. As one South African writer, Mark Gevisser, puts it, "We need the world to love us again, sometimes it seems, before we can love ourselves." Barry Bearak, "South Africa World Cup Hopes Extend Beyond Playing Field," *New York Times*, June 11, 2010.

67. Hans N. Tuch, *Communicating with the World: U.S. Public Diplomacy Overseas* (New York: St. Martin's Press, 1990), 162.

68. See Watanabe Yashushi and David L. McConnell, eds., *Soft Power Superpowers: Cultural and National Assets of Japan and the United States* (London: M. E. Sharpe, 2008).

69. Ambassador John Bolton interviewed on Fox News, December 24, 2009. See Ben Armbruster, "Bolton: Strike on Iran Is No Problem as Long as It's Accompanied by a 'Campaign of Public Diplomacy,'" Think Progress (Blog), December 23, 2009, http://thinkprogress.org/2009/12/23/bolton-iran-public-diplomacy.

70. Walter Pincus, "Pentagon Reviewing Strategic Information Operations," *Washington Post*, December 27, 2009.

71. Daryl Copeland, "Guerilla Diplomacy: The Revolution in Diplomatic Affairs," *World Politics Review*, December 25, 2009, www.worldpoliticsreview.com/article.aspx?id=4867.

72. R. S. Zaharna, "The Soft Power Differential: Network Communication and Mass Communication in Public Diplomacy," *The Hague Journal of Diplomacy* 2 (2007): 221.

73. Jan Melissen, ed., *The New Public Diplomacy: Soft Power in International Relations* (London: Palgrave Macmillan, 2005), 22–23.

74. Kathy R. Fitzpatrick, "Advancing the New Public Diplomacy: A Public Relations Perspective," *The Hague Journal of Diplomacy* 2 (2007): 203.

75. See, for example, Jesse Lichtenstein, "Digital Diplomacy," *New York Times Magazine*, July 18, 2010, 25–29.

76. Shambaugh, "China Flexes Its Soft Power."

CHAPTER 5 DIFFUSION AND CYBERPOWER

1. Richard Haass, "The Age of Nonpolarity," *Foreign Affairs* 87, no. 3 (May–June 2008): 47.

2. Timothy Garton Ash, "As Threats Multiply and Power Fragments, the 2010s Cry Out for Realistic Idealism," *The Guardian*, December 31, 2009.

3. Alvin Toffler and Heidi Toffler, *The Politics of the Third Wave* (Atlanta: Andrews and McMeel, 1995); Esther Dyson, *Release 2.1: A Design for Living in the Digital Age* (New York: Broadway Books, 1998).

4. "Data, Data, Everywhere: Special Report on Managing Information," *The Economist*, February 27, 2010, 4.

5. Pippa Norris, *The Digital Divide: Civic Engagement, Information Poverty, and the Internet Worldwide* (New York: Cambridge University Press, 2001), 232. (Given the indirect nature of packet routing, this comment obviously refers to human, rather than technical, intermediaries.)

6. Stephen Krasner, "Sovereignty," *Foreign Policy* 122 (January–February 2001): 24ff.

7. John G. Ruggie, "Territoriality and Beyond: Problematizing Modernity in International Relations," *International Organization* 47, no. 1 (Winter 1993): 143, 155.

8. Steve Lohr, "Global Strategy Stabilized IBM During Downturn," *New York Times*, April 20, 2010.

9. Jason DeParle, "A World on the Move," *New York Times*, June 27, 2010.

10. Walter Laqueur, "Left, Right, and Beyond: The Changing Face of Terror," in James F. Hogue and Gideon Rose, eds., *How Did This Happen? Terrorism and the New War* (New York: Council on Foreign Relations/PublicAffairs, 2001), 73.

11. See Ellen Nakashima, "For Cyberwarriors, Murky Terrain," *Washington Post*, March 19, 2010, for an illustration of the tension between law enforcement and intelligence.

12. Daniel T. Kuehl, "From Cyberspace to Cyberpower: Defining the Problem," in Franklin D. Kramer, Stuart Starr, and Larry K. Wentz, eds., *Cyberpower and National Security* (Washington, DC: National Defense University Press, 2009), 26–28.

13. Stuart H. Starr, "Toward a Preliminary Theory of Cyberpower," in Kramer, Starr, and Wentz, *Cyberpower and National Security*, 52.

14. See Jack Goldsmith and Tim Wu, *Who Controls the Internet? Illusions of a Borderless World* (Oxford, UK: Oxford University Press, 2006).

15. Martin Libicki distinguishes three layers: physical, syntactic, and semantic. Martin Libicki, *Cyberdeterrence and Cyberwar* (Santa Monica, CA: RAND, 2009), 12. However, with applications added upon applications, the Internet can be conceived in multiple layers. See Marjory Blumenthal and David D. Clark, "The Future of the Internet and Cyberpower," in Kramer, Starr, and Wentz, *Cyberpower and National Security*, 206ff.

16. I am indebted here to Jeffrey R. Cooper and his unpublished work "New Approaches to Cyber-Deterrence" (2010).

17. Ellen Nakashima and Brian Krebs, "Obama Says He Will Name National Cybersecurity Advisor," *Washington Post*, May 30, 2009.

18. See Gregory J. Rattray, "An Environmental Approach to Understanding Cyberpower," in Kramer, Starr, and Wentz, *Cyberpower and National Security*, 253–274, esp. 256.

19. Franklin Kramer, "Cyberpower and National Security," in Kramer, Starr, and Wentz, *Cyberpower and National Security*, 12.

20. LTC David E. A. Johnson and Steve Pettit, "Principles of the Defense for Cyber Networks," *Defense Concepts* 4, no. 2 (January 2010): 17.

21. Libicki, *Cyberdeterrence and Cyberwarfare*, xiii. See also William A. Owens, Kenneth W. Dam, and Herbert S. Lin, eds., *Technology, Policy, Law, and Ethics Regarding U.S. Acquisition and Use of Cyberattack Capabilities* (Washington, DC: National Academies Press, 2009).

22. It is estimated that the Conficker worm first developed in 2008 has been used to construct a Botnet with more than 6 million compromised computers. Mark Bowden, "The Enemy Within," *The Atlantic* 305, no. 5 (June 2010): 82.

23. Interviews with U.S. government officials, March 2010.

24. Goldsmith and Wu, *Who Controls the Internet?* 180ff.

25. "Don't Mess with Us," *The Economist*, January 2, 2010, 31.

26. Robert F. Worth, "Opposition in Iran Meets a Crossroads on Strategy," *New York Times*, February 15, 2010.

27. As documented by the Open Net Initiative. Richard Waters and Joseph Menn, "Closing the Frontier," *Financial Times*, March 29, 2010.

28. Ronald J. Deibert and Rafal Rohozinski, "Risking Security: Policies and Paradoxes of Cyberspace Security," *International Political Sociology* 4, no. 1 (March 2010): 25–27.

29. Sharon LaFraniere and Jonathan Ansfield, "Cyberspying Fears Help Fuel China's Drive to Curb Internet," *New York Times*, February 12, 2010.

30. See Goldsmith and Wu, *Who Controls the Internet?* 115; and Jonathan Zittrain, "A Fight over Freedom at Apple's Core," *Financial Times*, February 4, 2010.

31. Lawrence Lessig, *Code and Other Laws of Cyberspace* (New York: Basic Books, 1999).

32. Goldsmith and Wu, *Who Controls the Internet?* 165.

33. General Keith Alexander, head of Cyber Command, testimony to the Senate Armed Services Committee. "Attacks on Military Computers Cited," *New York Times*, April 16, 2010.

34. McAfee Report, "Unsecured Economies: Protecting Vital Information" (paper presented at the World Economic Forum, Davos, Switzerland, 2009). See also Tim Weber, "Cybercrime Threat Rising Sharply," *BBC News*, http://news.bbc.co.uk/2/hi/business/davos/7862549.stm. Franklin D. Kramer cites lower estimates under $400 billion in *Cyber Security: An Integrated Governmental Strategy for Progress* (Washington, DC: Atlantic Council Issue Brief, 2010), 2.

35. Munk Centre for International Studies, University of Toronto, "Tracking GhostNet: Investigating a Cyber Espionage Network," *Information Warfare Monitor*, March 2009.

36. Sharon LaFraniere and Jonathan Ansfield, "Cyberspying Fears Help Fuel China's Drive to Curb Internet," *New York Times*, February 12, 2010.

37. Stanley Pignal, "US Presses Brussels on Terror Data Swaps," *Financial Times*, February 3, 2010. See also Ellen Nakashima, "European Union, U.S. to Share Banking Data to Fight Terrorism," *Washington Post*, June 29, 2010.

38. See Owens, Dam, and Lin, *Technology, Policy, Law, and Ethics*.

39. Richard Clarke, "War from Cyberspace," *National Interest*, October 27, 2009, http://nationalinterest.org/article/war-from-cyberspace-3278.

40. See, for example, John Markoff, "Old Trick Threatens Newest Weapons," *New York Times*, October 27, 2009; and Shane Harris, "The Cyberwar Plan," *National Journal*, November 14, 2009, 18ff.

41. Richard A. Clarke and Robert K. Knake, *Cyberwar* (New York: HarperCollins, 2010), chap. 1.

42. See Owens, Dam, and Lin, *Technology, Policy, Law, and Ethics*, 27.

43. Interviews with U.S. government officials, March 2010.

44. Mike McConnell, "To Win the Cyberwar, Look to the Cold War," *Washington Post*, February 28, 2010.

45. "Clash of the Clouds," *The Economist*, October 17, 2009, 81.

46. See Tyler Moore and Richard Clayton, "The Impact of Incentives on Notice and Take-Down," Seventh Workshop on the Economics of In-

formation Security, June 2008, http://weis2008.econinfosec.org/Moore Impac.pdf.

47. Testimony of Steven R. Chabinsky before the Senate Judiciary Committee Subcommittee on Terrorism and Homeland Security, November 17, 2009.

48. Frederick R. Chang, "Is Your Computer Secure?" *Science* 325, no. 5940 (July 2009): 550.

49. Chris Bronk, "Toward Cyber Arms Control with Russia," *World Politics Review*, January 19, 2010.

50. McAfee, *Virtual Criminology Report 2009* (Santa Clara, CA: McAfee, 2009), 12.

51. Clay Wilson, "Cybercrime," in Kramer, Starr, and Wentz, *Cyberpower and National Security*, 428.

52. Irving Lachow, "Cyber Terrorism: Menace or Myth?" in Kramer, Starr, and Wentz, *Cyberpower and National Security*, 450.

53. Robert K. Knake, "Cyberterrorism Hype v. Fact," Council on Foreign Relations Expert Brief, February 16, 2010, www.cfr.org/publication/21434/cyberterrorism_hype_v_fact.html.

54. Mike McConnell, quoted in Jill R. Aitoro, "Terrorists Nearing Ability to Launch Big Cyberattacks Against the U.S," *Nextgov*, October 2, 2010, www.nextgov.com/site_services/print_article.php?StoryID=ng_20091002_9081.

55. Olivier Roy, "Recruiting Terrorists," *International Herald Tribune*, January 11, 2010.

56. McAfee, *Virtual Criminology Report 2009*, 6. See also Project Grey Goose, "Russia/Georgia Cyber War—Findings and Analysis," October 17, 2008, intelfusion@hush.com.

57. Michael B. Farrell, "Iranian Cyber Army Hack of Twitter Signals Cyberpolitics Era," *Christian Science Monitor*, December 18, 2009, www.csmonitor.com/layout/set/print/content/view/ print/269741.

58. See Kathrin Hille and Joseph Menn, "Patriotism and Politics Drive China Cyberwar," *Financial Times*, January 14, 2010; John A. Quelch, "Looking Behind Google's Stand in China," *Working Knowledge* (Harvard Business School), February 8, 2010, http://hbswk.hbs.edu/item/6364.html. I am also indebted to unpublished notes by Roger Hurwicz (February 2010).

59. Mark Landler and Edward Wong, "China Says Clinton Harms Relations with Criticism of Internet Censorship," *New York Times*, January 23, 2010.

60. David Barboza, "China's Booming Internet Giants May Be Stuck There," *New York Times*, March 24, 2010.

61. Kathrin Hille, "Google Attempts China Rescue," *Financial Times*, June 30, 2010.

62. Jack Goldsmith, "Can We Stop the Global Cyber Arms Race?" *Washington Post*, February 1, 2010.

63. John Markoff, "Cyberattack Threat on Rise, Executives Say," *New York Times*, January 29, 2010. I am indebted to Robert Sheldon for pointing out that the data refer to perceptions, not numbers, of intrusions.

64. For an analogous situation with regard to energy and climate issues, see Robert O. Keohane and David G. Victor, "The Regime Complex for Climate Change," Discussion Paper, Harvard Project on International Climate Agreements (Cambridge, MA: Belfer Center for Science and International Affairs, 2010).

65. The metaphor is from James A. Lewis. See also "Securing Cyberspace for the 44th Presidency: A Report of the CSIS Commission on Cybersecurity for the 44th Presidency" (Washington, DC: Center for Strategic International Studies, 2008).

66. See Elinor Ostrom, Joanna Burger, Christopher Field, Richard Norgaard, and David Policansky, "Revisiting the Commons: Local Lessons, Global Challenges," *Science* 284, no. 5412 (April 1999): 278, for a challenge to Garrett Hardin's 1968 formulation of "The Tragedy of the Commons," *Science* 162, no. 3859 (December 1968): 1243.

67. Elinor Ostrom, "A General Framework for Analyzing Sustainability of Social-Ecological Systems," *Science* 325, no. 5939 (July 2009): 421. See also Roger Hurwitz, "The Prospects for Regulating Cyberspace" (unpublished paper, November 2009).

68. Deibert and Rohozinski, "Risking Security," 30.

69. Ethan Zuckerman, "Intermediary Censorship," in Ronald Deibert, John Palfrey, Rafal Rohozinski, and Jonathan Zittrain, eds., *Access Controlled: The Shaping of Power, Rights, and Rule in Cyberspace* (Cambridge, MA: MIT Press, 2010), 80.

70. Clarke and Knake, *Cyberwar*, 146.

71. See Jonathan Zittrain, *The Future of the Internet and How to Stop It* (New Haven, CT: Yale University Press, 2008).

72. Quoted in Nathan Gardels, "Cyberwar: Former Intelligence Chief Says China Aims at America's Soft Underbelly," *New Perspectives Quarterly* 27 (Spring 2010): 16.

73. See Melissa Hathaway, "Strategic Advantage: Why America Should Care About Cybersecurity," Discussion Paper, Harvard Kennedy School (Cambridge, MA: Belfer Center for Science and International Affairs, 2009). See also Barack Obama, "Remarks by the President on Securing Our Nation's Cyber Infrastructure" (Washington, DC: White House, May 29, 2009).

74. William J. Lynn, III, "Defending a New Domain: The Pentagon's Cyberstrategy," *Foreign Affairs* 90, no. 5 (September–October 2010): 100.

75. See Clarke and Knake, *Cyberwar*, for a discussion of the limits of arms control and possible norms.

76. Christopher Ford, "Cyber-operations: Some Policy Challenges," report on a CSIS meeting, Washington, DC, June 3, 2010.

77. Joseph Menn, "Moscow Gets Tough on Cybercrime," *Financial Times*, March 22, 2010.

78. Robert Axelrod, *The Evolution of Cooperation* (New York: Basic Books, 1984). See also David Rand, Anna Drebner, Tore Ellingsen, Drew Fudenberg, and Martin Nowak, "Positive Interactions Promote Public Cooperation," *Science* 325, no. 5945 (September 2009): 1272.

79. Joseph Menn, "US Cybercrime Chief Wary on Provoking China and Russia," *Financial Times*, March 5, 2010.

80. For a description of the gradual evolution of such learning in the nuclear area, see Joseph S. Nye, "Nuclear Learning and U.S.-Soviet Security Regimes," *International Organization* 41, no. 3 (Summer 1987): 371–402.

81. See Abraham Sofaer, David Clark, and Whitfield Diffie, "Cyber Security and International Agreements," *Proceedings of a Workshop on Deterring Cyberattacks* (Washington, DC: National Academies Press, 2010).

82. John Markoff, "At Internet Conference, Signs of Agreement Appear Between U.S. and Russia, *New York Times*, April 16, 2010.

83. Duncan B. Hollis, "Why States Need an International Law for Information Operations," *Lewis and Clark Law Review* 11, no. 4 (2007): 1059.

84. Goldsmith, "Can We Stop the Global Cyber Arms Race?"

85. Waters and Menn, "Closing the Frontier."

86. Richard Falkenrath, "Texting with Terrorists," *New York Times*, August 9, 2010. See also Miguel Helft and Vikas Bajaj, "When Silence Sows Anxiety: Blackberry's Security Stance Throws Others Off Balance," *New York Times*, August 9, 2010.

CHAPTER 6 POWER TRANSITION:
THE QUESTION OF AMERICAN DECLINE

1. Robert Gilpin, *War and Change in World Politics* (New York: Cambridge University Press, 1981), 239.

2. Arthur Waldron, "How Not to Deal with China," *Commentary* 103, no. 3 (March 1997): 48; Robert Kagan, "What China Knows That We Don't," *Weekly Standard*, January 20, 1997, 22.

3. John Mearsheimer, "The Gathering Storm: China's Challenge to US Power in Asia," Michael Hintze Lecture, University of Sydney, Sydney, Australia, August 5, 2010, www.usyd.edu.au/news/84.html?newstoryid=5351.

4. Richard K. Betts and Thomas J. Christensen, "China: Getting the Questions Right," *National Interest*, Winter 2000–2001, 17.

5. Ernest May and Zhou Hong, "A Power Transition and Its Effects," in Richard Rosecrance and Gu Guliang, eds., *Power and Restraint* (New York: PublicAffairs, 2009), chap. 1.

6. See Jack S. Levy, "Declining Power and the Preventive Motivation for War," *World Politics* 40 (October 1987): 82–107.

7. Barry Blechman and Stephen Kaplan, *Force Without War: U.S. Armed Forces as a Political Instrument* (Washington, DC: Brookings Institution, 1978), chap. 4; Gary C. Hufbauer, Jeffrey J. Schott, and Kimberly Ann Elliott, *Economic Sanctions Reconsidered*, 2nd ed. (Washington, DC: Institute for International Economics, 1990).

8. Piers Brendon, "Like Rome Before the Fall? Not Yet," *New York Times*, February 25, 2010. For interesting comparisons of America and Rome, see Cullen Murphy, *Are We Rome? The Fall of an Empire and the Fate of America* (Boston: Houghton Mifflin, 2007).

9. See Paul Kennedy, *The Rise and Fall of the Great Powers: Economic Change and Military Conflict Among the Great Powers from 1500 to 2000* (New York: Random House, 1987), 154, 203. See also Bruce Russett, "The Mysterious Case of Vanishing Hegemony," *International Organization* 39, no. 12 (Spring 1985): 212.

10. Corelli Barnett, *The Collapse of British Power* (Atlantic Highlands, NJ: Humanities Press International, 1986), p. 72.

11. Charles Dickens, *Martin Chuzzlewit* (1844), quoted in David Whitman, *The Optimism Gap: The I'm OK–They're Not Syndrome and the Myth of American Decline* (New York: Walker, 1998), 85.

12. Some observers believe that "debating the stages of decline may be a waste of time—it is a precipitous and unexpected fall that should

most concern policy makers and citizens." Niall Ferguson argues that numbers indicating a doubling of public debt in the coming decade "cannot erode U.S. strength on their own, but they can work to weaken a long-assumed faith in the United States' ability to weather any crisis." He argues that "most imperial falls are associated with fiscal crises," but in fact the most common cause of sudden collapse is often war, as was the case of the Romanov, Austro-Hungarian, and Ottoman empires. Niall Ferguson, "Complexity and Collapse," *Foreign Affairs* 89, no. 2 (March–April 2010): 31.

13. For detail on the earlier cycles, see Joseph Nye, Jr., *Bound to Lead: The Changing Nature of American Power* (New York: Basic Books, 1990).

14. Stephen G. Brooks and William C. Wohlforth, *World Out of Balance: International Relations and the Challenge of American Primacy* (Princeton, NJ: Princeton University Press, 2008), 1.

15. Gideon Rachman, "All Eyes Are on Davos as a Shift in the Global Balance of Power Makes Itself Felt," *Financial Times*, January 27, 2010.

16. David Roche, "Another Empire Bites the Dust," *Far Eastern Economic Review* 171, no. 8 (October 2008): 11.

17. Brooks and Wohlforth, *World Out of Balance*, 4.

18. National Intelligence Council, *Global Trends 2025: A Transformed World* (Washington, DC: GPO, 2008), iv. In contrast, only four years earlier an estimate about 2020 forecast American preeminence.

19. Ralph Atkins, "State of the Union," *Financial Times*, June 1, 2010.

20. Pippa Norris, "Global Governance and Cosmopolitan Citizens," in Joseph S. Nye and John D. Donahue, eds., *Governance in a Globalizing World* (Washington, DC: Brookings Institution, 2000), 157.

21. Chris Patten, "What Is Europe to Do?" *New York Review of Books*, March 11, 2010, 12.

22. Marcus Walker, "EU Sees Dreams of Power Wane as 'G-2' Rises," *Wall Street Journal*, January 27, 2010.

23. "Lessons from 'The Leopard,'" *The Economist*, December 12, 2009, 61.

24. Stefan Theil, "The Modest Superpower," *Newsweek*, November 16, 2009, 41.

25. Mark Leonard, *Why Europe Will Run the 21st Century* (London: Fourth Estate, 2005), 2.

26. Andrew Moravcsik, "Europe: The Quiet Superpower," *French Politics* 7, no. 3 (September–December 2009): 406–407.

27. "Weathering the Storm," *The Economist*, September 9, 2000, 23.

28. Robert D. Blackwill, *The Future of Transatlantic Relations* (New York: Council on Foreign Relations, 1999).

29. Andrew Batson, "A Second Look at China's GDP Rank," *Wall Street Journal* (Asian edition), January 22–23, 2010. Purchasing parity comparisons are good for comparing welfare; exchange rate comparisons are better for estimating power in external relations. Each is valid for different purposes. In terms of purchasing power parity, China became the second largest national economy in 2001. In terms of exchange rate comparison, China's per capita GDP is in one-hundredth place.

30. Hiroko Tabuchi, "China's Day Arriving Sooner Than Japan Expected," *New York Times*, October 2, 2009.

31. "Hour of Power?" *Newsweek*, February 27, 1989, 15.

32. Jacques Attali, *Lignes d'Horizon* (Paris: Foyard, 1990); George Friedman and Meredith LeBard, *The Coming War with Japan* (New York: St. Martin's Press, 1992).

33. Herman Kahn and B. Bruce-Biggs, *Things to Come* (New York: Macmillan, 1972), ix.

34. They were questioned by some; see, for example, Bill Emmott, *The Sun Also Sets* (New York: Simon and Schuster, 1989).

35. Paul Bairoch, "International Industrialization Levels from 1750 to 1980," *Journal of European Economic History*, Spring 1982, 14n.

36. Prime Minister's Commission, *The Frontier Within* (Tokyo: Cabinet Secretariat, 2000).

37. Hisashi Owada, "The Shaping of World Public Order and the Role of Japan," *Japan Review of International Affairs*, Spring 2000, 11.

38. Department of Population Dynamics Research, National Institute of Population, "Summary of the Japanese Population Projection: Population Projections for Japan, 2001–2050" (2000), www.ipss.go.jp/pp-newest/e/ppfj02/suikei_g_e.html.

39. See Bill Emmott, *Rivals: How the Power Struggle Between China, India, and Japan Will Shape Our Next Decade* (New York: Harcourt, 2008).

40. "Not Just Straw Men," *The Economist*, June 20, 2009, 63.

41. Tyler Cowen, "For Much of the World, a Fruitful Decade," *New York Times*, January 3, 2010.

42. Ding Zhitao, "Bricking a Regime," *Beijing Review*, July 2, 2009, 2.

43. David Rothkopf, "A Bigger Clubhouse," *Newsweek*, November 15, 2008, 54.

44. Brendan Kelly, "The BRICs' Monetary Challenge," *PacNet* (Pacific Forum) 46 (June 25, 2009). See also Laurence Brahm, "China Thinks

the Washington Consensus Is Dead!" *PacNet* (Pacific Forum) 65 (September 29, 2009).

45. Jim O'Neill, "BRICS Are Still on Top," *Newsweek*, December 7, 2009, 44. See also Goldman Sachs, *Global Economics Weekly*, no. 10/01 (January 6, 2010).

46. Clive Cookson, "Huge Shift in Bric's Scientific Landscape," *Financial Times*, January 26, 2010.

47. Mikhail Gorbachev, speech to Soviet writers, quoted in "Gorbachev on the Future: 'We Will Not Give In,'" *New York Times*, December 22, 1986.

48. Eduard Shevardnadze, quoted in Stephen Sestanovich, "Gorbachev's Foreign Policy: A Diplomacy of Decline," *Problems of Communism*, January–February 1988, 2–3.

49. Sergei Karaganov, "Russia in Euro-Atlantic Region," *Rossiyskaya Gazeta*, November 24, 2009, available in English at http://karaganov.ru/en/news/98. An alternative view is that Russian soft power helped pave the way for a desired change of government in Kyrgyzstan in 2010. Andrew Kramer, "Before Kyrgyz Uprising, a Dose of Russian Soft Power," *New York Times*, April 19, 2010.

50. Murray Feshbach, "Russia's Population Meltdown," *Wilson Quarterly* 25, no. 1 (Winter 2001): 15–21; Nicholas Eberstadt, "Drunken Nation: Russia's Depopulation Bomb," *World Affairs*, Spring 2009, 53, 58.

51. Dmitri Medvedev, quoted in Anders Aslund, Sergei Guriev, and Andrew Kuchins, *Russia After the Global Economic Crisis* (Washington, DC: Peterson Institute for International Economics, 2010), 259.

52. Michael Wines, "For All of Russia, Biological Clock Is Running Out," *New York Times*, December 28, 2000.

53. Igor Yurgens, personal conversation, January 21, 2010.

54. Clifford J. Levy, "Russian President Calls for Nation to Modernize," *New York Times*, November 13, 2009.

55. Katinka Barysch, "Can the EU Help Russia Modernise?" *Centre for European Reform Insight*, May 28, 2020, 2.

56. Peter Aven, quoted in Charles Clover, "Caught Between Modernity and Chaos, Russia: Special Report," *Financial Times*, April 14, 2010.

57. Vladoslav Inozemtsev, "Dilemmas of Russia's Modernization," in Ivan Krastev, Mark Leonard, and Andrew Wilson, eds., *What Does Russia Think?* (London: European Council on Foreign Relations, 2010), 47. See also Jeffrey Mankoff, *The Russian Economic Crisis* (New York: Council on Foreign Relations, 2010).

58. Li Jingjie, "Pillars of the Sino-Russian Partnership," *Orbis*, Fall 2000, 530.

59. Karaganov, "Russia in Euro-Atlantic Region."

60. Bobo Lo, "Ten Things Everyone Should Know About the Sino-Russian Relationship" (London: Centre for European Reform Policy Brief, December 2008).

61. Dmitri Medvedev, quoted in John Lee, "Why Russia Still Matters in the Asian Century," *World Politics Review*, January 19, 2010, www.worldpoliticsreview.com/articlePrint.aspx?ID=4958.

62. Sarika Malhotra, "The World Will Become Tripolar Around 2040," *Financial Express*, March 7, 2010. Also based on personal conversations, New Delhi, January 2010.

63. Vijay Joshi, "Economic Resurgence, Lopsided Reform, and Jobless Growth," in Anthony Heath and Roger Jeffrey, eds., *Diversity and Change in Modern India: Economic, Social and Political Approaches* (Oxford, UK: Oxford University Press, 2010).

64. Martin Wolf, "India's Elephant Charges on Through the Economic Crisis," *Financial Times*, March 3, 2010.

65. Neal M. Rosendorf, "Social and Cultural Globalization: Concepts, History, and America's Role," in Nye and Donahue, *Governance in a Globalizing World*, 122.

66. Joshi, "Economic Resurgence."

67. "The Engineering Gap," *The Economist*, January 30, 2010, 76.

68. Cookson, "Huge Shift in Bric's Scientific Landscape." See also Richard Levin, "Top of the Class," *Foreign Affairs* 89, no. 3 (May–June 2010): 63–75.

69. See Tarun Khanna, *Billions of Entrepreneurs: How China and India Are Reshaping Their Futures—and Yours* (New Delhi: Viking/Penguin, 2007).

70. Interviews with Indian government officials, New Delhi, January 2010.

71. Fernando Enrique Cardoso attributes the cliché to Stefan Zweig. See Fernando Enrique Cardoso, *The Accidental President of Brazil: A Memoir* (New York: PublicAffairs, 2006), 6.

72. Interview with Luiz Ignacio Lula da Silva, "No More Second Class," *Newsweek*, October 12, 2009, 50.

73. "Brazil Takes Off," *The Economist*, November 14, 2009, 15.

74. Jonathan Wheatley, "Size of State's Role Emerges as Key Factor in Brazil Election Battle," *Financial Times*, February 24, 2010.

75. "Getting It Together at Last: A Special Report on Business and Finance in Brazil," *The Economist*, November 14, 2009, 5, 18.

76. Interviews, Sao Paulo, April 9, 2010.

77. Mac Margolis, "The Land of Less Contrast: How Brazil Reined In Inequality," *Newsweek*, December 7, 2009, 22. See also "Getting It Together at Last," 16.

78. "In Lula's Footsteps," *The Economist*, July 3, 2010, 36.

79. Alexei Barrionuevo, "Brazil's President Elbows U.S. on the Diplomatic Stage," *New York Times*, January 23, 2009.

80. "The Samba Beat, with Missteps," *The Economist*, December 20, 2008, 57.

81. Sebastian Mallaby, "Brazil's China Headache," *Washington Post*, December 14, 2009.

82. Robert Fogel, "$123,000,000,000,000," *Foreign Policy* 177 (January–February 2010): 70.

83. Barbara Demick, "China Won't Bow Down," *Los Angeles Times*, February 16, 2010.

84. Michael Brown et al., *The Rise of China* (Cambridge, MA: MIT Press, 2000).

85. Martin Jacques, *When China Rules the World: The End of the Western World and the Birth of a New Global Order* (New York: Penguin, 2009).

86. "American Opinion," *Wall Street Journal*, September 16, 1999.

87. Ingrid d'Hooghe, *The Limits of China's Soft Power in Europe: Beijing's Public Diplomacy Puzzle* (The Hague: Netherlands Institute of International Relations, 2010).

88. Thucydides, *History of the Peloponnesian War*, trans. Martin Hammonds (New York: Oxford University Press, 2009), 62.

89. Media Eghbal, "Chinese Economy Smaller Than Previously Estimated," *Euromonitor* (International Monetary Fund), February 11, 2008, www.euromonitor.com/Articles.aspx?folder=Chinese_economy_smaller_than_previously_estimated&print=true.

90. Sam Roberts, "In 2025, India to Pass China in Population, U.S. Estimates," *New York Times*, December 16, 2009.

91. Figures were calculated using data from *CIA World Fact Book 2000* (www.cia.gov/cia/publications/factbook/) for purchasing power parities and the World Bank (www.worldbank.org/data/wdi2001/pdfs/tab1_1.pdf) for official exchange rates.

92. Aaron Friedberg, "The Future of U.S.-China Relations: Is Conflict Inevitable?" *International Security* 30, no. 2 (Fall 2005): 7–45.

93. "A Slow-Burning Fuse: A Special Report on Ageing Populations," *The Economist*, June 27, 2009, 14.

94. Robert Zoellick, quoted in "Can China Become the World's Engine for Growth?" A Symposium of Fifty Views, *International Economy*, Winter 2010, 9.

95. "Agricultural Bank's IPO: Agricultural Revolution," *The Economist*, July 10, 2010, 69.

96. Michael Pettis, "China Has Been Misread by Bulls and Bears Alike," *Financial Times*, February 26, 2010. See also Michael Pettis, "Sharing the Pain: The Global Struggle over Savings," Policy Brief 84 (Washington, DC: Carnegie Endowment, November 2009).

97. Geoff Dyer, "Beijing Has a Long Way to Go Before It Can Dislodge the Dollar," *Financial Times*, May 22, 2009.

98. Ambassador Charles W. Freeman, Jr., "China's Challenge to American Hegemony," Remarks to the Global Strategy Forum, January 20, 2010.

99. Henry Rowen, quoted in "A Wary Respect: Special Report on China and America," *The Economist*, October 24, 2009, 14.

100. Lee Kwan Yew, personal conversation, January 22, 2010.

101. Minxin Pei, "Think Again: Asia's Rise," *Foreign Policy* 173 (July–August 2009).

102. Susan L. Shirk, *China: Fragile Superpower* (Oxford, UK: Oxford University Press, 2008), 253.

103. Bill Clinton, quoted in "A Wary Respect," 16.

104. Thom Shanker, "Pentagon Cites Concerns in China Military Growth," *New York Times*, August 17, 2010.

105. Keith Crane, Roger Cliff, Evan S. Medeiros, James C. Mulvenon, and William H. Overholt, *Modernizing China's Military: Opportunities and Constraints* (Washington, DC: RAND, 2005).

106. Kenneth Lieberthal, quoted in Bruce Stokes, "China's New Red Line at Sea," *National Journal*, July 3, 2010, 43. See also Andrew Jacobs, "Stay Out of Island Dispute, Chinese Warn U.S.," *New York Times*, July 27, 2010.

107. Edward Wong, "Chinese Military Seeks to Extend Its Naval Power," *New York Times*, April 24, 2010.

108. Deng Xiaoping, quoted in C. Fred Bergsten, Charles Freeman, Nicholas Lardy, and Derek J. Mitchell, *China's Rise: Challenges and Opportunities* (Washington, DC: Peterson Institute, 2008), 1.

109. Jacques, *When China Rules the World*, 12.

110. David C. Kang, "Hierarchy in Asian International Relations: 1300–1900," *Asian Security* 1, no. 1 (2005): 53–79. See also Stefan Halper, *The Beijing Consensus: How China's Authoritarian Model Will Dominate the Twenty-First Century* (New York: Basic Books, 2010).

111. John Ikenberry, "The Rise of China and the Future of the West," *Foreign Affairs* 87, no. 1 (January–February 2008): 23–38.

112. Lee Kwan Yew, personal conversation, January 2010.

113. Kagan, "What China Knows That We Don't."

114. Edward Wong, "Vietnam Enlists Allies to Stave Off China's Reach," *New York Times*, February 5, 2010; also based on personal interviews with Vietnamese officials, Hanoi, January 13–14, 2010.

115. Zixiao Yang and David Zweig, "Does Anti-Americanism Correlate to Pro-China Sentiments?" *Chinese Journal of International Politics* 2 (2009): 457–486.

116. For a detailed analysis, see Bill Emmott, *Rivals: How the Power Struggle Between China, India, and Japan Will Shape Our Next Decade* (New York: Harcourt, 2008).

117. Kennedy, *The Rise and Fall of the Great Powers.*

118. Of course, there were many more causes of this complex phenomenon. See Ramsay MacMullen, *Corruption and the Decline of Rome* (New Haven, CT: Yale University Press, 1988).

119. Frank Newport, "No Evidence Bad Times Are Boosting Church Attendance," *Gallup*, December 17, 2008.

120. "A Public Opinion Review of the Bush Years," *Gallup*, January 12, 2009.

121. Derek Bok, *The State of the Nation* (Cambridge, MA: Harvard University Press, 1996), 376.

122. U.S. Census Bureau, "The Foreign Born Population of the United States," August 2004, www.census.gov/prod/2004pubs/p20–555 .pdf.

123. Kenneth Scheve and Matthew Slaughter, *Globalization and the Perceptions of American Workers* (Washington, DC: Institute for International Economics, 2001), 35.

124. Lymari Morales, "Americans Return to Tougher Immigration Stance," *Gallup*, August 5, 2009.

125. Eric Schmitt, "New Census Shows Hispanics Are Even with Blacks in US," *New York Times*, March 8, 2001.

126. Steven Holmes, "Census Sees a Profound Ethnic Shift in U.S.," *New York Times*, March 14, 1996, 16.

127. Nicholas Eberstadt, "The Population Implosion," *Foreign Policy* 123 (March–April 2001): 43–49.

128. Marjolaine Gauthier-Loiselle and Jennifer Hunt, "How Much Does Immigration Boost Innovation?" (London: Centre for Economic Policy Research, January 2009), www.cepr.org/pubs/new-dps/dplist.asp ?dpno=7116. See also William Kerr and William Lincoln, "The Supply Side of Innovation: H-1B Visa Reforms and US Ethnic Invention," Working Paper (Cambridge, MA: Harvard Business School, January 21, 2009).

129. Public Policy Institute of California, "Silicon Valley's Skilled Immigrants: Generating Jobs and Wealth for California," *Research Brief* 21 (June 1999): 2. See also Elizabeth Corcoran, "Silicon Valley's Immigration Problem," *Forbes*, May 3, 2007.

130. Lew Kwan Yew, personal conversation, January 22, 2010.

131. International Monetary Fund, *United States: Selected Issues* (Washington, DC: International Monetary Fund, July 2009), 3; Martin Feldstein, "America's Growth in the Decade Ahead," *Project Syndicate*, January 25, 2010. See also Alan Beattie, "IMF Warns US to Tighten Fiscal Policy More Rapidly," *Financial Times*, June 30, 2010.

132. "Can America Compete?" *BusinessWeek*, April 20, 1987, 45.

133. Xavier Sala-i-Martin and Jennifer Blanke, *The Global Competitiveness Report 2009–10* (Davos, Switzerland: World Economic Forum, 2009). The United States remained high on most "pillars" of growth, such as institutions, infrastructure, market size, and technological readiness, but dropped from its first-place position the previous year because of macroeconomic instability.

134. Adam Segal, *Advantage: How American Innovation Can Overcome the Asian Challenge* (New York: Norton, 2011), 247.

135. Amar Bhide of Columbia Business School, quoted in "Innovation in America: A Gathering Storm?" *The Economist*, November 22, 2008, 73.

136. Dale W. Jorgenson, "Innovation and Productivity Growth," Theodore Schultz Lecture, Atlanta, Georgia, January 3, 2010, 1–2. See also Dale W. Jorgenson, ed., *The Economics of Productivity* (Cheltenham, UK: Elgar, 2009).

137. Stephen Oliner, Daniel Sichel, and Kevin Stiroh, "Explaining a Productive Decade," in *Finance and Economics Discussion Series* (Washington, DC: Federal Reserve Board, 2007), 4–6. See also "Productivity Growth: Slash and Earn," *The Economist*, March 20, 2010, 75.

138. Alice Lipowicz, "U.S. Investment in Global Research and Development Falls," *Federal Computer Week*, January 19, 2010.

139. Michael Porter, "Why America Needs an Economic Strategy," *BusinessWeek*, October 30, 2008.

140. Fareed Zakaria, "Is America Losing Its Mojo?" *Newsweek*, November 23, 2009; Claire Cain Miller, "A $3.5 Billion Effort, Fearful the US Is Slipping, Aims to Help Tech Start-Ups," *New York Times*, February 24, 2010; "The United States of Entrepreneurs: Special Report on Entrepreneurship," *The Economist*, March 14, 2009, 9. See also ibid.

141. Roger Lowenstein, "The Way We Live Now: Should We Spend or Save to Rescue the Economy?" *New York Times*, October 14, 2009. For a more optimistic view of American savings, see Richard N. Cooper, "Global Imbalances: Globalization, Demography, and Sustainability," *Journal of Economic Perspectives* 22 (Summer 2008): 95.

142. Sylvia Nasar, "Economists Simply Shrug as Savings Rate Declines," *New York Times*, December 21, 1998. Harvard economist Richard N. Cooper points out that national accounts designed over sixty years ago in the industrial age are defined largely in terms of structures and equipment and do not include in savings such items of deferred consumption as education, research and development, training, and consumer durables. Richard N. Cooper, "Remarks for Yale Workshop on Global Trends and Challenges: Understanding Global Imbalances" (unpublished paper, January 2009).

143. Milka Kirova and Robert Lipsey, "Measuring Real Investment: Trends in the United States and International Comparisons" (Washington, DC: Federal Reserve, National Bureau of Economic Research, February 1998), 7.

144. Niall Ferguson, "An Empire at Risk," *Newsweek*, December 7, 2009, 28; Niall Ferguson, "A Greek Crisis Is Coming to America," *Financial Times*, February 11, 2010. See also Francis Warnock, "How Dangerous Is U.S. Government Debt? The Risk of a Sudden Spike in U.S. Interest Rates," *Council on Foreign Relations Report*, June 2010; www.cfr.org/publication/22408/how_dangerous_is_us_government_debt.html?excer.

145. "Repent at Leisure: A Special Report on Debt," *The Economist*, June 26, 2010, 14.

146. "Damage Assessment," *The Economist*, May 16, 2009, 84. See also C. Fred Bergsten, "The Dollar and the Deficits," *Foreign Affairs* 88, no. 6 (November–December 2009): 20–38.

147. U.S. Department of Education, "Educational Attainment of Persons 18 Years Old and Over, by State: 2000 and 2006," http://nces.ed.gov/programs/digest/d08/tables/dt08_011.asp.

148. "Universities in Europe," *The Economist*, April 25, 2009, 57.

149. Times Higher Education, "Top 200 World Universities (2009)," www.timeshighereducation.co.uk/Rankings2009-Top200.html; Institute of Higher Education of Shanghai Jiao Tong University, "Academic Ranking of the World Universities—2009," www.arwu.org/ARWU2009.jsp.

150. *The Economist: World in Figures (2009 Edition)* (London: Profile Books, 2008), 99; *World Bank Indicators 2008* (Washington, DC: World Bank, 2008), 314; "A Special Report on Managing Information," *The Economist*, February 27, 2010, 18.

151. White House, *The Economic Report of the President* (Washington, DC: GPO, 2009), 218. There was an improvement over the decade. See U.S. Department of Education, National Center for Educational Statistics, *The Condition of Education 2000* (Washington, DC: GPO, 2000).

152. Sam Dillon, "Many Nations Passing US in Education, Expert Says," *New York Times*, March 10, 2010.

153. Tamar Lewin, "Once in First Place, Americans Now Lag in Attaining College Degrees," *New York Times*, July 23, 2010.

154. White House, *The Economic Report of the President*, 236.

155. U.S. Census Bureau, "The Changing Shape of the Nation's Income Distribution," *Current Population Reports* (June 2000): 1, 10.

156. James Fallows, "How America Can Rise Again," *The Atlantic*, January–February 2010, 48.

157. Henry Kissinger, "America at the Apex," *National Interest*, Summer 2001, 15.

158. NBC/*Wall Street Journal* poll, cited in David Brooks, "The Tea Party Teens," *New York Times*, January 5, 2010; Pew Research Center Publications, "Distrust, Discontent, Anger, and Partisan Rancor," April 18, 2010.

159. William Galston, "In Government America Must Trust," *Financial Times*, March 4, 2010.

160. *Washington Post*/Kaiser Family Foundation/Harvard University Survey Project, 1996; Harris Poll, 1996; and Hart-Teeter Poll for the Council of Excellence in Government, reported in the *Washington Post*, March 24, 1997. See also Seymour Martin Lipset and William Schneider, *The Confidence Gap* (Baltimore, MD: Johns Hopkins University Press, 1987); and Jeffrey Jones, "Trust in Government Remains Low," *Gallup*, September 18, 2008.

161. Harris Poll, 1966–1996. "The Harris Poll Annual Confidence Index Rises 10 Points," *Business Wire*, March 5, 2009.

162. Rasmussen Reports, "80% Say U.S. Is Best Place to Live; 41% Say U.S. Lacks Liberty and Justice for All," July 3, 2008; "62% Say Constitution

Should Be Left Alone," July 1, 2010. See also Joseph S. Nye, Philip Zelikow, and David King, eds., *Why People Don't Trust Government* (Cambridge, MA: Harvard University Press, 1996).

163. U.S. Department of the Treasury, *Update on Reducing the Federal Tax Gap and Improving Voluntary Compliance* (Washington, DC: U.S. Department of the Treasury, July 8, 2009), www.irs.gov/pub/newsroom/tax_gap_report_-final_version.pdf.

164. World Bank, *Governance Matters 2009: Worldwide Governance Indicators, 1996–2008* (Washington, DC: World Bank, 2009).

165. Steven Holmes, "Defying Forecasts, Census Response Ends Declining Trend," *New York Times*, September 20, 2000; Sam Roberts, "1 in 3 Americans Failed to Return Census Forms," *New York Times*, April 17, 2010.

166. See Nye, Zelikow, and King, *Why People Don't Trust Government*, chaps. 9, 10, and Conclusion. See also Pippa Norris, ed., *Critical Citizens: Global Support for Democratic Government* (New York: Oxford University Press, 1999).

167. Robert D. Putnam, *Bowling Alone: The Collapse and Revival of American Community* (New York: Simon and Schuster, 2000). See also Robert D. Putnam, Lewis M. Feldstein, and Don Cohen, *Better Together: Restoring the American Community* (New York: Simon and Schuster, 2003).

168. Pew Partnership for Civic Change, *New Eyes on Community: Eleven Years of the Pew Partnership for Civic Change* (Richmond, VA: University of Richmond Press, 2003).

169. "What's Wrong in Washington?" *The Economist*, February 29, 2010, 11.

170. George Friedman, *The Next 100 Years: A Forecast for the 21st Century* (New York: Doubleday, 2009), 18.

171. Lawrence Freedman, "A Subversive on a Hill," *National Interest*, May–June 2009, 39.

172. Anne-Marie Slaughter, "America's Edge: Power in the Networked Century," *Foreign Affairs* 88, no. 1 (January–February 2009): 94–113.

CHAPTER 7 SMART POWER

1. See Joris Lammers, Adam Galinsky, Ernestine Gordijn, and Sabine Otten, "Illegitimacy Moderates the Effect of Power on Approach," *Psychological Science* 19, no. 6 (June 2008): 558–564. See also "Absolutely," *The Economist*, January 23, 2010, 75.

2. Dacher Keltner, "The Power Paradox," *Greater Good*, Winter 2007–2008, 17.

3. For examples, see Giulio Gallaroti, *The Power Curse: Influence and Illusion in World Politics* (Boulder, CO: Lynne Rienner, 2009).

4. That power later corrupted David after he became king, producing what has been called "a Bathsheba syndrome," a sense of adulterous entitlement to the wife of one of his soldiers. He understood what he did was wrong, but he just did not think restrictions applied to him. Small agile actors can also lose by failing to adapt their strategies to changing contexts. For the interesting case of César Chávez, see Marshall Ganz, *Why David Sometimes Wins* (Oxford, UK: Oxford University Press, 2009).

5. Jeremi Suri, "American Grand Strategy from the Cold War's End to 9/11," *Orbis* 53, no. 4 (2009): 620. Eric Edelman warns against oversimplifications of the 1992 Defense Planning Guidance in "When Walls Come Down: Berlin, 9/11, and U.S. Strategy in Uncertain Time," (paper presented at the Miller Center Conference, Charlottesville, Virginia, October 26, 2009). Zbigniew Brzezinski similarly criticizes the first three post–Cold War presidents for lacking a real grand strategy in *Second Chance: Three Presidents and the Crisis of American Superpower* (New York: Basic Books, 2007).

6. Gordon Craig and Felix Gilbert, "Reflections on Strategy in the Present and Future," in Peter Paret, ed., *Makers of Modern Strategy: From Machiavelli to the Nuclear Age* (Princeton, NJ: Princeton University Press, 1986), 871.

7. Assistant Secretary of State Andrew J. Shapiro, "Political-Military Affairs: Smart Power Starts Here," keynote address to ComDef (September 9, 2009), in U.S. Department of State, *Diplomacy in Action* (Washington, DC: Department of State, 2009), www.state.gov/t/pm/rls/rm/128752.htm.

8. See examples in Watanabe Yasushi and David McConnell, eds., *Soft Power Superpowers: Cultural and National Assets of Japan and the United States* (Armonk, NY: M. E. Sharpe, 2008).

9. John Pomfret, "Newly Powerful China Defies Western Nations with Remarks, Policies," *Washington Post*, March 15, 2010.

10. Deng's statement has been translated with a variety of words but always with the same sense of prudence. See Erik Beukel, "China and the South China Sea: Two Faces of Power in the Rising China's Neighborhood Policy," May 2010, www.diis.dk/sw92785.asp.

11. Robert Kennedy, "The Elements of Strategic Thinking: A Practical Guide," in Gabriel Marcella, ed., *Teaching Strategy: Challenge and Response* (Carlisle, PA: U.S. Army Strategic Studies Institute, 2010), 6.

12. Walter A. McDougal, "Can the United States Do Grand Strategy?" *Orbis* 54, no. 2 (Spring 2010): 173.

13. See John Lewis Gaddis, *Strategies of Containment: A Critical Appraisal of Postwar American National Security Policy* (New York: Oxford University Press, 1982).

14. Assessing such changes requires contextual intelligence. Anthony Mayo and Nitin Nohria of Harvard Business School have defined contextual intelligence as the ability to understand an evolving environment and to capitalize on trends in changing markets. In foreign policy, contextual intelligence is the intuitive diagnostic skill that helps align tactics with objectives to create smart strategies in varying situations. On the attributes and dimensions of contextual intelligence, see Joseph Nye, *The Powers to Lead* (Oxford, UK: Oxford University Press, 2008), chap. 4. See also Anthony Mayo and Nitin Nohria, *In Their Times: The Greatest Business Leaders of the Twentieth Century* (Boston: Harvard Business School Press, 2005).

15. Charles Krauthammer, "The Bush Doctrine: ABM, Kyoto, and the New American Unilateralism," *Weekly Standard*, June 4, 2001.

16. The most recent American National Security Strategy identifies as the "challenges of our times—countering violent extremism and insurgency; stopping the spread of nuclear weapons and securing nuclear materials; combating a changing climate and sustaining global growth; helping countries feed themselves and care for their sick; resolving and preventing conflict, while also healing its wounds." White House, *National Security Strategy* (Washington, DC: White House, May 2010), www.whitehouse .gov/sites/default/files/rss_viewer/national_security_strategy.pdf.

17. See Michael Mandelbaum, *The Case for Goliath: How America Acts as the World's Government in the Twenty-First Century* (New York: PublicAffairs, 2005).

18. See Charles P. Kindleberger, *World Economic Primacy: 1500–1990* (Oxford, UK: Oxford University Press, 1996), 223ff.

19. Robert O. Keohane, *After Hegemony: Cooperation and Discord in the World Political Economy* (Princeton, NJ: Princeton University Press, 1984). See also Duncan Snidal, "The Limits of Hegemonic Stability Theory," *International Organization* 39, no. 4 (1985): 580–614.

20. See the critique in Carla Norrlof, *America's Global Advantage: US Hegemony and International Cooperation* (Cambridge, UK: Cambridge University Press, 2010), chap. 3.

21. John Ikenberry, "When China Rules the World: The End of the Western World and the Birth of a New Global Order (Review)," *Foreign Affairs* 88, no. 6 (November–December 2009): 152–153.

22. On the early stages, see Robert Putnam and Nicholas Bayne, *Hanging Together: The Seven-Power Summits* (Cambridge, MA: Harvard University Press, 1984).

23. Robert Fauver, quoted in Peter Baker and Rachel Donadio, "Group of 8 Is Not Enough Say Outsiders Wanting In," *New York Times,* July 10, 2009.

24. See Robert O. Keohane and David Victor, "The Regime Complex for Climate Change," Discussion Paper 10–33, Harvard Project on International Climate Agreements (Cambridge, MA: Belfer Center for Science and International Affairs, January 2010).

25. Leonardo Martinez-Diaz and Ngaire Woods, "The G20—the Perils and Opportunities of Network Governance for Developing Countries," briefing paper, November 2009, www.globaleconomicgovernance.org.

26. Anne-Marie Slaughter, "America's Edge: Power in the Networked Century," *Foreign Affairs* 88 (January–February 2009): 99.

27. William Inboden, "What Is Power? And How Much of It Does America Have?" *Holidays,* November–December 2009, 24–25.

28. After the United States rose to global power early in the twentieth century, the tension was exemplified by the contrasting realist vision of Roosevelt and the idealist vision of Wilson. In his study of diplomacy, former Secretary of State Kissinger argued that Wilson won the contest for the minds of the American public and noted that even Richard Nixon hung Wilson's picture in his office. Henry Kissinger, *Diplomacy* (New York: Simon and Schuster, 1994), chap. 2.

29. Henry A. Kissinger, "Realists vs. Idealists," *International Herald Tribune,* May 12, 2005.

30. Robert Ellworth, Andrew Goodpaster, and Rita Hauser, cochairs, "America's National Interests: A Report from the Commission on America's National Interests" (Cambridge, MA: Harvard Center for Science and International Affairs, 1996), 13.

31. Walter Russell Mead, *Special Providence: American Foreign Policy and How It Changed the World* (New York: Knopf, 2001).

32. Harvey Sapolsky, Benjamin H. Friedman, Eugene Golz, and Darly Press, "Restraining Order: For Strategic Modesty," *World Affairs* 172, no. 2 (Fall 2009): 85. See also Barry R. Posen, "The Case for Restraint," *American Interest,* November–December 2007.

33. Mancur Olson, *The Logic of Collective Action: Public Goods and the Theory of Groups* (Cambridge, MA: Harvard University Press, 1965).

34. For a full discussion of the complexity and problems of definition, see Inge Kaul, Isabelle Grunberg, and Marc A. Stern, eds., *Global Public Goods: International Cooperation in the 21st Century* (New York: Oxford University Press, 1999). Strictly defined, public goods are nonrivalrous and nonexclusionary.

35. Barry Posen, "Command of the Commons: The Military Foundation of U.S. Hegemony," *International Security* 28, no. 1 (Summer 2003): 5–46.

36. "High Costs Weigh on Troop Debate for Afghan War," *New York Times*, November 14, 2009.

37. Zaki Laidi, "Europe as a Risk Averse Power: A Hypothesis," *Garnet Policy Brief* 11 (Sciences Po) (2010): xi.

38. Richard A. Clarke, "How to Win the War on Terror," *Newark Star Ledger*, November 21, 2004.

39. Sarah Lyall, "Ex-Official Says Afghan and Iraq Wars Increased Threats to Britain," *New York Times*, July 21, 2010.

40. For more detail, see John Gaddis, *Strategies of Containment* (Oxford, UK: Oxford University Press, 1982).

41. Melvyn Leffler and Jeffrey Legro, "Dilemmas of Strategy," in Melvyn Leffler and Jeffrey Legro, eds., *To Lead the World: American Strategy After the Bush Doctrine* (Oxford, UK: Oxford University Press, 2008), 265.

42. Philip Seib, *America's New Approach to Africa: AFRICOM and Public Diplomacy* (Los Angeles: Figueroa Press, 2009), 19.

43. Ibid.

44. Thom Shanker, "Command for Africa Established by Pentagon," *New York Times*, October 5, 2008.

45. David Milliband, quoted in David Allaby, "We Underestimate the Value of Soft Power," December 22, 2009, www.publicservice.co.uk/print_fdeatureds.asp"type=news&id=13333.

46. Center for U.S. Global Engagement, *Putting "Smart Power" to Work: An Action Agenda for the Obama Administration and the 111th Congress* (Washington, DC: Center for U.S. Global Engagement, 2010), 15.

47. William Matthews, "Rumsfeld: U.S. Needs Online Strategic Communication Agency," *Defense News*, January 23, 2008.

48. Patrick Cronin and Kristin Lord, "Deploying Soft Power," *Defense News*, April 12, 2010.

49. Paul Kennedy, "Rome Offers Obama a Lesson in Limits," *Financial Times*, December 30, 2009.

50. David Sanger, "A Red Ink Decade," *New York Times*, February 2, 2010. See also White House, *National Security Strategy*.

51. Anthony Cordesman, quoted in Edward Luce, "Obama Doctrine Hinges on Economy," *Financial Times*, May 28, 2010.

52. Stephen Walt, *Taming American Power: The Global Response to U.S. Primacy* (New York: Norton, 2005).

53. Niall Ferguson, "The Decade the World Tilted East," *Financial Times*, December 28, 2009.

54. Richard Haass, "When World Is in Transition, Can Great Countries Have Good Policies?" *Sunday Times*, May 23, 2010, www.sundaytimes.1k/100523/International/int_05.html.

55. See Fareed Zakaria, *The Post-American World* (New York: Norton, 2008) for a thoughtful discussion.

INDEX

Shawn G. Henry

Joseph S. Nye, Jr., is University Distinguished Service Professor and former dean of the Kennedy School of Government at Harvard University. From 1977 to 1979 he served as deputy undersecretary of state for Security Assistance, Science, and Technology and chaired the National Security Council Group on Nonproliferation of Nuclear Weapons. In 1993–1994 he was chairman of the National Intelligence Council, and in 1994 and 1995 he served as assistant secretary of defense for International Security Affairs. In all three agencies, he received distinguished service awards. He also served as U.S. representative to the UN Secretary-General's Advisory Committee on Disarmament Matters, 1989–1993.

Joe Nye is a fellow of the American Academy of Arts and Sciences, the American Academy of Diplomacy, and the British Academy. He is an honorary fellow of Exeter College, Oxford, and a Theodore Roosevelt Fellow of the American Academy of Political and Social Science. He is a recipient of Princeton University's Woodrow Wilson Award, the Charles Merriam Award from the American Political Science Association, and the Distinguished Scholar Award from the International Studies Association, as well as France's Palmes Academiques. He received his bachelor's degree summa cum laude from Princeton University, was a Rhodes Scholar at Oxford University, and earned a Ph.D. in political science from Harvard. He has taught as a visiting professor in Geneva, Ottawa, London, and Oxford and conducted research in Europe, East Africa, and Central America.

PublicAffairs is a publishing house founded in 1997. It is a tribute to the standards, values, and flair of three persons who have served as mentors to countless reporters, writers, editors, and book people of all kinds, including me.

I. F. STONE, proprietor of *I. F. Stone's Weekly*, combined a commitment to the First Amendment with entrepreneurial zeal and reporting skill and became one of the great independent journalists in American history. At the age of eighty, Izzy published *The Trial of Socrates*, which was a national bestseller. He wrote the book after he taught himself ancient Greek.

BENJAMIN C. BRADLEE was for nearly thirty years the charismatic editorial leader of *The Washington Post*. It was Ben who gave the *Post* the range and courage to pursue such historic issues as Watergate. He supported his reporters with a tenacity that made them fearless and it is no accident that so many became authors of influential, best-selling books.

ROBERT L. BERNSTEIN, the chief executive of Random House for more than a quarter century, guided one of the nation's premier publishing houses. Bob was personally responsible for many books of political dissent and argument that challenged tyranny around the globe. He is also the founder and longtime chair of Human Rights Watch, one of the most respected human rights organizations in the world.

.   .   .

For fifty years, the banner of Public Affairs Press was carried by its owner Morris B. Schnapper, who published Gandhi, Nasser, Toynbee, Truman, and about 1,500 other authors. In 1983, Schnapper was described by *The Washington Post* as "a redoubtable gadfly." His legacy will endure in the books to come.

Peter Osnos, *Founder and Editor-at-Large*